ANTONIN BESSE OF ADEN

ANTONIN BESSE OF ADEN

*The Founder of St Antony's College
Oxford*

David Footman

M in association with
St Antony's College, Oxford

© Estate of David Footman and St Antony's College,
Oxford, 1986

First published 1986

Published by
THE MACMILLAN PRESS LTD
Houndmills, Basingstoke, Hampshire RG21 2XS
and London
Companies and representatives
throughout the world

Printed in Hong Kong

British Library Cataloguing in Publication Data
Footman, David
Antonin Besse of Aden.—(Political culture
and Communist studies)
1. Besse, Antonin 2. St. Antony's College
—History 3. Businessmen—Biography
I. Title   II. Series
378.425'74   LF741.S3
ISBN 0-333-38508-X

Contents

Acknowledgements

This book is based mainly on Antonin Besse's letters and other records kindly made available by the late Mme (Hilda) Besse at Le Paradou, Cavalaire; and, in Aden, by A. B. Besse who also enabled me to consult the original Courmont memoir. I have to thank Jean Selignac, his nephew, for AB's early letters to the family; and Edward Mayne and C. W. H. Fenn for certain letters and records of the twenties and thirties.

A full list of those whose help has made the compilation possible would be inordinately long, but in particular I wish to mention R. N. Bagadia, Sir David Barran, A. Benoit, Mlle Germaine Bernard, P. R. Besse, A. D. Bethell, William Cave, Sir Reginald Champion, G. W. S. Clucas, R. A. H. Clyde, H. J. Collins, Mme Collins-Besse, Sir William and Lady Deakin, I. Di Domenico, G. P. Dwyer, Lord Godber, Mme Godefroid, Dr Kurt Hahn, Viscount Hall, Sir John Hathorn-Hall, A. J. Jolly, J. R. Kynaston, Mohamed A. Luqman, Duncan Mackintosh, Mme Ina Marek, R. C. Martin, Sir John Masterman, Prabhulal Mehta, William Merson, Hugh Millar, Mohamed Aly, M. G. Patel, William Sands, Maganlal T. Shah, Sir Douglas Veale, Maurice Weerts, Sir Henry Willink, and J. M. Wisocky.

Many of the above are no longer with us. Most of this book was written before the British evacuation of Aden and the revolution in Ethiopia – events that have brought about the obliteration of the old order on either side of the Bab al Mandab.

Throughout AB's voluminous correspondence his comments on collaborators and associates are apt to be scathing and often unjustified; and in certain cases I have suppressed the names.

Responsibility for all that is written here remains my own.

The author and publishers wish to thank The National Trust for Places of Historic Interest or Natural Beauty, for permission to reproduce "If" by Rudyard Kipling from the *Definitive Edition of Rudyard Kipling's Verse*

DAVID FOOTMAN

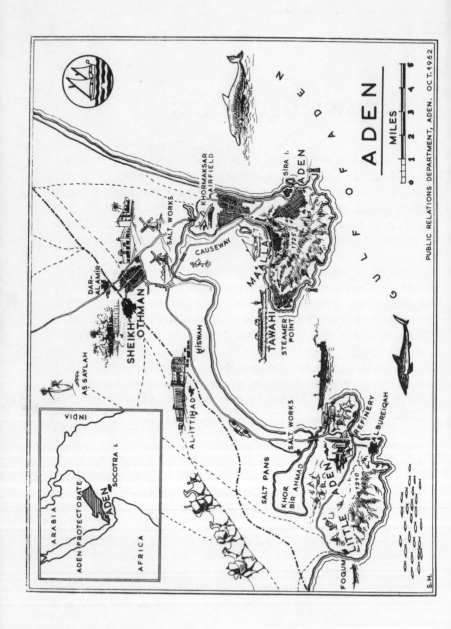

Map 1 The Federation of South Arabia, 1959–67

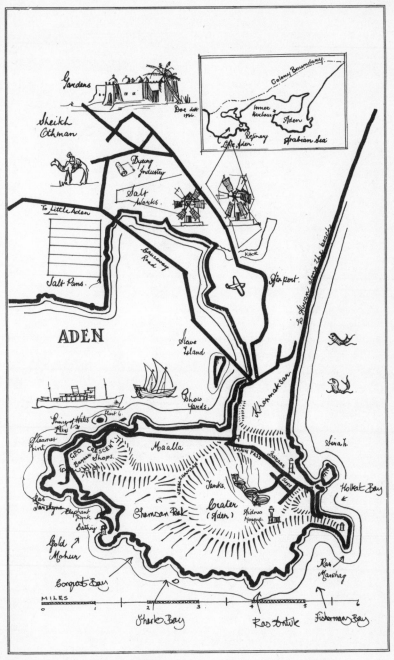

Map 2 Aden Colony c. 1956

1   1899

I

In 1899, when Antonin Besse first arrived there, the Settlement of Aden[1] had been, for over sixty years, part of the Bombay Presidency of the Government of India. North and East lay the Protectorates. Lahej, the Settlement's immediate neighbour, had a fair number of European visitors: there was nowhere else for Aden residents to go to. Further East the various Sheikhdoms saw little or nothing of the Protecting Power or of its nationals. Even Mukalla was not to have a British adviser for nearly forty years. At the turn of the century the Hadhramaut, and indeed most of the interior, was for Europeans a *terra incognita*.

To the North of Lahej the Yemen still formed part of the Ottoman Empire. The boundary line, where Turkish suzerainty should end and British influence begin, was still a matter of uncertainty and argument; and indeed little attempt was made effectively to control the hill country on either side of the frontier. But Turkish garrisons kept order in the larger towns, and Hodeida, the Yemen's main port, housed a small European trading community.

On the African side, though frontier demarcation was still proceeding, the map had, by 1899, assumed the pattern it was to keep for nearly forty years. The three Somalilands, Italian, British and French, were already established; and the French were at work on their newly chosen capital, Djibouti. Eritrea was an Italian colony. Menelik was on the throne of Abyssinia. Since his victory over the Italian army at Adowa (in 1896) he had become a figure in international politics and international finance. The first British Minister to the Ethiopian Court had been appointed in 1897. French interests had already acquired a concession for a narrow gauge railway – Chemin de Fer d'Ethiopie – to connect Djibouti with Addis Abeba. Work was in hand, but the line was not even to reach Diredawa till 1902.

The corner of the world where Antonin Besse was to operate was an area of vast distances, primitive communications, and, for the most part, sparse population and abject poverty. Away from the Ethiopian highlands the combination of extreme heat and high humidity made the climate exhausting. Centres under effective European administration were few and small; and from them, to quote a contemporary writer, 'one may step straight from this modern age of bustle and chicanery into an era of elemental conditions; where faithful friendship is jostled by the blackest treachery and the crude facts of a semi-barbaric life are encountered at every turn'.[2]

II

The Aden peninsular is a tangle of rocky volcanic hills, joined to the mainland by a narrow strip of sand. Rainfall is negligible. It is waterless and devoid of vegetation. There are hotter areas – the maximum summer shade temperature rarely rises above 110°; but the intense humidity can make the spring and summer extremely trying.

By the time of the British arrival Aden had long lost its importance of ancient times. Lieutenant J. R. Wellstead RN noted in 1835 'a few minarets, about a hundred houses and some disjointed remnants of its walls, the rest being occupied by tombs, mounds, heaps of rubbish, roofless walls of older dwellings or the wretched habitations of the present residents'.[3] The first census to be held under the British, in 1839, showed a local population of 1297, out of which the Jewish community numbered no less than 558.

With Pax Britannica the port began to revive. There was no other deep-water harbour capable of accommodating ocean-going ships for many hundreds of miles in any direction. Ocean-borne imports for Southern Arabia and for a large segment of Eastern Africa – cotton goods, sugar, kerosene – must be brought to Aden and there transshipped into dhows for carriage to the little ports on either side of the narrows. Local produce for the outside world – coffee, hides, gums – was exported along the same route in reverse. In 1853 Aden was declared a free port. By 1860 the population had grown to 20 000 and Aden was an important station on the route to India, via Alexandria and overland across Egypt to Suez. Inevitably the opening of the Suez Canal in 1865 gave a decisive impetus. Aden became one of the major coaling ports of Asia.

By 1899 the population was about 40 000.[4] Of these some 4000 were Indians – traders, clerks, craftsmen, minor government employees. There was still an appreciable Jewish community. There were half-a-dozen consulates, a branch of The National Bank of India, a number of shipping and coaling firms. The garrison consisted of fifty British and nineteen Indian officers, and 1200 British and 1050 Indian Other Ranks. The chief executive (under Bombay) was the Resident; five or six of his senior officials were British. Administration was simple and economical. The total cost of the Aden Police in 1897 was 56 640 rupees, or about £4250. This was Rs615 more than it had been in 1896 – the increase, as the Resident explained in his annual report, being due to a rise in the price of food grains and the cost of escorting lunatics to Bombay.

Water was obtained from a primitive distillation plant on Sira Island, or brought in from the North by sea or by camel cart. Domestic sanitation was on the system of the 'Big Drop'. There was no electric light or power. There were no modern insecticides. There was no public transport, no library, no newspaper. Letters from Europe took at least a fortnight. There were the psychological concomitants of living in a small, isolated community in an exacting climate. At the same time the Union Club was well established. There was tennis, cricket and golf. There was an active social life. Passengers from passing ships who came on shore for a couple of hours were often surprised to meet residents who were not unhappy at being stationed there.

III

The salt deposits – Aden's one natural asset apart from its harbour – were worked by an Italian firm. Indeed it would seem that at the turn of the century the port's commercial possibilities were of little interest to the higher British establishment. Aden rarely figures in proceedings of the Bombay Chamber of Commerce: though in 1900 a proposal, from Aden, for the construction of a public wharf was rejected by Bombay on financial grounds. And yet, with the South American plantations not yet productive, the Yemen was still one of the world's largest coffee producers. The trade in hides and skins from the African side was already important and ripe for considerable expansion.

Of course business in these commodities is tricky. Cleaning, sorting, grading, storing and packing involve a number of operations to be carried out under strict supervision. There were unending transport difficulties. There was the human element – the rich variety of local techniques for getting the better of a stranger. All this in a part of the world where things are very apt to go wrong, and where heat and humidity sap energy and initiative. For the time being the non-official British kept to their shipping and coaling, and the entrepôt trade was largely in the hands of Indians – Parsees and Gujeratis – and Hadhrami Arabs. But in 1865, on the opening of the Suez Canal, a young Frenchman came out from Marseilles to found the import – export firm of Riès. Some years later his example was followed by another Frenchman, one Bardey, who today is best remembered for having employed, at different times, Arthur Rimbaud and Antonin Besse.

2   The Youngest Corporal

Local records show that all four grandparents of Antonin Besse were of French nationality and Catholic faith. Pierre Besse, his father, was born in Carcassonne on 10 March 1839, son of Joseph Besse and of Jeanne, née Pommier. In due course he married Marie Bonnafous and became the father of four boys and three girls – Antonin, born on 26 June 1877, being the third son and fourth child. In the early eighties Pierre Besse's health began to fail, and he moved with his family to Montpellier where he hoped to get better medical attention. He died in 1884, when Antonin was seven. His widow stayed on in Montpellier, which, rather than Carcassonne, for the younger children at any rate, came to be the family home.

Pierre Besse had a small leather business, supplying local saddlers and shoemakers. He had little to leave his widow, but he cannot have left her destitute. There is no question of her having to find work. The boys went to secondary schools. Jeanne the eldest daughter, had a dowry of 10 000 francs[1] when she married Joseph Selignac, a young Montpellier lawyer. Her two sisters also married well. They were good looking girls, but it would have been most surprising in French provincial society of that time, for young professional and business men to marry outside their class. Mme *Veuve* Besse had enough to enable her to be accepted socially by the Montpellier bourgeoisie. But the struggle to keep up appearances must have been grim, bitter and unrelenting.

Antonin attended the Montpellier Lycée but failed to obtain his baccalaureat. We have no details. Many years later he was to write to a friend 'Intellectually I lack foundation, my schooling was inadequate.' Much later still, in a letter to his second wife Hilda, he looked back on 'the unbounded and naive admiration I had for the clever boys at school, the boys who knew all the answers and passed all the examinations. I was well aware that I had no chance of competing with them. Luckily, in my case, circumstances gave me a jolt . . .'. The same letter

5

went on to note with some satisfaction that these clever boys, as far as he could check, had all become bogged down in the monotonies of schoolmastering or the intrigues of the civil service.

II

Failure to obtain a *bachot* no doubt influenced his decision, in 1895, to volunteer for four years' military service. The normal age for the call-up was twenty-one and the period with the colours three years. But one could volunteer *par devancement d'appel* from the age of nineteen. (AB of course was only eighteen, so one suspects a wangle.) By volunteering for four years a man could choose his regiment, and was entitled to a small gratuity, half to be paid on joining and half on release. In 1895 Antonin had no job in view, no qualifications and no idea of what he wanted to do. He was very conscious that his mother was too poor to support him. To wait for the normal call-up meant having to wait till the age of twenty-four before he could start a career. By volunteering at eighteen he would be free of all military obligations by the time he was twenty-two.

AB was posted to an infantry regiment in Lyons. In early 1896 he was promoted *caporal adjoint*. In after life he would claim to have been the youngest corporal in the French Army. This may well be true: at his age, according to the regulations, no Frenchman had any business to be in the army at all.

We have a letter to his sister Josephine dated 18 May 1896. The regiment was then on the move and he had been detailed to the advance party. This was a strenuous assignment: he would start at 3 or 4 a.m., cover up to twenty-five miles in full marching order, and then see to it that provisions and stores were purchased and ready by the time the main body arrived. The family at Montpellier had sent him a small bottle of menthe, for which he was deeply grateful: 'it was of real help to me and to my exhausted friends'. He describes in some detail the countryside through which he had passed: he had already a keen eye for scenery. And, as in all his letters home, there is insistence on being given detailed news of what every member of the family was doing, and concern at the hardships they were having to face. 'Poor sister, forcing herself to be gay in order to make others happy. If only I could help you.'

The next letter, dated 24 May, is from Modane with a full description of the town and its setting. He seems to have been rather proud of

it. 'Keep my letter to be read again. I have not written to anyone else.'
The country round Modane impressed him. The town itself and its
inhabitants less so. There were too many Italians. Furthermore, 'the
women nearly all have goitre. No chance here to fall in love'.

Then there is a gap of nearly a year in the letters preserved. On 13
April 1897 he wrote: 'I have been ill, and did not write because I know
you love me and it would have pained you.'

III

AB's illness was an infection of the lungs, accentuated by the life of an
army conscript and the unwholesome air of the Lyons barracks. He
was seriously ill for some weeks, attended throughout by Major
Raymond Bernard, the regimental doctor. When sufficiently recovered for light duty Bernard had him transferred to his own Medical
Section where he remained for the rest of his military service.

We have already quoted from a letter he wrote to his wife in 1934 –
'Luckily, in my case circumstances gave me a jolt.' This letter goes on:

> I had been very ill, I was forced to forge myself a will, I had known
> abject poverty and had to struggle; and I met Bernard whom I bless,
> for he taught me to hold up my head and never to compromise when
> honour or dignity are at stake. If I am, to quote Stoner's lawyer, 'stiff
> in the backbone' I owe it to Bernard who has this quality to a degree
> I shall never attain.

Raymond Bernard was a man of high professional competence who
in due course became Chief Medical Officer of an Army Corps. He had
been brought up a strict Catholic; in his early army days he lost his
faith, and thereafter evolved an austere creed of absolute and uncompromising integrity which he imposed upon himself and on those
around him. Any lapse from his rigid standards he would punish by
complete withdrawal. We are told of one occasion when senior officers
were asked to a meal at his quarters. Their interest might have helped
his career; his wife was anxious to do more than could easily be
managed on her very modest household budget, and borrowed some
money from friends. Bernard became suspicious and taxed her with
borrowing. She was frightened and denied it. When, later, he discovered she had lied to him he stopped speaking to her. Over incidents
like this the two little daughters naturally sided with their mother. But

difficult as their father might be they were, and remained, intensely proud of him.

With AB as we have seen, admiration was reinforced by gratitude. It was, he felt, to Bernard that he owed his education, his sense of purpose, his confidence and his standards. In some respects the two men were alike. There was a self-effacement about Bernard that had little counterpart in AB's exuberant personality. Bernard's influence, as assimilated by his pupil, was not always a happy one. But AB, up to the end, felt for him a devotion and a veneration he felt for no one else.

The two men met only rarely once AB had left for Aden. Bernard spent long periods of service in the colonies. Even when the two were in France together it was not always easy to arrange a meeting. Only one of Bernard's rare letters has been preserved. He had been expected at the Besse home in Provence, and had not turned up. Hilda feared she might have in some way offended him, and he wrote back to her to explain:

I have always known I am disagreeable. When I was ten I was called a little horror. I have since been made aware I am neither attractive nor amiable. Age has not improved me. I cannot change my looks or my skin. I can and do love my friends and am worthy of their love. But not at too close quarters. I do not blame anyone who does not understand all this. But you must leave me as I am. This kink of mine makes me unhappy, but to try to force me out of it would make me more unhappy still. It would not be possible. Think of Bernard the Hermit condemned to live in his shell. And forgive me.

Bernard died in 1935 in the Val de Grace Military Hospital in Paris, following two serious operations. Towards the end he said he wished to be buried near his father in the graveyard of their village home; furthermore he wished to die, as his father had died, in the Catholic faith. He asked for a priest to be called and received the last sacrament. AB did not see Bernard during his last illness, and when in due course he heard of the manner of his end he was furious. Bernard's precept and example had been, as it were, a support of his own determined atheism. He accused Marthe, Bernard's elder daughter, of exploiting a moment when his mind was failing to trick her father into a cowardly surrender. The evidence was all the other way. Bernard's mind had been perfectly clear throughout, and Marthe knew he was not a man she could hope to influence. But AB would never speak to her again.

IV

There is no mention of Bernard in the letters we still have from Antonin's army days. It may well be that the experience was too intimate to be shared even with his family.

In late April 1897 he wrote to his mother. 'How I long to be free of military service, to come and be near you and repay you in love and devotion for all the trouble I have caused . . .'. What this trouble was we are not told. But later there is mention of a debt to the regiment, and it seems he was put to the bitter necessity of appealing to his hard-pressed family for small sums of money. In May he was writing:

> Thank you for what you sent me. I needed it because for the last two months I have only had the ten francs you sent me before. Now I shall get a few cutlets and some bottles of wine which I believe to be the best remedy there is for my state of fatigue. But do not send too much. I can do without.

In August he wrote that his debt was half paid off. So 'do not send anything. Your need is greater than mine'.

The letters are nearly all to Josephine. She was his favourite sister and nearest to him in age. His eldest brother never took the slightest notice of him. The second brother seems to have disliked him, and Antonin certainly disliked Marcel. Jeanne – five years older than Antonin – was fully taken up with her approaching marriage. Emile, the youngest brother, and little Marie-Louise do not seem to have been letter writers.

After August 1897 there is a gap in the correspondence up to 29 March 1898 when AB wrote from Lyons in more cheerful mood:

> My dear Josephine, Once upon a time in the sunny South there was a dark-haired girl who had the bad luck to have a brother. This brother would have been the happiest of mortals if only he had some braces to hold up his trousers. (Band strikes up *La Marseillaise*.) One fine day when it was raining he had a parcel from his sister who had second sight and guessed his need. The braces so ardently longed for! He was amazed at their colours – red, yellow, brown, white, grey. I do not know what. Worthy of an Art Gallery. Alas the beauty was only on the surface! After a few hours of wear the leather snapped. The buckles broke. A real debacle. What tears! Moral: Never buy braces at 19 sous (9½d.) . . .

In June 1898 he was writing from Valbonne. The weather was rainy and the little town was dull, but at least he had time to read. It seems he was by now the avid reader he was to remain for the rest of his life. We can guess that most if not all of the books had been lent to him by Bernard. And Bernard's influence comes out in the list of rules he here composed for little Marie-Louise in her first year at a secondary school.

Set yourself a standard of conduct and never depart from it. Be an egoist. Do not give your friendship to the first comer. Be on good terms with everybody, but do not have too many friends. Always be dignified. That is the only way to win respect.

Work hard and try and learn quickly. Learn much, listen much, remember what is essential and forget the rest.

Talk as little as possible. Do not listen to the malicious gossip so common in the town. Go out alone only when it is unavoidable. Dress correctly, neatly, unpretentiously.

On coming home in the evening think over the day's work and keep safe in your memory the little you have learned. After that read. Read books chosen by your sister or by my friend Olivier. Do not read much poetry, because poetry makes one dream, and one should not dream.

In July the regiment was on manoeuvres and life was very full. There are descriptions of the countryside; of dishonest vintners who sold bad wine at high prices; of a kindly farmer's wife who provided good cheese at two *sous* a pound. And there is much of his own special duties in the Medical Section, with talks and demonstrations to be given to large detachments. Antonin claims he acquitted himself very well. No doubt he did.

Our last letter, again to Josephine, is from Lyons and dated 15 November. 'I do not want you to send me anything. But, I forget, if any socks should come your way . . .' (AB was always very hard on his socks). There seems to have been fresh trouble at home, and he tries to offer comfort.

Life is not always unhappiness. Have faith, I do not yet know in what. Have hope. I have confidence in myself and in my energy. Put hope in that. Every day brings me nearer to my day of liberation – 108 days more. Oh, that day! As it draws nearer I have my very real anxieties. But I have hope, and I have my strength.

3 Passage to Aden

I

We can be sure that the 'very real anxieties' to which AB refers in his letter home were concerned with the finding of a suitable opening in civil life.

There is a legend in the Bernard family that when AB was first admitted to hospital Bernard asked him what he intended to do on release from the army. AB had said 'My mother thinks something in a lawyer's office', and Bernard had replied 'That is complete nonsense. It is not what your mother thinks, it is what you yourself decide.'

The matter was frequently discussed as the two came to know each other better. It is clear from what AB said many years later that his admiration for his mentor was such that he conceived the ambition to become a doctor. But that for the moment was out of the question; there was no money to pay for his training. Bernard throughout encouraged him to go overseas. There was more scope for a young man in the colonies than there could be at home; and desert air would be good for his lung. But there was still the question of an opening. AB's poor school record, not to mention his temperament, ruled out government service. There remained business. However to get into business one must get in touch with a firm with a job to offer. Bernard the Hermit was the last man to be expected to have commercial contacts. The impoverished family in Montpellier were no better placed. In the event it was not until a fortnight before his demobilisation that AB had his opportunity; and that he had it at all was due to Joseph Selignac, the young Montpellier lawyer who had recently married his sister Jeanne.

At that time the two hardly knew each other. AB's letters all start *Cher Monsieur Selignac*; it was not for some years, when he himself was well established, that he would write *Mon cher Joseph*. But Selignac from the start was ready to be helpful. He had a friend in business circles in Lyons, and wrote to ask him to do what he could for his brother-in-law. What next transpired is described in a long letter, dated 29 March 1899, from AB in the Lyons barracks to Joseph Selignac in Montpellier.

At 5 o'clock on a Friday afternoon AB received a message in the barracks that Joseph's friend was ready to see him. He hurried off and was told there was a vacancy for a junior employee in a French firm in Aden. For particulars he must apply to the firm's Lyons agents, Messrs Jomain Frères & Andouard. It was now half-past-six and the Jomain office was closed. AB went back to barracks 'to consult a friend'.

This friend was Bernard, though AB, characteristically, does not mention his name in his letter. But we know of the interview from Bernard's younger daughter, then aged six. She was called into her father's study and found him there with a young corporal. 'This young man', Bernard told her, 'intends to go to Aden and does not know where it is. Show him.' Little Germaine had been coached by her father in geography: embarrassed but very gratified she pulled out the atlas and found Aden. Bernard must have encouraged AB to go ahead for next morning, Saturday, (the letter continues) he put on his civilian suit and called at the Jomain office. He had to answer a lot of questions about himself and was told something about the terms of employment. But there was one difficulty. Jomain was merely the agent. The principal, a Monsieur Bardey, had already left Lyons for Marseilles where he was due to embark for Aden the next day (Sunday) in the afternoon: AB should write to him fully and at once in the hope that a letter would reach him before he sailed.

AB was urgently anxious to get the job and said he would go to Marseilles in person. Jomain did not dissent, but insisted that in any case he should write. So AB went back to barracks; wrote his letter and posted it; called on Bernard again to get leave of absence and borrow his fare to Marseilles; and finally caught the 11.20 p.m. train from Lyons, arriving Marseilles at 5 o'clock in the morning. He washed, tidied up, waited about and finally called at the hotel at eight. At nine, Bardey was able to see him. But the interview was inconclusive as the post had not been delivered and Bardey had never heard of his visitor. It was arranged that he should call again at two.

AB walked round Marseilles; inspected the Old Port; and took the formidable climb on foot to Ste Marie de la Garde. He had something to eat and was back at the hotel in good time. By now the post had been delivered: as well as Antonin's own letter there was a report, apparently a favourable one, on him from Jomain. The matter did not take long to settle. Bardey explained the terms of the contract AB would have to sign. It was not a 'brilliant' contract: in particular there was a 'draconian' clause that AB hoped later to have modified. But he wanted the job very badly and knew he had no experience and no qualifications.

So he made no attempt to argue, and undertook to embark on a steamer leaving Marseilles for Aden on 16 April. By 4 o'clock that Sunday afternoon he was in the train on his way back to Lyons.

He offered his warmest thanks to his brother-in-law for his good advice and his so effective help.

II

All this was only the first part of his letter of 29 March, the part that Selignac was to pass round the family to keep them in the picture. The second part was to be strictly confidential between the two of them. It was a matter AB could only bring up because the future was now assured.

He was due, he explained, to be demobilised in nine days' time. But he would have to stay in Lyons a little longer to sign the contract and fix up details with Jomain. This stay would cost money. He had to buy clothes for Aden and a trunk to pack them in. He had his small debt to repay to his *chef-de-service* (i.e. Bernard). And there was brother Emile. Emile had got a job as assistant in a chemist's shop in Lyons. Marcel had promised to send him 100 frs to start him off, but had not sent it. And Emile had been silly: instead of arranging with a small restaurant to have all his meals there and pay at the end of the month he had been paying as he went along. He had now got himself into debt and only Antonin could help him.

Antonin's own resources amounted to 40 frs which he had earned by giving private English lessons to two small girls. (He had never told his mother about these lessons for fear she might imagine things.)

Such was the position. He could not ask his family to help him. His brother-in-law would understand why. In his four years' military service he had never asked his family for a centime.[1] For the last two years he had not received a sou from anybody.

There follows a paragraph which remains obscure, as we have no clue as to the identity of the friends to whom AB was referring. He had, he told his brother-in-law, certain friends from whom he hoped he might one day be able to borrow a substantial sum. There was more chance of their agreeing to lend him a large sum than a small sum. In fact he felt he could not ask them for a small sum. 'I would be giving them the impression of not being what they believe me to be.'

He was therefore reduced to appealing to Joseph Selignac. The sum involved was 400 frs (£16) for himself and 100 frs (£4) for Emile. He would repay at the rate of 100 frs a month, from 1 May to 1 September inclusive. Perhaps, if Joseph was not in a hurry, he could pay back 50 frs a month: there might be unforeseen expenses on arrival in Aden. It was for Selignac to fix the rate of interest.

> Please telegraph if you are unable to help me.... Whatever your answer to my request, it will make no difference to our relationship. It has cost me a great deal to ask you this. It has hurt my pride. It is the first time I have done such a thing. I did not even hint at it before my future was settled as things then were going round in a vicious circle.

Joseph Selignac agreed by return of post, and AB's next letter (of 31 March) is full of relief and gratitude. He had cleared up the small debts. He was busy with his shopping. Most of it could be done in Lyons, and this would avoid the risk of the family at Montpellier interfering. After all 'I have enough initiative to avoid being robbed.' His mother might see to his underclothing, but that was all. Of great importance was the trunk. It would probably, in the end, be more economical to buy one of the best quality, specially designed to resist damp. Perhaps tropical kit had better be bought in Marseilles.

III

AB also sent his brother-in-law a close summary of the contract which he signed in the agent's office in Lyons. It contained six clauses.

1. Duration of the contract to be three years from the date of arrival in Aden. Remuneration to be 150 frs (£6) per month for the whole term. Food and lodging to be provided by the firm.[2]
2. At the end of three years the employee is entitled to a holiday of four to six months. Fare to Marseilles to be paid by the firm. Whether or not the employee is entitled to remuneration while on leave to be decided later.
3. If for reasons of health the employee is unable to continue to reside and work in Aden, this contract is cancelled. The firm would not demand a refund of the original fare from Marseilles, but the employee would himself pay for his journey home.
4. Misbehaviour, disobedience or inefficiency on the employee's part automatically cancels the contract, and the employee must leave Aden by the next boat at his own expense.

5. Should the firm, for reasons of its own, wish to terminate the contract before its expiry, the firm will pay second class fare to Marseilles and award a gratuity of 300 frs for every completed year of service.
6. The employee undertakes not to enter the service of any other firm and not to set up in business on his own account in the Aden area for a period of five years after leaving the firm of Bardey.

This last was the 'draconian' clause which was causing Antonin misgivings. The contract includes a reminder that he is to embark at Marseilles on 16 April, and terminates with some general remarks. It is hoped that he will, in due course, attain a good position in the firm; but this will entirely depend upon his aptitude, his good will and his constitution. The climate of Aden is healthy because it is dry (*sic*). But the heat can be trying. Absolute sobriety is essential.

IV

Antonin's first letter to his brother-in-law from Aden is dated 14 May 1899. He had arrived safely, but unpleasant boils were developing under his armpits. Bardey thought he should see a doctor. He had called on the French Consul to see that his papers were in order. The consul was on bad terms with Bardey but was perfectly polite to Antonin. Aden seemed rather remote. One got news of the outside world from a daily bulletin issued by Reuters (Reuters, he explained, was something on the lines of Havas.) Bardey received *Le Journal*, sent out to him by every mail. If Selignac could send him out some papers Antonin would be most grateful: postage on newspapers was very cheap. What was of particular interest to him then was the Dreyfus case. 'If anyone still believes Dreyfus to be guilty they must be blind'. AB went on to ask for family news and for any recent photographs. Of his brothers he says 'Emile is like a tortoise, slow but sure. But Marcel is a rabbit and will never get anywhere.'[3]

The most difficult part of the letter he kept to the end. Bardey was advancing small sums for his current expenses, but was retaining the bulk of his salary to be paid out in a lump sum in December. That meant that the repayment of his debt to his brother-in-law would have to wait till the end of the year. 'Or should I go back to Bardey and make a fuss?'

AB's early letters from Aden tell us little about his daily life there, either in or out of the office. It must have been a difficult period. He was not happy with Bardey. Normally he would take his meals with his employer; but when the latter had guests he had to eat in the kitchen with the servants, an indignity which rankled. The boils persisted. In October he was lanced for a second time, and was sure the doctor had bungled. In November he wrote that he was doing his own dressings. He needed a tonic and the Aden chemists had no cod liver oil: there was, however, something called 'Scott's Emulsion' that he hoped might help. He thanked his brother-in-law for his encouragement. 'But do not be anxious. I have courage, and I do not easily lose heart.'

But a letter of 3 January 1900 is more cheerful. A cheque (of Bardey's) for 600 frs had been sent off to settle his debt and leave a little over to help Josephine and Emile. And he is filled with delight to hear of the arrival of the first Selignac baby. 'The best, the strongest and the most moral satisfaction that a man can have is to be able to bring up those he loves along the right path. Believe me that for myself this is my dearest dream.' The prosperity of Bardey's firm largely depended on the judicious buying of Yemeni coffee as it came on the Hodeida market; and it was here, in the early summer of 1900, that AB first came to grips with the commodity that was to play so important a part in his business career. A letter to his brother-in-law from Hodeida and dated 10 June 1900 is unusually informative.

He was, he wrote, getting up at half-past four and working right through till six in the evening.

> The pressure is enough to break one's back. One must always be taking the initiative, no time to stop and think, one must work as it were by instinct. Big deals and little deals are settled by one word. The whole time one has to take one's courage in one's hand, and always, always press forward.... We have up to a hundred people working for us – Goanese (to whom I talk English), Banians, Hindus, Arabs. They are much like children, well, *enfants terribles*. Thieves and liars. One must be strict with them, keep a constant watch on them, never allow the slightest approach to familiarity. All the time one must keep up a stern façade, never relax, no little jokes, no smiles, all the time be firm, unbending, ready to find fault ...

The intense heat, he explained, abated a little after 6 o'clock, and that would be the time to write letters. But then one was seized by a sort of oriental lassitude, a moral and physical exhaustion. If one took a walk along the shore the hot damp breeze coming off the sea was like the breath of a wild beast. But one was so busy that the days passed quickly. He did not mix much with the European community. Many of them were Italians. They had no serious conversation and were given to jealousy and intrigue. A good deal of their time was spent in spreading malicious stories about their neighbours and competitors. Lack of society made him look forward all the more eagerly to letters from France.

Soon he would be having his twenty-third birthday. He had now been in the tropics for more than a year. He had completed his second term of six months. A further cheque of Bardey's for 600 frs in favour of Joseph Selignac was now on its way. Apart from the small monthly payment to Emile it should all be passed to his mother.

4 The Firm of Besse

On the expiry of his contract in the spring of 1902 AB took the big decision of breaking with Bardey and setting up on his own as a coffee exporter in Hodeida. Apart from a few letters to Selignac we have no documentary evidence of this period. AB obviously felt there was little point in continuing with his employer. In after years he used to say that he had disagreed with Bardey's methods, that he had told him so, and that Bardey had refused to take his advice. Bardey for his part seems to have been unable, or perhaps had reasons for being unwilling, to enforce the 'draconian' Clause 6 of the original contract. In any case the break was made.

AB's first need was to find working capital. He had nothing of his own; as we have seen, all he could save from his meagre salary was sent home to pay off his debt to his brother-in-law and to help his family. Now once again it was Joseph Selignac who proved to be the friend in need. Joseph (as we know from the family) advanced 10 000 frs (incidentally the amount of Jeanne's *dot*) on the understanding that the whole should be repaid within one year. But this was only the beginning. In the late summer AB was back in France, and on 30 September 1902 he signed an agreement for a substantial loan from the Montpellier branch of the Comptoir National d'Escompte. We do not know the exact figure, which must have been more than 30 000 frs. That AB at the age of twenty-five, was able to negotiate such a loan speaks much for his personality and persuasiveness. But a decisive factor was that the loan was guaranteed by a Monsieur A. Guirand, *ancien avoué* of Montpellier. We know nothing of Guirand. He may well have been one of the friends to whom AB referred in his letter to Selignac at the time of his engagement by Bardey. Family legend makes him out to be a close friend of Josephine's. In any case the loan from the Comptoir made all the difference to AB's position. He could pay off his brother-in-law. He had the funds to operate from Aden as well as from Hodeida. And he could bring out his favourite brother Emile to help him in the business.

II

At first all went well. AB was on the way to acquiring his formidable expertise in the matter of coffee. He was later to write: 'No man in Aden, Hodeida or Ethiopia knows coffee as I know it. At a single glance I can differentiate between the growths of each district, can distinguish the different aromas in the cup, and blend the various qualities as no one else can do.' He was, too, becoming an expert in an equally intricate aspect of the coffee export business, the pitting of wits against producers, middle-men and competitors on the Hodeida market.

But after a year or so something went wrong. We have no details, and the stories current in later years are inconclusive. Forward sales of coffee were apt to be risky, as there were no facilities in Hodeida for hedging against fluctuations in the world price. In any case early in 1904 AB was seriously behind in his payments to the Comptoir. We have two letters from him to Selignac with a printed heading 'A. Besse, Aden-Hodeidah'. They are undated, but obviously written in late 1904 or early 1905. In the first he speaks of himself as 'working from three in the morning till ten o'clock at night with only a few minutes off for meals; and with but one hope – liberation from this accursed debt'. There was, however, one consideration that was very present in his mind: to pay off the debt too speedily would leave him without adequate funds with which to operate. In the second letter he announced he had just arranged for two payments to the Comptoir, for 1300 frs and 3700 frs respectively: he hoped shortly to arrange a further remittance. Emile, he said, wished to clear off the debt as soon as possible. 'But I feel it better to retain a little capital.'

The Comptoir were not satisfied with the progress of repayment, and early in 1905 started proceedings against AB and Guirand in the Montpellier Commercial Court. AB was represented by his brother-in-law. The fact that his only tangible assets were in the Red Sea may well have weighed with the bank; in any case in July Selignac advised AB he was hoping to reach a settlement under which the Comptoir would consent to a reduction of the debt in consideration of an immediate final payment. At the end of the month he cabled to Aden that a settlement had been agreed.

AB's reply dated 2 August is characteristic.

I have your telegram – *Réduction acceptée Selignac*. You could just as well have telegraphed '6000', and omitted your signature. This

would have saved you the cost of two words in the cable and have
confirmed the exact figure.... The Mokha affair – Emile is there at
the moment – is not yet completed, but you will be getting the sum of
6000 frs.any day now if it has not reached you already ...

He goes on to thank his brother-in-law in the warmest terms for all he
had done for him. The letter concludes with his estimate of his own
position and prospects now that he had passed the first milestone of his
career in business on his own:

I still have some difficulties to face but on the whole I am very
optimistic. My first payment (to the Comptoir) was on 13 April,
1904, and including the final remittance of 6000 frs.that makes a
total of 29 000 frs.paid in sixteen months. On top of that I have sent
large sums home to the family, carried out improvements to the
house here and opened up new agencies.... The turnover for the six
months January to June 1905 was 800 000 frs. I am quite alone,
with no staff.... If I can hold out against the strain for another year
there is a hope of my coming back to France with a little fortune.
This thought gives me courage.

In due course Joseph Selignac sent him a copy of the final receipt
from the Comptoir:

Reçu de M. Antonin Besse à Aden-Hodeida des mains de Me.
Selignac avoué à Montpellier la somme de 6000 francs pour solde de
tout compte à ce jour, étant entendu que le dit versement libère
complètement M. A. Besse de tous les engagements résultants ou
ayant résulté pour lui *vis-à-vis* du Comptoir du compte qui lui a été
ouvert le 30 septembre 1902 sous la garantie de Me. A. Guirand
ancien avoué à Montpellier donné par acte du 29 du même mois. Le
Comptoir déclare renoncer moyennant le dit versement à toute
réclamation concernant les frais du procès evacué par le Tribunal
Commercial à Montpellier entre M. M. Guirand, Besse et Le
Comptoir d'Escompte Montpellier.

le 12 août 1905

III

We know little of AB's daily life as a bachelor. Life in Hodeida under
Turkish rule was far easier for Europeans than it was to become in an

independent Yemen. AB got on with the Turks. On at least one occasion he went up to Sanaa to visit the Governor. He played tennis; in Turkish days there was a flourishing tennis club. We are told that in Hodeida he lived with an Arab girl: and this may well have helped him to his fluent and forceful, if individual, command of spoken Arabic. But as time went on he spent more and more of his time in Aden, and here social conditions were different.

Fifty years previously Richard Burton had found much to dislike in Aden 'where social intercourse is crushed by "gup", gossip and the scandal of small colonial circles ... where briefly the march of mind is at a dead halt and the march of matter is in double quick time to the hospital'[1]. Burton of course had bees in his bonnet and times had changed since his day. But there was still the rigidity and the exclusiveness of a small Victorian outpost of empire. It was a world of 'we' and 'they' – the 'we' comprising the officials, the officers, and, as a matter of favour, the bank manager and a few of the leading shipping agents. AB's attempt to join the Union Club was rebuffed. We do not know if he was put up and blackballed or was advised to withdraw his candidature. All he said in later years was 'They would not have me.' But the humiliation rankled and continued to rankle. The Union Club became for him the symbol and focus of all he most disliked in the British officer class – snobbishness, heavy drinking, lack of any intellectual or cultural interest.

Meanwhile AB, as indeed all his life, was working very long hours at very high pressure. He was alone except for Emile, and Emile was mostly in the Yemen. But his remarkable vitality left scope for other interests. Gramophones were still too primitive to satisfy his love of music, but now that he could afford to buy books he read widely and voraciously.[2] Then, too, there was his passion for absolute physical fitness, doubtless reinforced by Bernard's precepts and confirmed by what he had seen of the Europeans in Aden.[3] He played tennis, he rode; and, true to the Nietzschean principle of living dangerously, he had his long swims in unprotected waters, regardless of the sharks, and his climbs along the crumbling cliffs of the volcanic hills around Crater.

IV

Early in 1907 AB was in France. His little nephew Jean Selignac, aged eight, remembers his uncle, aged thirty, as an important man and one who knew he was important. AB was by then entirely supporting his mother, and arranged for her to leave Montpellier and settle in

Breteuil. The old lady was seeing a good deal of Marcel, and one of AB's letters complains that a visit to her had been taken up in having to listen to Marcel's praises. Back in Aden, in May, he reported that business prospects were good and the days were passing quickly. Emile was working very hard at Hodeida and determined to make a success. But his health was feeling the strain and he might have to come home to recuperate. Emile did in fact return to France for a few months and in September AB wrote to his sisters:

> I am sure that little by little Emile will win you over, but he must not take my place in your hearts. I will squeeze and squeeze to make a little room for him there. But that is all. Send me news of his health and his progress. He must come back here with his mind broadened, and with more confidence in himself and in us.

To his brother-in-law he wrote: 'I am awaiting Emile's return in order to take what is perhaps a very serious decision. But in any case I will be coming back to France before the end of the year.'

The nature of this decision is no mystery. When in France at the beginning of that year (1907) AB met by chance in a train Mlle Marguerite Hortense Eulalie Godefroid. She was two years younger than he was, Belgian, of a well-to-do bourgeois family in Brussels. AB's charm was irresistible. All through the year there was a warm exchange of letters. In the winter of 1907–8 he was back in Europe. In February he wrote from Brussels to Selignac that he had formally proposed and been accepted: he would like his birth certificate sent him for the marriage formalities. The wedding took place in Brussels on 1 April 1908. A fortnight later he wrote that he was planning a business journey with his bride – 'Antwerp, London, Hamburg, Frankfurt, Munich, Vienna, Trieste, Venice, Milan, Genoa, Cote d'Azur, Marseilles, Barcelona, Bordeaux, Montpellier, Lyons, Paris, Havre, Brussels – Ouf!' In mid-May he had to report that Marguerite was laid up with complete exhaustion. He could only hope that the peace and quiet of Brussels would set her right again.

V

Marriage was an important milestone both in AB's private life and in his business career. For the next few years it was Brussels, not the South of France, that was his headquarters in Europe. He was based on

Brussels when he first came across the motto that he was to make his own – *Plus est en vous*, from the Von der Aa family memorial in the Grathaus in Bruges. In the winter of 1908 – 9 he brought his wife to Aden; a daughter (Meryem) had been born in Brussels in January 1909. Eighteen months later they had a son (André).

The impact of his marriage on his business was decisive. Marguerite had a substantial private fortune which she readily agreed to invest in the firm of Besse. AB's formidable honeymoon itinerary was obviously designed to find new outlets which he was now in a position to exploit. Quite apart from expansion, the possession of adequate capital enabled him to choose his time to buy and to sell.[4] But it was in expanding the firm that his dynamism, his determination and his uncanny flair found their fullest scope. A chance meeting with Max Klein, a leading Hamburg importer, turned his attention to hides and skins. At the start it was tough going. Established dealers have ways and means of making things difficult for inconvenient newcomers. But AB persisted. 'By 1914', he was able to record, 'our firm was buying at least 90% of the Arabian salted hides available, which we shipped to Johann Geipl & Söhne in Bohemia.'

By the outbreak of World War I AB was handling the whole range of local export commodities. He was established on the African side of the narrows, with agencies along the Benadir coast – brother Emile took charge in Mogadiscio – and in the main market towns of Abyssinia. His share of the import trade was substantial enough to warrant the engagement of G. E. Davis, a young textile expert from Manchester to look after the business in cotton piece goods. Foreseeing that the supremacy of Lancashire was unlikely to last he made contacts with American and with Indian cotton mills. In the early days AB's business had been confined to Yemeni produce and the Yemeni markets. When Turkey came into the war the Yemen was completly shut off; but by then the firm was sufficiently widely and strongly established to take advantages of the opportunities that war conditions were to offer.[5]

AB's marriage brought him not only finance but a highly competent business partner. His wife kept the firm's books. On the subject of profits Madame Godefroid (on her divorce she re-assumed her maiden name) has stated that at the time of their marriage AB's net yearly income from the business was 20 000 frs (£800). For the first year the new capital began to show results it was 150 000 frs. By the outbreak of war it had risen to 500 000 frs.

Early in 1914 AB moved to his new headquarters, built to his own design, in the Aidrus Road in Crater. It is a massive and uncompromising building, of dark local stone, rectangular in shape and with a central courtyard. On the ground floor were warehouses and storerooms. The first floor houses the offices and living quarters for staff. On the roof, looking over Crater to the craggy hills beyond, was the penthouse, with AB's own flat and the enormous private office from which he ruled his empire till the end of his life.

5 World War I

In the summer of 1914 AB and his family were back in Europe. In late July Marguerite and the children were staying on in Brussels, and AB set off on a business trip to Germany. Just in time he realised that war was imminent and made for France. Marguerite and the children were nearly overrun by the German invasion. But after an adventurous journey – mostly by taxi – they too reached safety. The family were reunited in Montpellier where AB received his call-up papers as *soldat, deuxième classe*. He was posted to the local depot, and the family rented a villa on the outskirts of the town.

One anecdote survives of his brief second term in the army. His sergeant asked him what he was in civil life and he replied 'millionaire'. Early on he applied to the Ministry of War for his release in order to go back and resume charge of his business. Strings may or may not have been pulled, but it was patently absurd for a man of AB's calibre to spend his war doing fatigues in the Montpellier depot. By the turn of the year his application was granted and he embarked for Aden. Permission was also accorded for Marguerite and the children to follow him.

II

There is a memoir, written many years later, by Edouard Courmont who in the summer of 1915 was sent by the Messageries Maritimes to take temporary charge of their Aden office. First impressions were unfavourable. The Company's quarters at Steamer Point were verminous and over-run with cockroaches. In the safe, behind the piles of currency, his predecessor had left an album of fat naked women. Courmont was relieved his posting was not to be permanent, and that his wife was staying on in France.

War conditions meant that few ships were passing through, and that there was keen competition among local exporters for such cargo space as might be available. Courmont made a round of calls on the Aden merchants. In due course he was shown up to the penthouse in the Aidrus Road in Crater. He was impressed by a standard of taste and comfort he had not yet come across in Aden. There were good Persian carpets. He liked the pictures. There was a piano. Lighting and fans were run off the only private electrical plant in the Settlement.[1] AB himself was shortish, powerfully built, with thick black hair, a southern complexion and splendid teeth. He was meticulously laundered. As he explained the activities of his firm and the plans he had in store for it he seemed to exude vitality.

The two soon found they had much in common quite apart from problems of cargo space. Courmont was a man of culture. His taste in books was much the same as AB's. Both were then keen Wagnerians. AB now had a gramophone and was building up his library of classical records. Within a few weeks the two were close friends.

AB was alone at the time. Marguerite had taken the children to the Ethiopian highlands to escape the heat. (Courmont noted that mention was seldom made of them.) AB was obviously delighted at finding someone to whom he could talk in the evenings on his roof in the Aidrus Road or on climbs along the crags of Shamsan; Courmont had a good head for heights and was always willing to come with him. Both men were Left Wing Radicals and anti-militarist: some of their talk would have seemed subversive to official circles in Paris. True, Courmont, in view of the standing of the Messageries Maritimes, was made temporary member of the Union Club, and AB was apt to be sarcastic when he went there. But, Courmont explained, he only went to read the *Manchester Guardian* and the *New Statesman*. He never touched those 'gospels of English snobism and conformism', the *Sphere* and the *Tatler*. He was once invited to a guest night at a garrison mess, and his disapproval of the drink consumed, the horseplay and the unintellectual conversation was all that AB could wish.

The friendship had practical advantages for Courmont. AB had the best cook in Aden. He was always ready to put a Fiat at Courmont's disposal – a great convenience over the ancient Messageries horse cab on the long trek between Steamer Point and Crater. But what really mattered was that AB had taken to Courmont, and when he liked anybody his charm was irresistible. In the autumn Courmont was posted to Bombay where Alice, his wife, was to join him. His last evening in Aden he spent with AB.

III

In July 1915 a small Turkish force advanced from the Yemen, overran Lahej without meeting opposition and took up positions facing the British lines at Sheikh Othman. Apart from a minor flurry early in 1918 the front remained static until the Armistice. From time to time a few shells were exchanged, causing neither casualties nor damage. Caravans could cross the opposing lines without let or hindrance. Daily life in Aden went on unruffled; and no surviving letter of AB's makes any mention of this little local war.[2]

We have few details of the firm's activities during the war. We know AB was short-handed. There was his wife. There was G. E. Davis, the young textile expert, who was sent on visits to India to ensure the flow of Indian cotton piece goods. Emile Besse was in Mogadiscio. Relations between the two brothers were no longer as warm as they had been: AB in his talks with Courmont had been full of complaints about Emile. Much of the work in Aden and in the agencies was done by Hadhrami Arabs, Indians and Levantines. The war brought increased demand and increased prices for all the commodities handled, and the firm was making big profits. But transport remained a bottleneck, and AB was thinking of acquiring dhows of his own.

In 1917 on a visit to Djibouti he met the colourful Henry de Monfried, and the two agreed to build a large dhow for their joint ownership – AB to put up the capital and de Monfried to come over to Aden to supervise construction and provide the know-how. The dhow was nearly completed when she was commandeered by the British Navy. One story is that AB was warned by the authorities that de Monfried might put the dhow to improper uses. We do not know how much the Navy paid in compensation. De Monfried maintains he had difficulty in getting AB to reimburse him for his time and his work. But this matter was eventually settled, and for some years AB kept in touch with both de Monfried and his wife. At the end of the war when de Monfried was in trouble and detained in British Somaliland AB told his manager in Addis Abeba to find out if Mme de Monfried would care to come to Aden. However, a few years later he would explode in anger whenever his former associate was mentioned. This may well have been because of the picture of him in one of de Monfried's books.[3]

IV

Throughout 1916 AB and Courmont kept in friendly touch by letter.

Courmont was helpful in a number of small ways: in Bombay he could pick up spare automobile parts and other items not available in Aden, and send them on by friendly ships' captains. AB's letters complained of overwork: could not Courmont look round Bombay and find him some suitable assistant? Finally in the early summer of 1917 came a direct appeal to Courmont himself: 'Resign from the Messageries and come here. Fix your own conditions. I agree in advance.' Courmont hesitated. He was not happy in Bombay. The place was hot and noisy and he was hard put to keep up the position required of him on his present salary. He wrote back that he was now getting 18 000 frs (£720) per annum with certain perquisites. Possibly in Aden he could manage with rather less. What did AB suggest?

AB's reply gave no definite figure, but there was no doubt of his eagerness for Courmont to join him. 'Whatever the niche you most would like it is here waiting for you. As manager. As *chef de service*. As employee with a share in the profits. And all this until the day when you become my partner . . .'. In the same letter he went on to discuss his own personal future.

I myself have a problem not easy to solve. I am forty, active, physically young: and with my simple tastes I would find it hard to spend a quarter of the income from my capital if I chose to invest it. Do I retire, live in comfort and do what good I can in my own circle? Or do I remain in harness, create, expand, give scope and opportunity to my collaborators? When I am tired I incline to the first alternative.

A definite offer came only in January 1918. For the first year Courmont was to have a salary of 7500 Rs (or £500) with food, lodging and laundry. His wife (Courmont noted later) had misgivings. She had not met AB and thought his letters over-persuasive; also, knowing her husband, she did not like his giving up an assured career in the Messageries. But Courmont wished to take the plunge and in late February the couple arrived in Aden. Courmont's record of his association with AB is that of a man with a grievance. All the same it is borne out by other sources. For Alice Courmont the start in Aden was unpropitious. Their lodging turned out to be two gaunt rooms in the main Aidrus Road building, with the smell of naphthaline coming up from the store below. There were the inevitable cockroaches, and, after Bombay plumbing, the shock of the 'Big Drop'. On the day of arrival she was shocked by AB's obvious relationship with the children's governess. Alice was one of the few who felt no response to AB's charm.

Courmont meanwhile was immersed in finding his way about the complexities of the business. To be associated with AB was an exciting and stimulating experience. The two would go to the market, where bargaining for consignments of coffee or skins took place with Arab intensity and ferocity. AB was a natural actor. Crowds would collect to watch, while he in his forceful and individual Arabic assumed the leading role with immense verve and gusto, to a crescendo of laughter, imprecations and applause. (In comparison, marketing with Davis was rather dull. Davis was highly competent, but AB seemed to get the better bargains.) Through it all there was AB's obvious pleasure in having Courmont with him. They climbed the hills together. There was music. AB planned to make his house an oasis of culture in the Aden desert, and they discussed the formation of a library. AB felt literature should have a message. He approved of Romain Roland and Barbusse but not of Proust. In poetry he would go as far as Verlaine, but not Rimbaud and certainly not Baudelaire.

In early May AB went off to Addis Abeba with his wife and children. The final stretch of the Chemin de Fer d'Ethiopie had just been completed and the party travelled in the first train to reach the capital. Left in sole charge in Aden Courmont at first was apprehensive. But demand for all goods the firm was handling was insatiable. In July alone the business showed a profit of 124 000 Rs; and by that time Courmont was sufficiently confident of his future with Besse to turn down an offer of a well paid post in Indo-China.

Correspondence between the two men was voluminous and cordial. Current deals were covered in minute detail. But for AB, at that time, Courmont was more than a business associate; he was one to whom he could open his heart. In a long letter from Addis Abeba (in September 1918) he returned to problems of his own future. Should he, perhaps, follow up an early dream and qualify as a doctor? There were practical difficulties, the time required, the examinations to be taken. And then 'intellectually I lack foundation, my schooling was inadequate. The only quality I can claim is a certain talent for organising, reinforced by my liking to see a task well done . . .'. An alternative would be:

> to organise all the Red Sea, Arabia, Abyssinia, the Sudan, the Somalilands, British and German East Africa; acquire ships to bring out to these countries all that the natives can need; and convey back to Europe and America all that these countries can produce; estab-

lish agencies in London, Paris, Marseilles, Barcelona, New York, Hamburg.... But to go on working at the tempo I am working now, to find my burden growing ever heavier, this would be tantamount to the murder of all my aspirations in the fields of art and culture ...

And to take up social work 'would need the soul of an apostle which I do not possess. One would have to lack any feeling for art and beauty not to be terrified by the ugliness, the stupidity and the nastiness of those one is trying to help'.

A month later he wrote. 'I am delighted at the way you have mastered our work. Splendid. Now you may put your mind at rest as far as your own future is concerned.' In November, just after the Armistice, he came back to Aden and professed himself very satisfied. His plan was to stay in Aden for the winter. Courmont and Alice set out on a long business tour, first to India where there was a project (later abandoned) of acquiring a small steamer; and then on to settle a number of outstanding problems in France, Italy and England.

6 Stoner

I

The end of the war meant that AB could go ahead with his plans for expansion. Demobilisation eased the staff position; quite a number of young men were taken on during the winter. The firm's letter heading in early 1919 shows that the Yemeni agencies – Hodeida and Mokha – had been re-opened, and that, on the African side, the firm was established in Djibouti, Zeila, Bulhar, Berbera, Addis Abeba, Diredawa, Harrar, Mogadiscio, Merca, Brava, Itala, Mahaddei and Baidoa. AB's forthcoming trip to Europe intended to initiate more far reaching developments.

Throughout Courmont's extensive tour directives and advice arrived by every mail. 'As to B, be nice to him, even if you despise him utterly. Promise him everything till you have got all you can out of him. It is disgusting, but it is the only way.' Later a sharper tone came into the letters. On reaching London in January 1919 Courmont called on one Stoner, with whom AB had had a number of deals, and reported he was not impressed: Stoner was apt to get vague when asked to be specific. AB wrote back 'Allow me to say why not follow my instructions which are clear, simple and cause you no difficulties. As it is you make me write to you three times on the same matter, and you know how precious my time is.' Courmont's first year was nearly up, and in early February he wrote to ask for a formal contract. In due course came a reply offering 1000 Rs per month, plus 2·5 per cent of the profits in the first year, 3·5 per cent in the second and 5 per cent in the third – the arrangement subject to cancellation by either party at six months' notice. Enclosed was a second letter complaining of muddles in the Aden office for which AB held Courmont responsible. Courmont apologised for the muddles, accepted the terms offered, and assumed that the six months' notice clause would come into force at the end of the third year. AB noted the apologies; explained that the six months' notice came into force now; and concluded 'I ardently desire to see you at the head of the business, but after our experience we must have a further and longer period of trial.'

In the spring of 1919 AB left Davis in charge in Aden and took ship to Marseilles where he opened a branch office. In early June he joined Courmont in London. Any cloud threatening their friendship seemed to have rolled away and it was a happy interlude. Business was booming. As Courmont went round with AB he was struck by the effect of his charm and vitality upon all whom he met. Young candidates for the Aden office, hard-headed Scottish business men, old Baron Schroeder, head of the banking house all seemed to be won over. With women, he successfully exploited 'the salacity of being a Frenchman'. All this time AB was full of his plans for establishing a cultural centre for Aden in his house in the Aidrus Road; and he introduced Courmont to a Mrs Wilford, a middle-aged lady devoted to the arts, whom he had invited out for the winter in order to further the project.

In due course Courmont returned to Aden. AB left London for his house in Brussels. The exertions of the summer had been a strain even on his iron constitution. He was exhausted and his eyes were painful.[1] However in Brussels he had long conversations with General Dixon on the possibilities of opening up in Mesopotamia and Persia. He got through a great deal of correspondence with Stoner and others. We have letters of his to Davis in Aden, one long one on the question of staff. This, he explained, was particularly important as he intended to tackle British and German East Africa as well as Mesopotamia. Some of the new recruits in Aden seemed neither satisfied nor satisfactory: and AB was not entirely happy with the way Davis had handled them. 'I feel you do not give me credit for the good treatment of my staff, and this hurts me. . . . You might have trusted to my generosity or rather my sense of justice and waited patiently . . .'.

By the end of September AB was fit again. He seems to have felt he had completed the tasks he had set himself, and went off to Paris to see the de Coppets, whom he had got to know when de Coppet was French Minister in Addis Abeba. Mme de Coppet was great on good works. She also led an active social life, and had a number of friends in smart intellectual circles, prominent among whom was Mme Jules Siegfried, sister-in-law of André Siegfried. AB prolonged his visit. It was the first time in his life he had come into contact with such a milieu. His vitality, his charm and his reputed wealth and generosity ensured him a warm reception. He seems to have found the experience a little intoxicating. On 29 October he wrote to Courmont.

I have met some quite delightful people, such as one had never seen before, people who put you at your ease with their first words. You

seem to be up on their level, your heart glows, your spirits quicken, the best that is in you seems to blossom out. You discover in yourself all sorts of treasures you never knew of.... I have been to the Cantine Maternelle,[2] which, if I may say so, O support. I have been to see other institutions. I have been in touch with men and, in particular, with women of the very highest society unostentatiously engaged in most admirable social service. Their one thought is the good they are able to do. What wonderful people, and how one's spirits rise when one is with them. Meanness and feebleness are swept away. Anything, everything, seems possible. I have made some important resolutions and I now see more clearly how to arrange my life in future. This will cause pain to some. But it is necessary and I will not listen to the screams of my conscience...
[This last seems to indicate he had decided to break up his marriage.]

A fortnight after this letter AB paid a flying visit to London to sign his agreement with Stoner, and then took ship for Aden.

II

John Jacob Stoner was considerably older than AB. His family home was in Germany and his family name was Stein. As a young man he settled in London: and in 1894 he became a British subject by naturalisation and assumed the name of Stoner by deed poll. He was an agent and general merchant with interests in various parts of the world. His first contacts with AB must have been well before World War I; in the agreement it is stated they had been undertaking business on joint account or as agents for each other 'for many years'. The idea of partnership seems to have taken shape during AB's visit this summer. In August he wrote to Davis in Aden: 'It is most probable that I shall come to terms with Stoner instead of opening my own London office as had been my intention at one time'. A subsequent letter mentions an 'agreement with Stoner as to the working of both firms in America which should be satisfactory'.

We have a few letters between the two men dating from this period. Stoner writes 'My dear Besse', and AB replies 'Dear Mr Stoner'. Both were agreed on the supreme importance of transport. As AB wrote from Brussels on 18 August 1919 'The success of our enterprise may be greatly facilitated if we become independent for our shipping.' The two were shortly to place an order in Scotland for the construction of a diesel-engined ship of 1500 tons, and two small coastal vessels, with

semi-diesels, one of which to be fitted with twin decks for the transport
of cattle. But the immediate issue was the enormous American demand for hides and skins. The boom was on. AB was confident
that prices would rise still further. Stoner had contacts with American
tanners and glove makers. It was arranged that Stoner should cross the
Atlantic as soon as possible and open a branch or agency in Philadelphia or New York. On 8 September, when AB was recuperating in
Brussels, Stoner wrote him:

> I myself will take complete charge of the American venture .... My
> dear friend, for God's sake take a holiday and don't worry. I will
> manage the business and I want you to take life easily for the next
> three or four weeks. You need it. Do not play with your eyesight.
> Health is the most precious thing and money is nothing.

AB, in reply, urged Stoner to expedite his American visit; and himself,
as we have seen, went off to Paris.

III

The 'Deed of Arrangement for Joint Trading Adventure' between
John Jacob Stoner of 12 Mark Lane, London, and Antonie [*sic*] Besse
of 46 rue de la Tourelle, Brussels, was signed on 10 November 1919, to
come into force on 1 January 1920, be valid for seven years and
thereafter automatically renewable. Specific mention was made of The
South African Export Company, a venture of Stoner's, which was to
remain Stoner's exclusive concern. Stoner was to have a one-third
interest in the recently established Marseilles branch, AB retaining
two-thirds. Otherwise, it was laid down:

> the partnership shall comprise and include all business and trading
> transactions hitherto carried on by the partners individually or
> hereafter to be established and acquired by them ... the benefit and
> liability of all outstanding transactions and current contracts ... all
> trading transactions undertakings concessions obtained by one or
> either of them personally as if the same were expressly included and
> set forth in these presents.

Except as provided in the Deed, both parties were precluded from
undertaking any business other than that of the partnership. And

neither party might, at any time, assign, mortgage or charge his share in the partnership.

The Deed was drawn up by Stoner's solicitor. AB maintained afterwards that he had never read it; indeed if he had done so he would have insisted on his first name being correctly given. It did not occur to him to have the document vetted by a lawyer of his own. He trusted Stoner and that was good enough. It does not seem that at any time during the negotiations was it suggested that either party should produce an audited balance sheet.

IV

Back in Aden the winter of 1919–20 passed without marked incident. The strains in the Besse marriage were becoming increasingly apparent, and Alice's sympathies were all with Marguerite. Inevitably AB made advances to Alice, inevitably without success. And he must certainly have realised that her influence over her husband was stronger than his own. Both Courmonts were unhappy over AB's treatment of Little André. But, on the surface, all went smoothly. There was tennis, swimming, climbs up the hills. In the evenings there was gramophone music on the roof, or reading; AB enjoyed reading aloud and read well. There was a regular Sunday lunch in the penthouse – AB, Marguerite, the two small children (silent and timid), Mrs Wilford, the Courmonts and a newly joined European clerk. Oysters were always served on Sunday. AB would do most of the talking, with Mrs Wilford as a fulsomely appreciative chorus.

As far as the business went, demand remained brisk and AB was buying extensively. But optimistic as he always was, he felt Stoner was going too fast ahead in Tanganyika. On Christmas Day 1919, a week before their agreement came into force, he wrote to sound a note of warning:

You will have to deal with natives, half-natives and worst of all Levantines, and it is not on material of that kind that one can build anything healthy and productive. . . . it is not that I make it a financial question – it would be beneath me to do so. And I am quite prepared to stand a loss, even a big one. But I do ask you to put my letter on record.

Stoner made his trip to the States but returned without having made any definite arrangements. AB was disgusted. 'The fact', he wrote on 6 February, 'that you have backed out of your task simply means that I shall have to do myself what you have left undone. . . . There is only one way to carry out a scheme – to put one's whole heart into it.' So Davis was sent out to establish the American end of the partnership business. As the weeks went by the outlook became less rosy. Stoner, back in London, seemed always in need of liquid funds. The new Marseilles branch ran into difficulties. And brother Emile, in charge at Mogadiscio, chose the moment to announce he proposed to leave the firm and take his share out with him. He had brought no capital into the business, but now claimed 1 000 000 Rs. AB was angry. 'Having', he wrote, 'entirely by my personal efforts built up his fortune, I am not going to allow his greed to endanger my own.'

In early May 1920 AB left Aden for Europe.

7   The Crisis

It may well be that AB returned to Europe in the late spring of 1920
with his mind turned towards those exciting horizons opened up by his
Paris visit the previous autumn. Soon after arriving in Brussels he
wrote to Courmont that a turning point in his career might be at hand,
that he might be about to switch his activities to a less profitable but
more worth-while field: he wished he could be quite alone for a few
days to think things out. We have nothing more precise than this. But
for much of the summer he was constantly on the move about Europe
so that the Aden office had no idea from where his next letter was
likely to come. He seemed to be seeing a good deal of Mme Jules
Siegfried. It is possible that this was the one period of his life when his
preoccupation with his business was only intermittent.

On 8 June he informed Aden he was leaving Brussels for London for
discussions with the head office of the National Bank of India. In
Europe, he explained, everyone was talking about a slump. But a
slump, if it came, should at least cut out the weaker competitors and
put the world markets in a healthier state. After all the world was in
need of the goods that the house of Besse could supply. Aden and the
branches should go on buying whenever they could do so reasonably
cheaply, but they must be careful not to put themselves in the hands of
the banks. On 10 June he wrote from London that he had seen the NBI
and had secured a further advance, though the bank had been 'reluctant'.

Meanwhile the Marseilles branch was still in difficulties. The American end was hanging fire. Davis (in Philadelphia) had been told to
ignore Stoner and take instructions only from the Aden office or from
AB himself; but with the drying up of the American demand there was
little that Davis could do. There were delays and frustrations over the
ships under order in Scotland. An expert engaged by the two partners
to supervise the construction was proving unsatisfactory 'Kindly remember', AB wrote to Stoner, 'that you have to keep your eye on X

and check his expenses which I find exaggerated. I have received news from Aden about his friend Y who seems to be a first class rogue.' And the dispute with Emile continued. 'The greed of my brother' AB noted, 'passes all comprehension.... In our present state of affairs it would be folly not to fight for every penny we have – should we give in there will not be enough money left to continue the business.'[1]

A more immediate problem was Stoner. Stoner had been speculating (how disastrously AB did not yet know) and was drawing on the office in Aden to keep going. On 15 July AB (in London) noted. 'It pains me to see the financial position of Stoner is so weak.' A month later he wrote (from Brussels) 'At the moment Stoner is in a state of mind that makes it impossible to talk to him.' AB was now beginning to feel that once the slump was over it would be wise to think out means of dissolving the partnership. But on the world position he was not despondent. 'As to things in general I feel that Stoner as always is now exaggerating. I think the atmosphere is now more healthy, and if France had not been so mad as to support Wrangel things would be in part cleared up.'

In due course the July accounts arrived from Aden, showing that Stoner owed Besse the sum of 410 000 Rs. On 30 August AB wrote to Stoner:

> I wish very strongly that you should refrain from writing in your official correspondence that the current account in London shows any amount to my debit; you know very well that this does not correspond to the truth. Another thing I cannot approve of are your weekly drawings on Aden for trifles. As I have already told you my policy has been to tell the bankers in Aden, always and always, the whole truth, and whenever a remittance has been effected to London I feel certain Mr Courmont has told them for what it was meant. They therefore know the money was transferred to you and they cannot but feel surprised you are now drawing on me. The strength of my credit in Aden is now of such importance to yourself that you ought to do everything in your power to keep it intact.

On 12 October AB was in London and had an important interview with Baron Schroeder at the latter's bank. The following day he wrote to Courmont: 'Schroeder has specially called my attention to Stoner's character ... it would not be fair however to put the whole of the blame on the old man as a situation like the one we are in at present is altogether without precedent.' (This incidentally, is the last occasion on which we find AB finding any excuse for Stoner.) AB went on: 'I admit now I am much to blame on account of my optimism towards business and my confidence in Stoner's affairs, and there is no doubt but we shall have to pay very dearly for my mistakes.' There would have to be a drastic streamlining of the Aden end of the organisation. 'It may well happen also that we shall have to reduce the rate of salaries for everyone. Those who know me and the feelings of generosity that have always guided my actions will surely understand the great need of this. The others will be free to go.' He concludes 'If you have the impression that I am down-hearted it is a mistake. I have never felt more vividly my strength which is made up of yours and of the confidence and esteem of all who love me.'

At this stage AB made no attempt to terminate or to modify the partnership agreement, or even to clarify his position by taking legal advice. He took the first passage available for Aden, where he arrived at the beginning of November.

II

AB's first action on return to Aden was one that must have caused him much heart searching: he sold the Aidrus Road building constructed to his own design some six years previously. The purchaser was a substantial local Arab merchant with whom he was on friendly terms, and a condition of the sale was that the house be let back to AB at a reasonable rent. This arrangement worked smoothly and lasted till years after AB's death. His other real estate – the garage and workshops higher up the Aidrus Road, with the staff quarters there, and the godowns at Ma'alla remained AB's property.

Courmont was at once sent over to Africa to reorganise the firm's network in Abyssinia. On the way he contracted malaria and was laid up for a week at Diredawa. He has recorded a curious conversation with the Arab servant he had brought with him.

'When I get back to Aden,' Abdou remarked suddenly, 'Mr Besse will call me in and ask me questions. "What people did he see? Did he spend much money? Did he play cards? Did he have women?"'

'And what will you answer, Abdou?'

Abdou was silent.

III

Courmont reached Addis Abeba in late November and was soon joined there by his wife Alice. With every mail from Aden came a spate of explosive exhortation from AB. Courmont must first and foremost 'prevent a recurrence of the appalling waste that has characterised the agencies everywhere'. He must look into everything – catering, house-boys, cooks, horses, travelling expenses, office equipment. 'As for stationery, this, as you know, is wasted beyond all limits of common sense.' There was the problem of staff.

> 'You must point out to A' [acting manager in Addis Abeb] 'the number of times he has made fundamental mistakes in his judge-ment of men and things. A slight one in B, more serious in C, worse still in D' [three members of staff]. 'There is so much good in A and so little bad that we must strive, you and I, to make him see where he is at fault.' [Courmont must always take a firm line.] 'E is *not* a man to be handled softly – in fact very few are.'

Courmont was entirely in agreement. As he pointed out in his reply, the local accounts were in such a muddle that the exact position was difficult to determine. 'Our African agencies are like bottomless barrels where profits disappear with a rapidity that no firm could survive. There is something rotten in the State of Denmark.' He goes on:

> Either our recruiting is bad, or our way of working spoils the men we employ. The world is not entirely composed of incapable or dishon-est people. the great mistake has been lack of control. We have left too much liberty to our agents, and left too much money at their disposal.... One cannot get away from the fact that you made a mistake in giving F such undeserved confidence right at the beginning... what we lack is stability and continuity of personnel. That has been our great handicap. My friend, no more promises. They only tend to make people disappointed and to bring about in our staff a state of mind that we want to avoid...

The firm's organisation in Abyssinia had, of course, been entirely AB's work; one wonders whether Courmont realised how keenly he was apt to resent any criticism. The above quoted letter (dated 12 December) crossed two from AB. In one of them he wrote:

> I hope soon to organise the work here that each member of the staff shall receive such a comprehensive training that if at any time any of our men, however important, in the agencies has to be relieved, he could be replaced at once without a hitch.'

In the other he finds fault with Courmont's management in Aden during the summer.

> Since my return it has been my principal task to go into the details of the general office and house expenses. And I must tell you that the waste has been such on all sides that I am utterly appalled.

He takes Courmont to task for having raised certain salaries.

> At the end of the present month I shall inform the native staff that salaries will be reduced by one-third – those willing to stay at the lower wage being welcome to do so, and those who are not can leave the firm. If the crisis goes on for another month I shall do the same with the European staff.... I rely upon you to act with similar strength wherever you go.

At this time pressure from the bank was increasing. It was essential to dispose of the vast stocks in the Besse depots, and to collect sums owing from debtors. Courmont's task in Addis Abeba was to bring in funds to remit to Aden ... AB wrote to him on 29 November:

> If the £20 000 arrives here before the end of the month our overdraft with Gray (Aden manager of the NBI) will be under twelve lakhs for the closing of the monthly account. Gray, needless to say, is very pleased at the prospect. I shall continue to strive with all my might to reduce it to at most seven lakhs in order to have liberty of action in case of emergency.

Ten days later he wrote: 'The last private letter I had from Stoner shows a state of depression that augurs ill for our future. He appears to be literally at his wits end.' (Stoner however seems to have made some sort of proposition because on 22 December AB noted: 'I know Stoner and his foxy tricks too well to do anything for him before studying the situation myself'). The hoped for remittance from Addis Abeba was not forthcoming. On 28 December AB wrote to Courmont. 'I shall have to go to Gray again and tell him tales, an altogether hateful task for me as you will realise. News arriving each week from Stoner, from Tempier (at Marseilles) and Davis (in America) grows steadily worse and the future looks positively hopeless.' And, on 11 January 1921: 'The position is hopeless. I cannot possibly remit the £15 000 required at once. The worst can happen now ... and I am utterly helpless.'

IV

Helplessness was not one of AB's traits, but the strain came out in the increasing asperity of his letters. In any case correspondence was handicapped by the haphazard local postal service; it might be six weeks before an answer was received to any particular query. There were plenty of minor irritations. In January Courmont had a letter from an Indian in the Aden office whose pay he had raised in the autumn.

> I beg to lay down the exact words given to me by Mr Besse today at about 9.45 a.m. 'Look here, I did not know your salary was so big and so I cannot keep you any longer in the firm.' On account of my being fool to trust your words which are not worth to me at present even a single penny I lost my job.... I sincerely apologise if this letter contains any ridiculous mirror to reflect your ideas.

And then there was D, a young Frenchman in the Addis Abeba office who had turned out to be unsatisfactory. In a letter from AB his shortcomings were said to include 'criminal carefulnessless [*sic*], if not more'. Courmont asked AB to delete this phrase, but AB refused. D got hold of the letter and started proceedings in the French Consular Court. In spite of efforts to have the case stopped it came on: the Court found in favour of D, awarded him damages and ordered the firm to pay his expenses back to France.

By the new year Courmont was moved to remonstrate at the tone of AB's letters.

> Your letters do not show the calm and the sangfroid now so essential. I would like you to be convinced, once and for all, that I am not one of those in need of continual prodding. All that your reproaches – unmerited – can effect is to cause me distress. Neither you nor I can afford the time for this sort of correspondence.

To this AB made no comment.

Meanwhile Courmont still felt himself to be AB's main collaborator and adviser. He was not, of course, aware of all the ramifications of the Stoner connection; but was convinced that once that affair was settled the firm of Besse should be completely reorganised. He worked out a scheme in some detail and sent it over to Aden in a long letter dated 11 January 1921. Assuming that the firm would come out of the crisis with a capital of 1 500 000 Rs what then? He suggested that only Aden and

Mogadiscio should import and export. The smaller branches, like Djibouti, should become mere buying agencies. Aden and Mogadiscio would each require a capital of 400 000 Rs. Marseilles would need almost as much – say 350 000 Rs. This would leave something over for operations in America and in Djibouti, Hodeida, Berbera and Bombay. Abyssinia was a problem that would have to be considered on its own. The Abyssinian business, even with first-class management, would need a capital of half-a-million rupees.

AB never welcomed unsolicited advice. Again he made no comment. In his letter of 18 January he wrote:

I notice you are in the habit of using the small i for your dates. As this is not unlikely to lead to misunderstandings I feel it advisable you should use either the l or the capital I.

A fortnight later he wrote:

Another point which we differ is the necessity for an expert accountant. These so-called experts do nothing but complicate the work. Up to your arrival to take charge of Aden three years ago I was able, single handed, to run my business and keep my own books. I can come to no other conclusion but that all complications must be done away with.

A more serious difference was that over salaries. AB was and always remained convinced that an employee's loyalty to the firm should entail willing acceptance of a reduction of salary when times were bad. Courmont thought otherwise, and his own case was complicated by family commitments in France. On 13 February AB wrote reproaching him for delay over salary cuts in Addis Abeba. He himself had gone ahead in Aden with most of the Europeans. A had agreed to a cut, so had B. X, Y and Z would make no difficulties. 'And so,' AB concluded; 'there remains only yourself. And my spirit is making every effort to reject the conclusion that logic seems to impose.' Courmont replied rather sharply that he believed the agreement of the individuals named had been extorted by pressure; and that in his own case he would not agree to a reduction.

AB was due to leave for Europe in the Spring of 1921. Early in March Courmont received, along with other mail, a copy of a telegram from Aden to Mogadiscio from which it would appear that Emile Besse was to take over the management in Aden during AB's absence. Courmont was deeply hurt. On 15 March he wrote:

Mon ami.... Before you leave I would like to know what role in the business you wish me to fill. I would very much prefer to have a long talk with you. I feel that for the last few weeks we have no longer been working in the harmony that is so necessary. I have the impression that you have doubts, not only of my capacity but even of my devotion to your interests. It is this, especially, that pains me. Our collaboration must be based on absolute mutual confidence – without which it will fail. I am ready as you will know to go, and to stay, wherever you feel my presence would be useful. Allow me only to remind you that as I defended your interests against those of your brother at a time when those interests were opposed, it is quite impossible that he (Emile) should be well disposed towards me.

He concluded *'À bientôt, j'espère.'*

Courmont was at Diredawa on his way back to Aden when he received AB's reply dated 24 March:

'*Mon cher Courmont,* I have received your little note of the 15th. I find it very difficult to reply to you; although my frankness has sometimes made a void all round me I cannot change my ways which are the logical outcome of my character. In accordance with this directness I feel I must tell you that even if it is still possible for us to work together one can no longer count on this absolute and *disinterested* friendship and confidence: those feelings I fear have been tarnished – for always.... I have no idea what role in the business I can keep for you.... Be, like me, patient, and, if you can, have confidence.

We have no details of the two men's talks in Aden. The idea of Emile Besse was dropped, and it was agreed that Courmont should remain in charge. But it is clear from Courmont's record that the old friendship and confidence was tarnished, and that he realised his days with the firm were numbered. He seems to have stipulated that AB should be back by June when he proposed to take Alice, his wife, to France. He was anxious about her health and did not wish her to face another Aden summer.

At the beginning of April 1921 AB embarked, leaving Marguerite behind in Aden. He arrived in London to find Stoner penniless and a broken man, and debts of the partnership amounting to £550 000, of which more than half was unsecured.

8   The Settlement

As against the unsecured liabilities amounting to nearly £300 000 Stoner had certain unpledged assets which, it was hoped, might realise £20 000. Debts owing to the partnership came to £7000, but only some £3000 had any prospect of being collected. The creditors could be divided into five groups. There were the small creditors – some twenty of them – with claims totalling £6500. There were the shipbuilders: Thorneycrofts for the MV *Elizabeth Stoner* and the Montrose Shipbuilding Co. for the two small coastal vessels. The debts here were secured on the ships themselves, though there was room for much argument over a mortgage that Stoner had managed to raise on the bigger ship. By far the largest claims were those of the banks – Barclays, the National Provincial, the London County & Westminster, the Bank of British West Africa, the National Bank of India, Schroeders and the Swiss Bank Corporation. There was a substantial sum due to a group of West of England tanners and glove makers, for advances to Stoner on account of hides and skins. Finally there were the rubber firms: Stoner had been speculating heavily and disastrously in rubber futures.

The natural course for anyone in AB's position would have been to apply for bankruptcy. But for AB the firm of Besse was too bound up with his whole being, with his pride, with his Nietzschean image of himself as a creator. The humiliation of surrender was unthinkable. And so he deployed his formidable determination and resource for the hardest struggle of his whole career. He had throughout the friendly advice of Baron Schroeder, who, he recorded many years later, 'showed the attitude of a father rather than a banker'. But it was AB alone who thought out his scheme and who, single handed, carried through the prolonged and arduous negotiations involved in enforcing its acceptance by a mixed collection of hard headed business men who agreed only in their suspicion of any proposition put up by a partner of J. J. Stoner. When, in July, AB walked into the City office of William

Cave, of Martin and Son, Solicitors, the matter was already settled. What he required of a lawyer was not to negotiate on his behalf, but to put into legal form the result of the negotiations he had concluded. Stoner had no say in the settlement: he had merely to sign his name where he was told to sign it.

What most struck those who met AB at that time was his bearing. It may have been, as he afterwards told a friend, that the Yeovil glove makers looked at him 'as butchers look at a pig', but there was no hint of the diffidence or defensiveness that one might expect in a man who owed vast sums which he had not got. He exuded self-confidence and self-importance. As always he insisted on going to the men at the top. As always he paid no heed to the convenience of anyone else. He would then turn up when it suited him, as often as not without an appointment, and expect to be received at once and with due consideration. In his talks he was prepared to agree that the present position was unfortunate, but the fault lay with those who had been naïve enough to advance Stoner all that money. He now proposed to help them save something from the wreck.

AB produced balance sheets purporting to show that his firm's assets in Aden and the various branches were worth £100 000. This sum he proposed to pay over to the creditors, in complete settlement of all liabilities, in quarterly instalments of £5 000 each over five years. If this idea did not appeal, then the creditors could make him bankrupt and take over his assets: it was for them to choose. The deciding factor in the negotiations was undoubtably the impression made by AB's personality. But his case was helped by the nature and location of his assets. A stock of perishable produce in a godown in Hodeida or Diredawa is not very easy for anyone in London or Yeovil to turn into cash. The creditors – wisely as the event was to show – preferred to trust AB.

II

The final document or Indenture is dated August 22nd, 1921, and was registered at the Supreme Court on 29 August. The parties to it were AB, Stoner, the various creditors and three Trustees. These last had the task of receiving the remittances from AB and arranging for their distribution. All three were eminent chartered accountants, nominated respectively by the banks, the West of England tanners and the rubber interests, and approved by the creditors as a whole.

The preamble to the Indenture refers to the Deed of Arrangement of November 1919 – 'Whereas the said partnership business has not been successful and its liabilities at the present time exceed the value of its assets ... '. And later it lays down:'The claims of the said Antonin Besse by reason of large advances made by him for the benefit of the partnership and otherwise far exceed those of the said John Jacob Stoner as the said John Jacob Stoner hereby acknowledges ... '.

The next clause does not entirely tally with the wording of the original Deed of Arrangement:

Whereas the assets of the business with headquarters at Aden and with branches or agencies in various parts of Arabia and Abyssinia and elsewhere in Africa which belonged to the said Antonin Besse prior to the execution of the Partnership Deed were never treated or intended to be treated by the said John Jacob Stoner and Antonin Besse as brought into or as forming part of the said partnership business as the said John Jacob Stoner hereby admits and acknowledges. . .

Later it is expressly stated that the Marseilles branch had been established and financed exclusively by Besse from Aden.

Schedules attached to the Indenture set out the various assets and liabilities. Note is made of the declaration by Stoner that he possessed no private means outside the partnership. The crux of the settlement is contained in Clauses 5 and 10.Clause 5 runs:

The said agency or business at Marseilles and the said business of the said Antonin Besse with headquarters at Aden and the branches and agencies thereof and all the assets thereof shall be and remain vested in the said Antonin Besse for his own absolute use and benefit. And in consideration thereof the said Antonin Besse hereby covenants with the Trustees that he will pay to the Trustees out of his own moneys the sum of One hundred thousand pounds by twenty equal quarterly instalments of five thousand pounds each the first of such instalments to be paid on the thirtieth day of November 1921.

Clause 10 runs: 'In consideration of these premises the creditors do and each one of them does hereby release and discharge the said John Jacob Stoner and the said Antonin Besse and each of them from all debts due.'

Other clauses provide for the dissolution of the partnership; an undertaking by Stoner to engage in no form of business whatsoever in Arabia or in East Africa for the next ten years; and for absolute discretion for AB to run his business as he saw fit, though he must submit accounts to the Trustees if and when required by them to do so. The small creditors were to be paid out in full. With regard to the others, the Trustees should handle claims on the lines laid down by the Law of Bankruptcy – but they 'will retain the fullest discretion to adjudicate upon and determine without appeal the amount (if any) that each creditor is to receive'. In the event of disagreement among the Trustees the ruling of the majority was to prevail.

III

With the signature of the Indenture Stoner passes out of the picture. In due course he went back to Germany and managed to open up a small business in Hamburg. According to one story he spent much of his time there complaining of the harsh way AB had treated him.

Meanwhile AB's mission was not yet completed. To meet his commitments to the Trustees he needed substantial working capital. All he had was a heavy overdraft with the National Bank of India. The Bank was unhappy about the whole position. But, not unlike the Stoner creditors, they were faced with the choice of losing their money or taking a risk and trusting AB to make good. Once again it was AB's tenacity and force of character that prevailed. A special meeting of the NBI board was summoned, and AB called in to put his case to the tough Scottish directors in person. The decision taken was to grant an unsecured credit of fourteen lakhs of rupees.

In late September AB embarked for Aden.

IV

It had been a trying summer for those left behind in Aden. Exceptional heat and humidity put nerves on edge. Marguerite was in any case under the strain of the imminent collapse of her married life. Courmont was caught up in both business and personal anxieties.

The big overdraft with the Aden branch of the National Bank of India was secured on the stocks in Aden and in the various branches. Courmont's task, as acting manager of the whole firm, was to sell these stocks as and when he could and pay in the proceeds to keep the bank happy. In the early summer he discovered that two of the more important branches were making sales on their own and remitting the proceeds to an account of AB's in London and to Emile's account in Marseilles; on his demand for an explanation the branches replied they were acting under AB's express orders. Courmont was indignant at orders being passed to his subordinates behind his back, and at being put in a false position *vis-à-vis* the NBI. He wrote protesting to AB in London. Meanwhile June had come with no date yet fixed for AB's return; and Alice was so affected by the Aden summer that Courmont sent her across to stay with the branch manager in the more bearable climate of Diredawa.

AB took no notice of the matter of sales by the branches, but for the time, his letters to Courmont were friendly. He wrote at length (and with justification) of the 'superhuman' task on which he was engaged. He counselled patience and hoped to be back in Aden in a matter of weeks. In early August he wrote: 'I am distressed to see that you have had, once more, to undergo the trials and sorrows of this grim crisis. You will be able to boast of having overcome obstacles that come to a man only once in a lifetime.' When this letter arrived Courmont was in Diredawa: Alice had to undergo an operation for peritonitis in the rather primitive local hospital. The operation appeared to be successful. Courmont's one idea now was to take her back to France, and he wrote urgently to ask AB whom he should leave in charge at Aden, and to request permission to take an advance on his salary.

AB replied by return.

... although I shall soon be back in Aden I do not feel, in view of your insistence, that I can ask you to wait. You may therefore hand over the management to my wife. I would have liked to consent to your taking an advance, but I am living here with the strictest economy and in my present position any sum, however small, might be vital. I am therefore forced to refuse.... I feel you are full of rancour so I prefer, at the moment, not to say what I think. This crisis has enabled me to judge the real worth of my collaborators. I have learned, late, how much I can rely on the devotion and disinterestedness of each. The lesson will not be lost....

In late September Courmont was handing over in Aden when another telegram summoned him back to Diredawa. Septicaemia had set in. A week later Alice was dead. Courmont did not return to Aden and was never again to see AB. On 11 October 1921, when he was in

Djibouti awaiting a passage back to France, AB disembarked in Aden. That same evening AB wrote Courmont a little note of sympathy. But two days later, just as he was embarking for France, Courmont was handed a typewritten letter to the effect that he owed the firm some 8000 Rs for advance of salary, travelling expenses, doctors' fees etc. This sum, AB continued, should be paid to the firm's Marseilles agents at the rate of four francs to one rupee. AB concluded: 'I regret to trouble you at a moment when one should perhaps leave you to your grief. But as this did not prevent you from taking the money I hope it will not prevent your repaying it.'

Courmont was nettled; all the more as he calculated that, under the terms of his contract, some 35 000 Rs was due to him as his share of the profits. His ship called at Port Said in late October and he replied, rather sharply, that this was purely a matter of bookkeeping and would be adjusted when the final settlement was made. He was back in France when he received a further letter from AB dated 29 November:

> ... what various witnesses have told me of the outward signs of your grief led me to believe that your moral aberration was only temporary. Your letter shows me I was wrong. Its impudence adds to your dishonesty. Please note I have issued a writ and have had impounded your cases on the Messageries Maritime quay. The writ is a civil one, but I shall start criminal proceedings as soon as it is possible to apprehend you.

The writ was duly served in France. Courmont instructed his lawyers to put in a counterclaim for his share of past profits. Proceedings were still pending when, in late January 1922, AB wrote again to Courmont:

> 'It is not a simple difference about money. If there is anyone who could testify to my disinterestedness it should be yourself. If it were merely a financial matter my attitude would be entirely different.... When left in charge of the office you systematically allowed things to go to pieces, you ignored my instructions and took the opportunity to rob me of a substantial sum.... It is my task to inflict upon a dishonest man – a man I had heaped with kindness and whose feebleness and incapacity are notorious – a punishment that will make clear to all my collaborators the fate awaiting those who abuse my confidence....

In due course the case came on. Courmont had not brought with him extracts from the firm's accounts. His counterclaim lacked documentation. AB's lawyers produced a new set of figures drawn up by an Indian accountant in Aden whose certificate was signed in the presence of a junior Indian official of the Residency. The case trailed on, but the ultimate issue was not in doubt. Faced by mounting claims for interest, Courmont, on 27 October 1924 signed an agreement under which he was to pay 5500 Rs and 11 000 frs in final settlement.

So ended an unhappy story. The facts are not in dispute. But what it was that aroused AB's vitriolic resentment during the twenty-four hours following his return to Aden is unlikely ever to be known.

9   The Early Twenties

The year 1922 marks a watershed, both in AB's private life and in the history of the firm. Marguerite Godefroid successfully petitioned for divorce, though the ultimate financial settlement was to provoke much legal argument and lasting acrimony. It was Marguerite's investment that had turned a small firm into a big one. But in 1922 and for many years to come AB had to carry the weight of a huge overdraft. It was only after his death, in 1951, that the matter was finally settled to the satisfaction of all concerned.

As soon as the divorce proceedings were completed AB married Hilda Crowther. Hilda came of a Yorkshire father and a Scottish mother. The family had a financial set-back during the war, and she decided to earn her own living. She was employed by AB during his stays in London, and, in the early summer of 1921, came out to work in the Aden office and wait for him there. Her effective partnership and unswerving devotion and loyalty were to be an essential element of the rest of AB's life.

Meanwhile within a few months of Courmont's departure all the firm's European employees, apart from Davis, either resigned or were dismissed. General demobilisation and the impact of the slump now made it easy to find replacements.

AB and HB (as Hilda came to be known) regularly spent their summers in Europe – Davis being left in charge in Aden. Brussels of course was no longer the European base. For a time the couple had a house in Kent, Barfield, between Chislehurst and Bickley. But Barfield was cold and draughty, and a residence in England provoked the curiosity of the British Inland Revenue. For two summers the couple were at St Cloud outside Paris. But St Cloud, too, had its disadvantages. HB wanted somewhere in the South of France. AB objected that the Midi was relaxing and enervating. HB was quietly persistent. In the summer of 1925 there was the chance of renting a farm, Le Paradou, near Cavalaire between Toulon and St Raphaël. AB was induced to make the experiment – a rare instance of his being persuaded against his will. The stay was a success and when, two years later, the property came on the market AB bought it. Once it was his own his pride and delight in the place became absolute.'Like Mohamet' he was to write, 'on the subject of Damascus, I feel that if there is a sky in Paradise, if there are gardens in Paradise, they cannot excel these here.'

AB and HB had five children – Ariane, Joy, Peter, Tony[1] and Monna. When the question of their education arose HB found a house on the outskirts of Toulon so that they could go to Toulon schools. But Le Paradou, added to as the family grew, was always the family home. André meanwhile spent a few terms at Tonbridge, and in due course came out to Aden to work in the firm. Meryem too came out; from the age of seventeen she was very much a full-time employee, besides keeping house for her father when HB was in France looking after the younger children.

II

In the early twenties the firm of Besse assumed the shape and pattern it was to retain, in spite of its spectacular development, right up to AB's death in 1951. An attempt to describe it will inevitably entail over-simplification. But broadly speaking both imports and exports were under the direct and absolute control of the Aden office. In the case of imports, the agencies and branches, in Africa and Asia, put up their requirements to Aden, and it was Aden who ordered the goods, from origin, and arranged for their consignment to the ports concerned. The granting of credit to local customers was the responsibility of local managers acting, of course, under Aden's close supervision. As to exports, Aden would issue directives to the branches to govern their purchases of local produce – laying down, in general terms, quantities, qualities and prices. But the actual export of this produce was the concern of Aden. For instance Aden would advise Addis Abeba that a consignment of skins of specified qualities and weights was to be made up and despatched to Djibouti by the Chemin de Fer d'Ethiopie in time to be loaded on such and such steamer due at Djibouti on such and such date. It would be for the Besse manager in Djibouti to supervise the actual loading.

AB did not like branch managers to know the amount of profit accruing to the firm on any consignment of local produce bought by the branches for export. Accordingly the standing instructions were that on despatch of each consignment a cost invoice should be sent to Aden including a commission just sufficient to cover branch overheads. Similarly branches were not credited with the full profit on imports. The larger branches such as Addis Abeba, Mogadiscio and Djibouti kept their own profit and loss accounts and transferred their trading results to Aden at the end of the year. Smaller branches and agencies like Hodeida, Mukalla and Zeila transferred the trading results of each consignment: branch expenses and commissions were transferred at the end of each month.

Finance of course was the concern of Aden. In the case of exports to the United Kingdom, Aden would draw bills – usually 90-day or 120-day bills – on the Besse office in London and discount these bills with the Aden branch of the National Bank of India. NBI (Aden) would forward the bills to NBI (London) who would present them to Besse (London) for acceptance. Besse (London) would sign and hand to NBI (London) a Trust Receipt, take over the goods on arrival and dispose of them. Proceeds of the sales would be used to pay the bills on maturity, and the Trust Receipts would be surrendered. Imports were financed by similar arrangements in the reverse direction – Besse (London) drew bills on Besse (Aden) and discounted them with NBI (London); in due course Besse (Aden) would hand over a Trust Receipt to NBI (Aden), and take over and dispose of the goods.

Banks played only a minor role in the work of the branches. In those early days, apart from the NBI in Aden, well established banks had not yet opened branches in the Besse area. (The State Bank of Ethiopia was used by the Addis Abeba office mainly as a safe deposit to store Maria Theresa dollars.) AB's policy was for the branches to keep as far as possible imports and exports balanced; Mogadiscio, for instance, would use the proceeds of sales of piece goods and in due course kerosene for the purchase of skins and other local produce. If at any time branches needed additional funds the practice was to sell drafts on Besse (Aden) to local Indian brokers.

III

The larger branches had a European manager, though his authority was not always complete. For many years Seyid el Baharoon, a Hadhrami Arab, played a leading role in the affairs of Addis Abeba. In Hodeida Sheikh Omar Basuedan, another Hadhrami, was always the most important figure, whether or not a European was in residence.

Smaller branches and agencies were run by Arabs, sometimes by Levantines, either salaried or on a commission arrangement. Everywhere the accountants and bookkeepers were Indians: the endemic Arab–Indian incompatibility was an assurance to AB against collusion.

A Besse branch manager had plenty of problems. Conditions varied from post to post. Addis Abeba was one of the few with a congenial climate. But the town then, as now, was of great expanse; and even when not on trek to the outlying sub-agencies the manager would spend much of his time on horseback. He would open his office at 7.30 a.m. and then do a round of the hide and skin dealers. There were no means of foretelling what he would find. Peasants and farmers up country had no programme of marketing. They would load up their wares as and when they needed the money. The donkey (or more rarely) camel caravans would take days and weeks to reach the capital, and the drivers themselves on setting out had little idea when they would arrive. But in due course the hides or skins were unloaded and stacked in piles round the dealer's compound. It was for the Besse manager to assess, to select and, after protracted bargaining, to agree a price. The deal concluded he would, before going on to the next compound, mount sentries over the piles he had chosen to guard against pilfering and substitution until such time as a Besse truck arrived to collect. Next day the dealers would turn up at the Besse office for payment – each dealer, if the sale had been at all substantial, with his party of coolies with leather sacks to take away the heavy silver Maria Theresa dollars. (The weight of the MT dollars had one advantage – large sums could be sent to the State Bank by a string of porters without armed escort: the burden was such that no bandit could make a quick get-away). Meanwhile the hides purchased were cleaned, weighed and sorted under the supervision of the branch's expert sorter, and stacked in piles, according to quality and weight in the Besse godowns awaiting export. 'Sorters', AB was later to write, 'are a small cog in our big machine, but nevertheless vital.' It was up to the manager to know the sorter's job as well as the sorter himself, and to keep a constant eye on him.

On AB's visits to a branch he usually occupied the manager's house. More often than not he brought his butler, Mohamed Aly, to the great relief of the manager's wife. Mohamed Aly would take complete charge of the local servants, and ensure that the coffee was properly made and everything done according to his master's wishes. On the first day of a visit to Addis Abeba AB would call on the Emperor and on certain notables, and have a long confidential talk with Seyid el Baharoon. On the second day it would be for the manager to make himself busy elsewhere, while AB took over his private office and interviewed the whole staff, one by one, down to the drivers and storekeepers. In due course the manager would be told of as much of these conversations as AB considered he should know.

IV

In Aden there was the main building in Crater – stores on the ground floor, offices and living quarters above. In due course hides and skins were to be stored and handled at Ma'alla, but coffee, incense and myrrh continued to be treated, graded and packed in the Aidrus Road. Further up the road, near the big mosque, was the garage with its workshops and additional staff accommodation. In Ma'alla were the godowns, solidly constructed of the dark local stone and covering an ever-increasing area as the firm's activities grew.

In Ma'alla, too, was the dhow port. By the early twenties AB had his own dhow fleet, built, for the most part in his own yard on the traditional pattern with timber he himself imported from the Malabar coast. Timber amounted to half the cost of construction as local labour was cheap; a skilled carpenter would expect two and a half to three rupees a day and a labourer one rupee. AB's dhows, like so many Aden dhows, were *sambuks* with low curved stems and higher sterns; he also had a few *zaruks*, smaller, double-ended and undecked. Carrying capacity of a dhow is reckoned in packages of Basra dates of 180 lbs each. A large *sambuk* could take 2000 packages.[2]

V

In the main office HB, from the start, played an important role as AB's aide Davis, diffident, cautious and indispensable, took charge when AB left for Europe for the summer. At other seasons he was in the States or elsewhere on the firm's business. It was largely due to Davis that America, as the slump receded, became so important a customer for hides and skins. The Aden office was organised in departments, mostly with a European in charge. Clerks were Indians or Arabs; much of the firm's correspondence was in Arabic. The Accounts Department was entirely Indian. T. A. Parekh had arrived from India in 1918 as junior bookkeeper. By the early twenties he was Chief Accountant, a post where his immense capacity and resource were to have great influence on future developments. The financial secrets of the firm were known only to AB and Parekh.

Office hours were seven in the morning to four, with a break for lunch. AB was firm in his insistence on physical fitness, and at four the Europeans were expected to take exercise – tennis, swimming, climbing. Golf and cricket were not favoured: these games of course take time. Anyone with work on hand was expected back in the office in the evening to complete it. The weekly P & O from home reached Aden on the night of Saturday to Sunday, and Sunday morning was devoted to the opening, distribution and discussion of the mail. Sunday afternoon was a half holiday.

AB was always accessible, always ready to discuss any problem however minute. Newcomers soon learned it was a mistake to admit to ignorance when asked a question; much better make a guess and trust to luck. It was possible to disagree with AB. There would be a storm, but, unless he suspected some implied criticism of himself, the storm would blow over. Sometimes next day he would approve the idea that had been put to him. Sometimes he would bring it up as his own. It is not on record that anyone was ever unwise enough to remark 'But that is what I said yesterday.'

VI

Every day AB set out on his climbs up the rocky hills, his muscles taut and tough as those of an athlete in training. He read voraciously – sitting for hours at his desk, marking, copying, doodling, polishing up his translation into French of Kipling's *If*. There were his letters to HB, when she was in France with the children. 'You have chosen,' he wrote her 'very large writing paper for me. Was it intentional? I love chatting with you by letter, but I do not know that I shall always have the time to fill five of these pages.' But nearly always he did. And any delay in the arrival of a letter from HB would provoke a flurry, sharp enquiries to the Aden Post Office and the P & O, and, on occasion, an angry telegram to Marseilles.

In the firm AB seemed ubiquitous – in every department of the office, on the quays, in the godowns, in the dhow yard. Woe betide any employee not seen to be working at full stretch; or, indeed, anybody using two words in a telegram where AB thought one would suffice; or forgetting to turn off his electric fan before going to the loo. AB disliked waste. All this time he himself was working at a tempo that would have broken most men in a few months. He would get up very early, sometimes at three or four in the small hours. Mohamed Aly, his butler, with uncanny prescience, would sense his stirring; coffee was on his desk by the time AB arrived.

VII

Tension, in the early twenties, was increased by AB's ever present consciousness of his commitments under the Stoner settlement. One of his more elaborate doodles has been preserved. It is a pyramid, shaded brown and going up in twenty steps. The bottom layer shows in black ink the total outstanding – £100 000 – and in red, the date, 1 December 1921. The next layer shows £95 000, and the date, March 1922; and so on up to the summit, where the debt has been paid off. Above is a five-pointed star (one of AB's favourite markings) and on either side a quotation: 'Though deep yet clear, Though gentle yet not dull; Strong without rage, Without o'erflowing full.' In the spring of 1925 HB, expecting a baby, left Aden early, and AB wrote to her:

Life goes on here as you have lived it. Not an hour of respite, driving on and on, a new decision to be taken every instant. As you so rightly said, my work is 'greedy', enormously so. I have moments of loneliness which frighten me. This constant tension, this constant state of war, can build up in me another self, can deaden those finer qualities of heart and brain which I feel ready to blossom out in me but which I insistently have to repress even though I am afraid I am killing them. When I think you have already been away a fortnight I am terrified. Time presses on and in spite of this ceaseless activity one feels one is not living. In fact it is true that one does not live: one acts without any consciousness of acting. Well, another eighteen months and perhaps – perhaps – I shall be beginning to get myself clear of this pitiless involvement. By the time this letter reaches you I shall be ready to mount one more step – the fifteenth – of this long and painful climb. And then I shall be looking with anguish at the five steep distant steps to come. No one can understand what this pyramid means to me: and I started to go up with so light a heart and so full of strength and confidence! Never mind: I shall reach the top.

But before this letter was written and long before reaching the top of his pyramid AB had launched out on a new venture, involving him in a new and very heavy commitment.

10　Shell

I

In the years immediately following World War I the consumption of
petrol in the areas where AB traded was small; motorised transport on
any scale was yet to come. Of far greater interest to the big oil
companies was kerosene (paraffin), for which the demand was already
substantial. In 1922 the local market was dominated by the Standard
Oil Company of New York. There were, as yet, no shipments in bulk.
Supplies were shipped in 'units', a unit comprising two four-gallon cans
packed together in a wooden case or crate. From 240 to 300 gallons
(according to the product) made up a ton. SOC products were despatched, two or three times a year, in very large consignments, from
Port Arthur in Texas. Most of the units were landed at Aden where
SOC had a large warehouse. Some went on to Hodeida. At Aden (and
Hodeida) cases were loaded on dhows, or on the minute and aged
steamers run by Cowasjee Dinshaw, for conveyance to the smaller
Arabian and African ports. From there supplies for the interior were
sent on by donkey or by camel.

By 1923 the Texas Oil Company (now merged in Caltex) had
acquired a small share of the trade. The participation of the Anglo-
Persian Oil Company (now BP) was largely confined to bunkering at
Aden.[1] Shell's total sales in the whole area amounted to only seven
hundred tons a year.

At this time the marketing side of Shell was the Asiatic Petroleum
Company. The shipping side was The Anglo-Saxon Petroleum Company. Asiatic had a number of subsidiaries, such as The Shell Company
of Egypt. These subsidiaries all had offices in London alongside the
parent company. But the man who really counted, the senior executive
in charge, was the Shell Representative in Cairo, who, with his staff,
controlled Asiatic's activities (and, to a great extent, Anglo-Saxon's)
throughout the Middle East.

II

R. C. Martin was Representative in Cairo when, early in 1923, Shell
decided to appoint a new agent to handle their business in Aden, the
Protectorate, the Yemen and the Hejaz; and, on the African side, in
the three Somalilands, Eritrea and Ethiopia. Martin saw fit to visit
Aden and have a look at possible candidates on the spot. He had, he
recalls, two main requirements in his mind as he set out in May. It was
the peasants up country who wanted kerosene. An agent confining his
activity to a big port would miss most of the business. He must have his
network of subagents and traders deep in the interior, to get at the
villages. Furthermore he must be in a position to finance his operations. Shell, as was constantly asserted, were not moneylenders.

Martin's first impressions of Aden were unfavourable. The sea in the
harbour was slimy. Pitiless heat seemed to radiate from the ragged hills
behind. Along the dusty waterfront squalid little shops sold tourist
souvenirs. Mangy camels dragged rusty iron water tanks. The one
hotel was dingy and its celebrated stuffed mermaid quite revolting.
Martin went the round of the established shipping and trading firms in
Steamer Point, British and Parsee. They were prosperous: agency
work, lighterage and storage brought in a substantial income. What
appeared lacking was any aggressive urge to seek out and exploit new
business. From gossip in the hotel bar and in the Union Club the most
disliked man in Aden seemed to be a certain Besse. Martin called at the
National Bank of India to make enquiries. The manager told him he
was scared whenever Besse came in. The man was more bankrupt than
anyone he knew. But any money he wanted from the bank he could
have, any time he wanted it.

Martin took a cab to Crater. The Aidrus Road was dusty and
unkempt. Goats, hens and grubby little children scratched for finds
among the rubble. Up in the penthouse AB was sitting at a small desk
at the far corner of his huge office – short, dark, thickset, meticulously
laundered. To Martin he looked like a small and distant Buddha.
Martin explained he was looking for an agent to handle Shell products.
AB said he would undertake it. Martin went on that a considerable
outlay would be involved, and he understood the firm of Besse was
insolvent. AB flared up. But soon they were talking business again,
and before very long agreement was reached.

III

In October 1949 AB wrote one of his marathon letters to a senior
executive of Shell in London. Below are extracts.

I wish this letter, which is in the nature of a last testament, to be read with the respect due to a lifetime of tireless striving towards perfection of an organisation which I consider today to be almost complete, and during the building of which Shell interests have always been placed before those in my own firm.

It is now upwards of a quarter of a century since R. C. Martin called on me in Aden and offered me your representation. At that time, incredible though it may appear today, nobody knew anything about Shell. [There follow uncomplimentary remarks about previous attempts to sell Shell products].... To take over your agency in these conditions meant a great deal of uphill work, and the aim of introducing your brands widely appeared almost unattainable. My own task was rendered all the more difficult in that I had just lost everything I possessed through the swindle of a Jewish firm to which my affairs in England had been entrusted.

Having taken stock of the situation, and realised the obstacles to be overcome, I summoned all my Arab friends and asked for their support. But this was a failure. At that time, Standard Oil reigned supreme in these territories; they had no competition to contend with.... The idea of challenging and defeating such a giant seems preposterous; but fortunately for us we found a powerful ally in the vanity and stupidity of A, who felt so sure of himself that he never gave a thought to what I was doing until it was too late.

It did not take long to realise that practically the only weak spot in their armour was the landing of oil, in very large quantities at a time, at Aden and Hodeidah, whence it had to be transported all over the Red Sea by dhow, or by Cowasjee Dinshaw. The only means by which I could compete was to build a small ship myself, to ply between Suez, where Shell supplies were available and all the small Red Sea ports – Confudah, Loheya, Kamaran, Mokha, Khokha and also Mukalla, Sheher and Berbera.

I submitted my idea to your Head Office but they would have nothing to do with my scheme. So I set about scraping together all the pennies I could, obtained a loan from the NBI (my Bankers) and had the MV *El Halal* built. Being an utter layman in such matters, I foolishly allowed myself to be guided by the suggestions of B.... We had endless trouble. Not a voyage was effected without some mishap, and as there was no wireless on board the number of sleepless nights I spent, whenever the ship was overdue, were incalculable. Moreover, the running expenses were enormous, and the commission I earned on the sale of the oil did not cover half of them...

Nevertheless, due to the fact that all the small ports were now being supplied regularly with an excellent quality oil, fresh from your Suez installation and fully equal to the American product, in brand new tins and cases, the situation was rapidly changing in our favour...

It is perhaps necessary to point out here that both Aden and Hodeidah have very damp climates, and that unless tins are inspected and carefully greased at frequent intervals they rapidly deteriorate and considerable leakage ensues. The SOC had discovered to their cost that, when large supplies were landed at these ports, after a few months scarcely a tin remained undamaged. Many of them, indeed, lost more than half their contents, and their appearance when they were sold was anything but inviting. Very soon the native dealers, seeing that they could obtain supplies from us in new cases and bright tins, whose contents were still intact, ceased to take any interest in the SOC's product, even at reduced prices. Indeed, the position now was completely reversed, and instead of being obliged to accept one rupee less per case for the Shell product, I often obtained a rupee more.

As was to be expected, your trade expanded rapidly, and before very long I found that the one small ship I had had built was no longer adequate. I decided to build a second and larger unit, and this time London showed a better understanding of the problem and agreed, against a mortgage on the new ship as well as on *El Halal* and my business, to advance me the money necessary to build *El Amin*. No sooner was this vessel in commission than the field of our operations was extended still further, and she was kept busy plying up and down the Red Sea, until she ran aground on a rock off Suez. Getting her off was an expensive business, and the subsequent repair bill was crushing. The result of that accident was an immediate and sharp drop in Shell's Red Sea trade, and London, now fully awake to what was at stake, made no difficulty when I asked them for help to build my third ship, *El Hak*, under the supervision of your Superintendent Engineer.

With these three ships at my command we made wonderful headway, and the day dawned finally when I was able to write to London that we had 72 per cent of the whole of the Red Sea trade in our hands.

What stands out in all this is AB's vision: he saw at once that the crux of the problem was to get the product and its containers, in good condition, within reach of the customers.[2] And there is his courage in adding so substantially to his heavy liabilities by the construction of *El Halal*. To have ships of his own was of course of enormous advantage in AB's other business. But he had no need to point this out in a letter to Shell.

IV

As we have seen, before AB took over the agency Shell sales in his area were 700 tons a year. In 1928, thanks largely to *El Amin* they had risen to 5400. *El Hak* reached Aden on her maiden voyage at the end of 1929 and the figure for 1930 was 6700. This was to rise to 26 200 in 1935 and to 46 900 in 1945.[3] For the first few years supplies came from the Suez refinery. A few days before the arrival of a Besse ship at Suez a telegraphic order from Aden would specify categories and quantities. When loaded the ship would proceed down the Red Sea discharging at the various ports of call. (Every inch of space not required for oil products had of course to be utilised for other Besse cargo.) Timing and routing of the voyages was for the Aden office. Shell products were shipped on consignment: until sold they remained the property of Shell. Every month Aden would send Cairo a statement together with remittance for oil sold, less freight, lighterage, storage, leakage and damage, commission and other charges. Credits to local customers were AB's own concern, to be financed by him.

Arguments over freight rates were often heated and went on for years. In any case lack of port facilities make Red Sea rates abnormally high. 'It is a fact,' wrote a visiting Shell man in 1928, 'that *El Amin* sometimes has to waste three days unloading 2000 cases at some Yemeni port, which at an upkeep of 725 Rs a day means a loss for Besse on the freight quoted.' AB maintained he had built his ships for Shell and was losing money on them. From time to time he threatened to give them up and leave Shell to run them. It does not seem this threat was taken very seriously in St Helen's Court. Shell's handling of AB throughout was extremely skilful. 'Besse's motives', runs an internal memorandum, 'must always be assumed to be noble, whatever the actual sins of commission may be. . . . If he feels he is with friends he will give of his utmost.'

There was bound to be plenty of incident in any close association with AB. 'The Shell Statistical & Accounts Department,' he noted, 'has become an excrescence which saps the life of the firm and impoverishes its vitality.' And then the strictest economy on telegrams was always one of the pet bees in AB's bonnet. Shell's lavishness provoked indignant expostulation. We have a letter to Martin. 'I really think it my duty to draw your attention to the criminal waste of money Cairo is guilty of in the shape of totally unnecessary telegrams ... a system of wastefulness which makes my heart bleed.' Meanwhile, in Aden, AB and his staff spent hours in devising codes and streamlining outgoing cables, with results not always easy to decipher by the recipient. Shell offices resented the time taken up in trying to make out what AB meant, when the meaning would have been perfectly clear had he only been willing to spend an extra couple of shillings.

On the other hand AB never minded how long were his letters. These would be page after page of argument, protest, criticism and advice, going into the most insignificant detail. Reception at the Shell end was mixed. Some of the younger men were apprehensive. Others were interested to see what the old boy was up to now. Of course a suggestion might be sound enough from the limited angle of Aden, but not fit in with the world policy of the Shell head office. Then there was the time involved. Martin once told AB that he had not the time to read his letters. Other executives were less abrupt. AB was apt to reinforce his letters with long lectures to senior Shell managers whenever he called on them. Martin was asked to do what he could tactfully to discourage over-frequent visits to St Helen's Court.

But the association was a happy one. It became extremely profitable to both parties. Shell throughout showed tact and judgement. It became understood in London and in Cairo that inquisitiveness over AB's accounting might cause trouble. AB was impressed by the 'gentlemanly' aura that Shell rather consciously diffused. Towards the end of his life he was to write: 'The agency of Shell is invaluable to the firm for a host of reasons. It is at the same time a source of joy and pride to be associated with a concern whose leaders are so liberal minded, so fair and so easy of access.'

11 A Secondment

I

The technicalities of the oil business made it desirable that Shell should have one of their own men seconded to AB's office in Aden – all the more so in view of the organisational developments that were shortly to come. In 1928 Shell and Anglo-Persian agreed to merge their marketing. A new Company – The Consolidated Petroleum Company – was formed to implement the agreement. Management was to be in the hands of Shell; and so Shell's Cairo Representative became Representative for Consolidated and Besse became Consolidated's agent. Shell sales and Anglo-Persian sales in his area were integrated under his Aden office. Shell meanwhile decided to establish an ocean depot at Port Sudan, and, when this was completed in 1930, Shell products in their Gazelle containers were shipped from there and no longer from Suez. Anglo-Persian products, in cans marked with a Palm Tree, were shipped from Abadan. It was also about this time that the Standard Oil Company of New York merged with Vacuum Oil to become Socony Vacuum.

II

One of Shell's problems in dealing with AB which lasted for the whole of their association, was the selection of men to work in the Aden office. It was not a question of competence: the Red Sea business was far too important for Shell to nominate anyone they were not convinced was up to the job. It was purely a matter of personality. And here AB was quite unpredictable. Three days after X's arrival Cairo might receive a cable 'This man is a swine.' Y on the other hand might appear to have made a good start; and then, after a couple of months, AB would abruptly turn against him and demand his instant recall. No explanation would be forthcoming. As often as not AB would maintain that the man 'was not a gentleman'. But who would and who would not qualify as a gentleman in AB's eyes was something impossible to foretell.

Perhaps the most successful secondment of all was that of EM, who was in Aden from March 1929 to June 1930. He had heard of his predecessor's experiences, and so setting out he noted: 'I am lent to work with and under Besse. On the face of it there seems the slenderest chance of my pulling it off.' But he was over-pessimistic. Here are extracts from his diary:

10 March 1929	Mrs. Besse met me on the pier, and AB and she have been charming. Early afternoon we (AB, Mrs. and I) started off up to the spurs behind Crater. We walked and sweated and scrambled, steep mountains of basic volcanic rock, all along the southern face overlooking the sea till we dropped down to Sharks Bay.
11 March	Just back from dinner with Besse and his wife. We discussed the world of men after an excellent dinner. A *truly* remarkable man, Besse. A great idealist and man of imagination.
14 March	Besse and his wife have taken me some fascinating climbs round the volcano which is Aden... They are unfailingly charming to me.
8 April	Ride and climb and tennis.
10 April	The Besses continue charming and I sup with them regularly.
17 April	I am finding business all absorbing. (Later) Went for a heavenly ride with Mrs. B.
27 April	Mr. and Mrs. Besse and I ran round in the launch to Deep Bay. After supper we listened on the roof to the First Act of Tristan... Then AB read in old French the first part of the story ...
5 May	I have had lots to write but haven't: about the time AB got lost in the mountains and we were out till one o'clock searching with lanterns ...
9 May	This evening I ran from Crater to Sharks Bay, up at least 1000 feet and down to the sea, in exactly 45 minutes. This beats all records.
26 May	A delicious philosophical supper with the Besses. The last Act of Tristan.
30 May	AB leaves tomorrow or the next day.
31 May	AB wants me to run his business in a controlling capacity and has granted me full powers in writing.
2 June	AB and HB left today and I love them both a deal. I love AB as a second father and I wonder if it will last.

There were reasons for this happy state of affairs. EM was young. He came up to AB's strict standard of physical fitness. He was a good tennis player and a fearless climber. He was an accomplished swimmer. (A glimpse of lurking sharks made him chary of AB's favourite waters, but AB forgave him this.) He had an ardent and genuine appreciation of much that meant so much to AB – landscape, music, books, long discussions about life. Above all there was AB's charm, irresistible when he liked anybody and knew that that person liked him. We must also remember AB's insistently proclaimed dream of retiring from active participation in the business and devoting his life to culture and the arts. But rather than see his firm unworthily managed he would, as he so often asserted, 'pull down the whole edifice with his own hands'. Hence his quest for a successor. The Courmont experiment had been a failure. There was always the supremely competent Davis, but Davis in AB's eyes lacked the fire and the drive he considered so essential. He was now beginning to hope he had found what he wanted in EM.

That year, 1929, AB and HB returned from France in October. Their ship called at Port Sudan, and EM went there to come back to Aden with them. Here are further extracts from his diary:

19 October   (SS *Moldavia*) I have just turned down an offer of £1600 a year and a probable partnership. We sat side by side in Besse's cabin. (I had had two days to think it over – as a matter of fact I have been thinking for six months). . . . I went on to explain the pros and cons and we discussed them. He is a wonderful man. At times I had a lump in my throat.

27 October   (Back at Aden): Last night AB continued reading Tristan in marvellous French.

9 November   After supper with AB Louise and Petrouchka[1] joined us, and AB read aloud the latter part of Tristan and Isolde. I don't remember when I have been so moved. We went indoors and played the last piece of the opera, which finished me . . .

10 November   Learnt from Parekh the amazing story of the firm of Besse. 1920 and the other misfortunes surmounted. I feel an intense desire to take hold of the firm and guide it along the lines of its glorious tradition. If it was not for Aden and what Aden means[2] I think I would. What a unique and splendid business. And this is the man with all his enemies. Anyway I admire

and love him. .... As an average the firm now earns
£30 000 profit a year in bad times and twice or more
in good ....

11 December   This evening we had the Seventh Symphony after a
              climb in the hills, then supper and AB read 'Hyalis'
              by Albert Samain and other poems of his. Then we
              discussed poetry, English and French, and music ....

On Christmas morning EM found in his room a copy of Joseph
Bedier's *Tristan et Iseult* with an inscription in AB's handwriting:

'May this wonderful story, which we read together under our
splendid sky, remind you when you are far away of the peace
surrounding us, of our sincere and deep affection; and may it inspire
in you the will to live a dangerous and heroic life, the only life worth
living.'

Perhaps these last words should have been a hint to EM – then under
orders to visit Cairo for consultations – that AB never thought the
same again about a man who refused a chance to throw in his lot with
the firm of Besse.

To return to EM's diary:

27 December   In the afternoon one of the best climbs in the hills
              with AB and HB alone. I discovered a new way to the
              summit.
28 December   In the afternoon *El Hak* arrived.
New Year's   AB is getting through mountains of work – too much
    Day 1930 and his nerves are badly frayed. I don't like his
              continued depression. It makes him definitely less
              attractive.
18 January   Dined with the girls with the Besses on the roof and
              listened to ordinary sounding music of Debussy on
              the gramophone. ... To Cairo in a week today. I long
              to get to Egypt and away from Aden. Much though I
              love and admire AB I am profoundly glad I have not
              thrown in my lot here.
19 January   Had my first serious row with AB. I recognise and
              admire the motives from which he acts, but he can't
              walk roughshod over everybody. Answering insult-
              ingly a letter addressed to me. And he doesn't realise

he lets me down. Truly the great big Egos cannot keep men of character near them, but must surround themselves with nonentities. Now I am under a cloud and I feel that the friendship between me and them both is strained.

23 January (on SS *Rajputana*). The evening before leaving I had a long talk with AB, HB also in the room. It appears to them I have changed and that the frost of the last few days is mine and not theirs. So be it. . . . The thing that has done it is his monstrous egotism – the essence of great men, it seems to me. I always knew it, though it was never directed against me till the other day; I should have fought it to the death. It is a very good thing my instinct told me not to join him. . . . I wonder if he realises that if the spirit of the Maison Besse has been so pleasant on the whole it is in quite a measure due to me. I have a sort of youth and gaiety that they all lack.

EM spent a month in Cairo. In early March he was back in Aden and life seemed to renew its earlier pattern:

3 March Supper en masse on the Besse roof – music capped with the Prelude of Lohengrin.

17 March All day we climbed . . .

22 March Last night after a lovely afternoon on the hills, a delicious supper on the roof with the Besses, and music, such music . . .

For most of April EM was away on a tour of the African agencies.

29 April First day back in Aden – Joy of meeting people again, especially AB and HB. But after a delightful supper with the Besses, one of the staff tells me AB thinks I have been playing him false. Rage, Bitterness, inward tears and sorrow . . . .

1 May Of course I had it out with AB yesterday. He thinks no such thing. So the blow did not fall. He is fond of me – she also – but relations are not of the depth they might be – that they are in my imagination. . . . Last night a dull all-staff party on the roof.

EM was now finally recalled to Cairo. Here is the last entry in his Aden diary:

10 June — I love AB – I have said that before – for many reasons. The last days we have come together again nearer in sympathy. He has so much that is splendid. But I still feel that I could not live with him without suffering from the crushing weight of his personality. ... Last night when I went to bed late I found by my bedside a little note in rounded spidery writing and a cheque for £200. I slept on it tho' my emotion was great. ... I knew that I wanted a present from AB, not a slice of the money the firm needs so badly at present. I went up and put it to him. He was moved; and went and altered it to £100: then wouldn't budge. The last two evenings on the roof have been as beautiful as any. Delicious food, exquisite wine and coffee, a man I love and around us friends, the poetry of Samain or the music of César Franck, a soft clear moon, the high dark shoulders of the ridge ....

On the voyage back to Suez EM read, on AB's recommendation, the poems of Samain and *Thus Spake Zarathustra*.

12   The Depression

On 5 February 1930, AB wrote to one of his Shell friends in London:

> When *El Hak* arrived out here a few weeks ago the trade crisis
> assumed undreamed of proportions and one after another the
> products of these regions decreased to 50% of their recent value,
> Hides and Coffee (the main articles of export) dropping to one-third
> of the figures formerly obtained for them. This state of affairs
> naturally resulted in the reduction to almost zero of the native's
> purchasing power, and at present he is buying nothing but the bare
> necessities of existence, with the unhappy result that the sale – and
> consequently the transport – of your products (considered in the
> poor countries in which we are established still as a luxury) as well as
> of the large majority of Import goods, has fallen to a fraction of its
> former volume. Our ships are plying up and down the Red Sea,
> keeping to their itinerary, empty . . .
>
> To the heavy losses entailed by this state of affairs must be added
> those, just as crushing, which we have had to face on the stocks of
> merchandise which we have perforce always to keep at each of our
> many branches, and as all sales have to be effected on credit terms it
> is only by nursing the native merchant that we can hope to get our
> money back. Silver has depreciated so enormously, moreover, that
> his capital, which is in MT dollars, has dwindled by 33% – a factor
> which still further reduces his purchasing power and, incidentally,
> affects us very adversely at the end of each month when we calculate
> the amount of the remittance which has to be made to you . . .
>
> I can safely state, in short, that EVERYTHING has worked
> against us.
>
> The strain on the firm's finances is terrible, and I have been
> obliged to ask our bankers to increase their support, which means
> that we are no longer in a position to discuss as we should like to do
> the rates of exchange and interest they charge us on our Bills and our
> Overdraft . . .

AB was never one to understate his case, and the point of this letter was to get Shell to modify the conditions of the loan for the construction of *El Amin* and *El Hak*. But the depression hit the firm very hard. AB, as so often, was overtrading and his huge stocks showed an increasing loss as the market moved against him. There were contributory factors. The Halal Shipping Co. was going through its teething troubles, and the rapid turnover in ships' personnel did not help: in spite of the slump few really first class ships' captains or engineers seemed to want to serve in the Red Sea on the terms and conditions AB considered reasonable. There was also Soviet competition in the oil trade to the Yemen, where in 1931 the Russians secured 38% of the business as against Shell's 57%. AB visited the Yemen and sent a long report to Sir Stewart Syme (one of the few Aden Residents with whom he was on friendly terms). While there he had several talks with the head of the Soviet Trade Mission. 'Balkan is not an intelligent man in the real sense of the word. He is cute; he is shrewd. But he overdoes it.' AB was not perturbed about the long-term threat of Soviet competition; but he was disgusted when Consolidated, in view of the slump, came to an understanding with Standard Vacuum and Texas to stabilise their respective shares in the trade throughout the whole area. AB regarded this 'As Is' agreement as tying his hands in his battle with his main competitors: and for years there were angry rumbles in his correspondence with Shell.

The slump of 1930 did not hit the firm so hard as the Stoner affair of 1920. There was a joke going round the Indian brokers in Aden 'Mr Besse has pledged his trousers to the NBI', but Parekh's confidential balance sheets showed that at no time did the firm's liabilities exceed its assets. Steps were taken to meet the crisis. With *El Amin* (726 tons) and *El Hak* (1022 tons) in commission there was no longer need for *El Halal* and she was sold in 1931. Davis for two years volunteered not to draw his salary. Parekh drew up a scheme for a reduction of 20–25 per cent in the pay of all non-Europeans in the firm; and this was put into effect without a murmur from any of those involved. But it was not AB's nature merely to retrench and await events. He was, throughout, exploring every possibility for expansion. By 1932 the agencies held by the firm, apart from Shell, included Chrysler, Goodyear, Underwood and I. G. Farben; and the list was growing. He went into the sugar business in a big way, and was planning to cut out the London brokers by direct contact with Java ('thus freeing us of brokerage and avoiding the feeling that our business is communicated to everybody'). He went into the pilgrim trade, conveying the faithful from African ports to

Jedda for the annual pilgrimage to Mecca. A minor but profitable line was the trade in waste paper. There was a demand throughout his area for old newspapers which AB bought in London and shipped out. The actual trading transactions usually showed a loss; but the freight earned by the *El Hak* and the *El Amin* made the business very well worth while.

II

All this time AB was living his usual life, getting up very early and doing four or five hours of intensive work before breakfast. He would have his elevenses, thin buttered toast with plenty of salt, brought him by Mohamed Aly or by Meryem. In the afternoons he would climb in the hills. It was at this time that Evelyn Waugh visited Aden and took part in that all too strenuous expedition he was afterwards so delight-fully to describe.[1] Freya Stark came a little later, and was considerably impressed.[2] She got into AB's good books by her fearless climbing. 'Mrs Ingrams and Freya Stark', AB wrote to HB, 'followed me everywhere.'

But the period was one of strain. AB had fits of depression, and he missed HB when she was back in France with the children. He wrote to her:

I used to like being alone. It has helped to form my character. To be quite alone is bearable, but among all these young people here who cannot understand, with whom one has continually to strike an attitude (*plastronner*) – then it becomes painful. But I must not complain.... Perhaps these times when you and I are apart are necessary, a sort of shade to bring out all the brightness of when we are together.

By mid-1932 the business outlook was more favourable. Even the cautious Davis was optimistic; and in August AB wrote to him from Le Paradou.

You have yourself expressed the opinion that we were in for better time.... It is only fair if, indeed, we have turned the corner, that the staff throughout the firm, starting first and foremost with yourself, should have their salaries raised. If our hopes concerning the future do not materialize and it takes longer to free ourselves from the clutches of the NBI and pay our debt to the Anglo-Saxon than I had imagined, so much the worse.... The contentment of the staff, including yourself, has always been and will remain so long as I am at the head of the firm, paramount.

You are aware that I have not so much as a penny set aside myself, and, although I have seldom mentioned the subject to you, my indebtedness to the Bank and the Anglo-Saxon preoccupies my mind constantly. I shall remain in the firm, health permitting, until the position is absolutely sound and independent, but when that day comes there will have to be a change.... Having brought the ship safely into port, I shall leave the bridge for ever.

13   Staff

I

We have a letter, dated late 1927, from one of the French girl
secretaries in Aden, encouraging a friend of hers, Louise le Brozec, to
accept a job with the firm.

> ... I can only repeat I am very happy here, and so, I am sure, will you
> be. Monsieur Besse is sometimes rather difficult. He is human, but
> human also in the best sense of the word. He can make mistakes, but
> one must remember that he means well, and that he is really good
> and generous. Madame Besse's charm has nothing superficial about
> it – she is all kindness and graciousness.

In due course Louise joined the firm in Aden and was a great success.

Not all secretarial appointments worked out so happily. Years later
Ina Marek described her ex-employer as 'very much a Frenchman, and
a Southern Frenchman at that'. (HB was aware of and accepted this
aspect: their marriage was never in danger.) And so from time to time
there was an abrupt and unexplained resignation. Stories went round
Aden and some of them got back to London. In 1929 *The Times*
refused to accept the firm's advertisements for secretarial vacancies.
Passport officers and consuls were instructed to warn girls proceeding
to Aden to work for the firm. AB lodged an angry protest with the
Resident and received a non-committal reply.

When Ina Marek, Petrouchka as she came to be called, applied for a
visa at the British Consulate in Geneva she was duly warned. She
decided to take the risk, and did not afterwards regret her decision.

Petrouchka recalls (perhaps rather surprisingly) that her work in
Aden was not all that exacting; and after office hours there was tennis,
bathing, picnic parties. There were occasional staff dinners in the
penthouse – hors d'oeuvres in aspic, roast chicken with tinned peas,
tinned fruit with ice cream and a savoury. Unlike her male colleagues
she did not feel a sense of relief when AB embarked for France in the

spring; it seemed rather dull when he was away. 'He used', she says, 'to flirt with the girls, but the boys all had to be supermen.'

When she left to get married in 1931 AB gave her a small volume of Mistral's poems with an inscription in his spidery handwriting:

Mireille, hymn to the glory of Provence, where all is light, clarity and perfume. There every line is pure, clean, defined, vision is unblurred and thought precise and logical. May this book become a source of inspiration and support to the confused and wayward Slav soul to whom it is offered. Plus est en vous.

In later life Petrouchka worked for other self-made tycoons, and says it was all very much like working for AB.

II

The young men, for the first three or four years (and few of them lasted longer), were paid £150 a year with lodging, laundry and meals in the staff mess run on economical lines by Mohamed Aly. AB maintained this was ample. Cotton clothes, run up by an Indian tailor, subscription to the Tennis Club and petty expenses should not come to more than £5 or £6 a month. Swimming and climbing were free. Any idea of joining the Union Club (and all that that entailed) was not for members of the firm of Besse.

AB believed that he was generous. But the fact remains that his salaries to Europeans were lower than those of the other firms in Aden. His ships' officers were paid less than the corresponding grades in the Anglo-Saxon fleet. It is true there were ex-gratia payments and these could be substantial. When Jeff Collins went off on leave to Europe after his first three years on £150 p.a. he was given an envelope to open when on board; it contained a cheque for £750. All the same Maurice Weerts, who was with the firm for fifteen years and who rendered outstanding service during the Abyssinian crisis, reckons that his salary and gratuities combined were certainly not more than he would have had from another firm. But there is no record of resignation on the score of salary alone.

On AB's death Davis was to write: 'To him, to give someone work in his firm meant, if they did it thoroughly, an immense improvement in their life; and certainly he felt he was uplifting them as much as is possible in this world.' But there was the difficulty of communication.

AB relished the role of mentor to the young, and at one time in 1934, in spite of HB's misgivings, he inaugurated staff meetings to expound his philosophy of life. The experiment was short-lived. 'Alas,' he wrote to HB, 'one is too remote. Our words do not mean to these young people what they mean to us. When one talks to them they sneer. One reads it in their eyes.' It was a profound disappointment to him.

In two of AB's letters to Shell are tributes to his staff, and indeed the firm could never have developed and prospered the way it did without a number of highly competent people working for it. Yet a great deal of the firm's internal correspondence is taken up with AB's bitter complaints of staff shortcomings. In his weekly marathon letters from Le Paradou in the summer to Davis in Aden is often a paragraph listing individuals with a derogatory comment on each.

A: Lack of manners and refinement. Incurable habit of sneering and jeering. An undesirable influence. B: That he will make a mess of things is a foregone conclusion. A fatuous gasbag. C: Just the spoilt baby he always has been. D: Morally a very big question mark. E: No devotion to the firm – his interest revolves round his own unimportant little person.

And so on.

AB of course was a formidable personality. Paul Nizan, who spent a few unhappy months in Aden in the late twenties as tutor to young André, notes that his presence brought 'an atmosphere of grim foreboding (présage mortel)'.[1] Many of the young men were afraid of him, and this brought out the streak of sadism in his character. Sturdier spirits were up against his possessiveness, his urge to dominate, in and out of office hours. Collins wrote to a colleague in 1933: 'The one thing he can't stand is that things should work smoothly without his continual interference.'

But perhaps the most important factor in the constant staff turnover lay in AB's sudden, often inexplicable, revulsions of feeling. Up to the last few years of his life he turned against every European working for him, and that, for the individual concerned, was the beginning of the end. Oddly enough, in view of his frequent invocation of the Nietzschean precept 'Be Hard', AB was apt to avoid a head-on clash. The task of dismissal would be delegated to a branch manager, or the subject needled into resignation. There were cases where a man first learned he was to go by seeing a newspaper advertisement for his successor.

Quite a number of men who worked for Besse went on to highly successful careers elsewhere. Apart from Jeff Collins' CBE there is no recorded comment by AB on such cases. For him the discards were failures, to be written off. For the men themselves bitterness was often lasting. An enquiry to one of his former senior managers brought the reply: 'My years with Besse are those I am most anxious to forget.' But on the other hand Charles Fenn (of whom more later) was to write in after AB's death:

His stimulating leadership went far beyond the limits of the work; and for my part I know that his influence lasted a very long time after I left Aden. There is an awkward pride that prevents one making such admissions in a man's life-time. But they remain none the less true.

14   The Title Deeds

It was in early 1933 that two of AB's young men, Charles Fenn and Jeff Collins, staged the nearest approach to a successful revolt that ever took place in the Besse office. AB went off for a tour of his African agencies. Before leaving he told Collins to buy a dhow that was coming on the market, and named the price. There was unexpected competition and Collins had to go above the figure given: to miss the dhow would have been thought a major calamity. The deal was reported by letter to AB.

In due course AB returned to Aden in one of his ships. Collins and Fenn went on board to meet him. While waiting they had a word with the captain and asked (as one usually did) about the state of the weather. Captain Z said it was very stormy: AB had been furious about the price paid for the dhow and violently abusive of Fenn and Collins. This, the young men felt, was grossly unfair and called for some reaction. AB had the habit – taken over perhaps from Bernard – of refusing to speak to someone who had displeased him. Fenn and Collins decided to do likewise. They hurried off the ship before AB emerged, drove back to the house independently, refused an invitation to dine in the penthouse and, in the office, maintained a wall of silence.

AB was unperturbed. He seems to have felt that sooner or later the unruly children would come to heel: but the first approach should come from them. AB and HB had desks in the big room where Fenn and Collins worked, and, for the time, AB refrained from speaking directly to either. 'Hilda', he would say in a voice audible throughout the room, 'please tell Mr Collins . . . '. HB would pass on the message. 'Hilda, will you give this letter to Mr Fenn . . . '

AB seemed to be expecting one or both of them to seek a private interview. They did not do so. Finally he sent for Fenn and asked point blank what it was about. Fenn told him what they had heard from Captain Z.

'I did not speak like that to Z.'

Fenn was silent.

'Do you accept my word that I said nothing of the sort to Z?'

Fenn said nothing.

'Or do you mean to tell me that I am deliberately lying to you?'

Fenn still said nothing.   'Go and fetch Captain Z.'

In due course Fenn came back with a very embarrassed and uncomfortable Captain Z. Of course, Z explained, he had not said anything at all and even if he had said anything it was obviously a joke. Z was dismissed and Fenn left alone with AB.

There was a pause.

'I had better resign', said Fenn.

AB's face broadened into a smile and the magnetic charm came on again.

'Fenn, you stay.'

II

AB was continually asserting his desire to retire from active management. That he would ever do so was open to doubt; but his unrelenting quest for Men (or Messiahs as the young men called them) was more or less part of the office routine. In the early thirties both Collins and Fenn were given to understand, at different times, that they were being groomed for leadership. So far from this leading to rivalry the two of them adopted and transcribed a little French rhyme on the theme of the blue-eyed boy. This document became The Title Deeds.[1] It was held by whoever happened to be in favour at the moment; to be formally transferred, over a whisky and soda, to the other party whenever the wind changed.

In the summer of 1933 Fenn was recalled from Aden for a spell in the London office, where he envisaged his life as 'a scramble between catching up the threads of current business and interviewing future Messiahs'. AB of course was in France at the time, and Fenn was invited to break his journey at Le Paradou. We have a letter of his to Collins:

'Miss Archer the new English governess was there to meet me with the five very self-possessed and Bessic infants – and I had a full twenty hours of the most beautiful scenery, the most excellent bathing and, well yes, several tots, I think, before AB turned up seething with suppressed excitement with a splintered windscreen and a brand-new Ford,[2] badly dented after an attempt to get past another bloke who was there already.

After supper and seven sides of his latest pianoforte solo played in terrifying stillness and semi-darkness, the rest of the household were packed off to bed and my sympathetic ears were opened to a flood of woe ...'

This letter crossed one from Collins:

AB's letter on the London staff just about made my blood boil. What is the man thinking of? He has a reasonably decent staff and because he has 'too much ego in his cosmos' he sets in to upset somebody. Well, believe me, he had succeeded beyond his wildest expectations this time.... As for me I really feel I cannot go on any longer ....

Judging by the tone of AB's letter you are once more the Messiah and since your eyes are now definitely bluer than mine, I propose, as soon as I can find them amongst my papers, to send you the Title Deeds to which, and Young agrees with me, you now have prior claim.

A fortnight later Fenn replied:

Times there are, my lad, when the London office can make even a sane man think wistfully of an enamelled cot and a Marelli fan. If you can find the Title Deeds tie them to a lump of gum, myrrh or a large cockroach and deposit them, with appropriate ceremony, down the Big Drop.

III

Fenn, during his stay in London, was apt to take an independent line; and AB's reaction to this attitude is of interest. In early November 1933 AB was back in Aden, and Fenn saw reason to criticise his instructions over certain deals in skins. AB replied in a marathon letter dated 22 November.

... When a man believes he has acted for the best and feels he has given everything that is in him he should be impervious, sentimentally, to criticism, and merely consider it in so far as it is likely to help him on similar occasions. You are probably, I should say almost certainly, right about this question of prices. But do you really believe it serves any purpose to waste precious hours writing at such length as you did on this matter? Has it helped you? Has it helped me? ... I have not the slightest doubt in my mind and I am glad to state it here that you have given your best. I am also glad to add that your best is good, and this should suffice.... *Allied Kid Co*: I was probably wrong in refusing the large offer.... *British Tanners*: I was also wrong in believing in Mr. A's friendly sentiments ... I am fully aware that you and every other member of the staff will criticize my actions as regards *Allied Kid*, as regards *British Tanners*, as regards everything. But this does not matter. As I repeatedly told you I shall always prefer to sin by commission rather than to sin by omission. I shall continue to preserve the same humility before my big task, knowing fully well that many of my decisions will again be errors of judgment. Through errors I have always contrived to reach the truth in the end, and I am afraid that I shall continue to do so up to the last. But if you know of better hands than mine to hold the rudder of our ship by all means name him and it will not be long before it is entrusted to him ...

This crossed a letter in which Fenn seems to have raised some question of staff responsibility. AB wrote back on 29 November. After dealing with coffee deals, skins, sugar, banking facilities and the Marseilles agency he goes on:

> I would have also preferred to delay answering your letters until I felt better. But, if I allow you to continue as you are doing at present, I fear it may lead us both to the irreparable ...
>
> To excuse the incompetency, the colossal blunders, the stupid errors and lack of efficiency of a department by stating that it is managed by a young man who has no experience is to admit that everything was left to him and no supervision was exercised by the man in charge and, therefore, responsible. From here I have had to direct my adverse criticizm to the department concerned but, behind it all I saw the head, and nobody else.
>
> Next week will doubtless bring me another of your fulminations in answer to our letters about sugar, though events have proved how entirely misled I have been and how superficial is the knowledge you have in London of the circumstances affecting this delicate market ...

When covering his subordinates a man may have two aims. One is popularity. But, God forbid that you should ever think of riding this old and vicious nag as it has broken every bone of its riders and destroyed irremediably their soul. To be 'pally' as the young generation says, with our subordinates or, in fact, with anybody, is to abandon one's own dignity. Our sole presence ought to be a tonic, create the desire to give of our best, do our utmost and not cause a relaxation of the effort, indispensable if we are to win the battle. The other reason, a nobler one, is the desire to shelter the weaker brother and bear the brunt of a punishment which would have fallen on his shoulders. I have known heroic and at the end, alas! tragic examples of the result caused by this attitude. But have you paused to think of the results?

One thing only matters to me, and this is, the welfare of the firm. Above the people I love dearest, above my health and, I think I can say, above my life, this belief stands unquestioned. How many times have I faced the possibility of giving up the fight and taking a deserved rest, God and my wife only know. But the firm is for me, to-day, like a huge beehive, with many thousand souls living upon it, this hive clinging to a single branch, an old and already half broken one, hence the tragedy. Hence also my intense desire, since I know too well my days are counted, to create men, develop their energy where it already exists, give them the desire for a more risky, hazardous but fuller life and, in the end, enable me to hand over the torch to better hands than mine in order to prevent the destruction of a life's work. Your way, on the contrary, will create slaves and there are enough of those on the earth. You wish to be a shield, please yourself. I prefer to be a spear . . .'

IV

There were circumstances about the departures both of Fenn and Collins that were to wound AB where he was very sensitive; and if later he referred to either of them it would be with abusive contempt. Fenn became increasingly restive under his employer's dominance, and in 1934 he tendered his resignation. AB took it well. The parting was correct if not particularly cordial; AB gave him £100 gratuity. But three months later Louise le Brozec, AB's favourite secretary, also resigned. It transpired that she had been secretly engaged to Fenn and was leaving in order to marry him.

Collins stayed on four years longer. On many occasions he was on the verge of revolt, but, as so often, exasperation melted away in face of AB's charm. In the autumn of 1938 when AB returned to Aden from France Collins informed him that he and Meryem, AB's eldest daughter, had decided to marry; and Collins was on the next boat to Marseilles. Meryem, foreseeing what was likely to happen, had found some excuse for staying on in France that autumn. The young couple were married and there came a son and a daughter. Meryem and her father were reconciled, more or less, in 1944. Some six years later AB expressed satisfaction on hearing that Collins had been awarded a CBE and there were hopes the two might come together again. But AB died before that was possible.

15 The Indians and the Arabs

In December 1936 AB wrote to the manager of his London office:

> I presume it is impossible to make you realise that the strength of the firm resides in our magnificent native staff, which it has taken me a lifetime to select. If I had been helped by the London office, we should today have had a European staff imbued with the same lofty ideas, the same sense of devotion, the same loyalty, the same efficiency.

Indeed the record of AB's Asian staff is in striking contrast with that of the Europeans. Of the scores of Europeans whom AB took on at different times, a bare half dozen were ever with him for as much as five years; while at the time of his death there were double that number of Asians in responsible positions, whose service went back for more than twenty. Incidentally there were a number of Arabs and Indians whose association with AB proved extremely lucrative; whereas with one (or perhaps two) exceptions the Europeans all left AB as poor as when they joined him.

Indians and Arabs working for AB received higher wages than they would have got in other Aden firms. Sir Tom Hickinbotham writes:

> He treated his labour more liberally than any other employer. He took a personal interest in their living conditions. . . . His men could speak personally to him, but having done so must accept his decision or clear out. He paid well but he got the best men and that paid him dividends.

But there were factors of more importance than pay packets. There was AB's sincere (and known) sympathy with and respect for Arab and for Indian culture. There was his accessibility. Above all there was the strength of his personality – he was one in whose leadership a man could take pride. Furthermore the difference in race, religion and background was an effective shield against those psychological strains and stresses in Aden and elsewhere which so bedevilled AB's relations with his Europeans. How far he could have kept his hold on his local staff in the unsettled atmosphere of the 1960s is another matter. But in his lifetime it was his personality rather than his payroll that paid the dividends.

II

AB had a natural sympathy for Arabs and the Arab way of life. As we have seen he acquired, very early on, a fluent knowledge of spoken Arabic. He insisted that his staff should learn the language. Whatever the pressure of work he never grudged the time spent in talks or correspondence with his Arab contacts. He was always accessible. Guests at dinner were apt to find proceedings interrupted by the appearance, unannounced, of a bearded Arab with whom AB would have an animated conversation for as much as forty minutes. All this meant that 'al Biss' (the cat) as the Arabs called him acquired a standing in the local community that few Europeans and no other business man had ever attained. He was on terms of intimacy and of complete confidence with the older generation of Arab merchants; and this not only brought business, but kept his finger on the pulse of current trends and moves.

Apart from AB himself, perhaps the most striking personality in the household was Mohamed Aly. He arrived as junior house boy, from a mountain village in the Yemen, in 1918. Before long, with his untiring devotion to AB's service, he was made head boy. It became natural to ask his advice when further servants were needed. Invariably the newcomer would be from Mohamed Aly's own village, or be someone with whom he had some tribal or family connection. It was the same when subordinate staff were required for the office; and, in due course, for the Soap Factory, and the Crescent Hotel. They were all, in a sense, Mohamed Aly's men. He became a sort of Sheikh, with an intelligence bureau of house boys in all the Besse establishments and indeed in nearly all the households, clubs and offices outside. There is of course a cleavage between Yemeni Arabs and Arabs from Aden: non-Yemenis in the Besse service, while of unquestioned loyalty to AB, were prepared to call down curses on Yemenis in general and on Mohamed Aly in particular. But Mohamed Aly's hold on his little private empire remained unshaken.

As AB was leaving Aden for the last time in the spring of 1951 he called in Patel, the Chief Accountant[1] and charged him, whatever happened, to look after Mohamed Aly 'who has done more for me than anyone else'. And Mohamed Aly has given the following note on his late master:

> Mr A. Besse was one of the best people, modest and merciful to all, whether big or small. He used to talk and listen to everybody and on any matter. He was industrious and hard-working. He would rise at midnight from his bed to attend to any important task of his, and normally start his working day at 5 a.m. when every one else was asleep. He was gentle and kind to his employees. Mr Besse used to stop his car when he noticed any of his employees, to speak to them and find out if he could offer them any assistance. He was a human in every sense.

The firm owed much, especially in the earlier years, to the successful operation of AB's fleet of dhows. Here his gift for dealing with Arabs was manifest. His heart was in his dhows. He was constantly in the building yard, looking into everything, talking to everybody. The launching of a dhow would be a tremendous occasion, the workers there *en fête* and AB's appearance greeted with thunderous applause. As often as not on the eve of departure he would turn up on the quay, his car packed with provisions, come on board and have a meal with all the crew. At sea the role of the *nakhudas* (or captains) was decisive. There was of course no wireless; once a dhow left port she was out of touch, perhaps for weeks. On every voyage it was the skill, the judgement and the integrity of the *nakhuda* that made all the difference between disaster and success. AB treated and regarded his *nakhudas* as his friends. On return to port they would come straight to his private office, where all other business would be set aside to make way for a discussion of the minutest details of the voyage. Most of them stayed with AB for years.

Mention has already been made of Arab contribution to the work of the outlying branches and agencies, of Sheikh Omar Basuedan of Hodeida and of Seyide Baharoon of Addis Abeba. There were also Abdulla Basuedan in Dessie; Abdou Hashem in Mogadiscio; Sheikh Omar Badeeb in Hargeisa; Mohamed Salem Shamakh in Zeila; and many others. Some of these were salaried, some on a commission basis. AB knew them all, and on their visits to Aden there were endless and amicable palavers in his private office. Inevitably, in the outlying districts, a resourceful Arab agent could find opportunities for personal gain by some private combination with a local dealer. Occasionally these opportunities were taken. In some of these cases AB took prompt and drastic action. In others he did nothing at all, to the indignation of his young Europeans who had reason to believe that substantial sums were being pocketed on the side. For the most part AB would listen in silence to their protests. But on one occasion there was the following exchange:

'You say this man has been cheating us.'
'Yes.'
'For how much, in the last six months?'
'Perhaps ten thousand rupees.'
'What profit have we made from his work?'
'About fifty thousand.'
'Well?'

III

AB was not exaggerating when, towards the end of his life, he wrote: 'Our Hindu staff should be considered as the sinews of the firm.' Indians were an important element in all offices in Aden. Their standard of living was modest, and they would accept far lower salaries than Europeans with corresponding qualifications. They were immensely industrious – long hours and overtime they would take in their stride. For the employer they had the further advantage of being a closed community, immune from unsettling European influence and from Arab intrigue. In the firm of Besse the whole of the growing and ever more complicated accountancy apparatus was in Indian hands. So was much of the import–export business. And during World War II it was an Indian, Prabhulal Mehta, who was in charge of the vitally important department dealing with Shell products.

It would be hard to overestimate the role played by Tarachand Amritlal Parekh, who was taken on as junior bookkeeper in the early twenties. He combined an infinite capacity for work and great technical efficiency with considerable resource and an uncanny sense of timing. Within a very few years he was Chief Accountant. Vacancies in the firm were filled by young recruits from his home district in India, with whom he had family or other connections. By the late thirties there were few Indians in the office who had not some tie with Parekh. But his private empire (and his intelligence network) stretched far beyond the firm of Besse. He became the most influential figure in the Indian community in Aden, with contacts in the offices of AB's business competitors and in the government offices with which AB had to deal,[2] and, indeed, in most of the little ports along the African shore. In the Aidrus Road his word of course was law for all the Indians. He kept the personal accounts of the European staff. Up till the late thirties AB only rarely handed out cheques: the usual procedure was for sums to be credited to the employee's personal account with the firm. To know where one stood one had to go to Parekh, and applications for permission to withdraw went through Parekh. It was sometimes felt that the image of Parekh loomed rather too large.

Not untypical of how things happened is the case of R. N. Bagadia. He was still a schoolboy when he first met Parekh (then on holiday in India) shortly before the outbreak of World War II. Parekh was known throughout the area as the one to whom young men had best apply for advice or help; and on leaving school in late 1940 Bagadia wrote to him in Aden. In due course came an offer of a post of junior clerk. Bagadia joined up in early 1941. The salary was modest, one hundred rupees a month out of which he must keep himself. But it was more than he would have got if working for a local Indian firm. He shared quarters with three other Indians, and, as junior, had all the domestic chores to do. What struck him at once was the feeling of his room-mates for AB, for HB and for the firm of Besse. It was, as it were, *their* firm. To work elsewhere would be quite unthinkable.

After six months he was transferred to Addis Abeba and it was on AB's visit to the branch the following summer that he had his first real contact. 26 June was AB's birthday. The whole staff assembled, and, one by one, made appropriate little speeches. It was an occasion quite outside the very young Bagadia's experience, and when it came to his turn he blurted out: 'In my village at home a rich man marks his birthday by giving alms to the poor.' There was an awkward silence. Some present seemed embarrassed. Some suppressed a laugh. AB alone appeared to understand. 'Go to the cashier,' he said, 'and bring me a hundred and fifty dollars.' Bagadia went off and returned with a heavy bag of thalers. Next day he was summoned to AB's presence. The bag was intact. 'I have been thinking of what you said to me', AB told him. 'But I have found no one to whom to give. Take the money back to the cashier.' Young Bagadia pondered deeply over the incident. It must, he felt, contain some lesson. And he concluded that AB had meant him to understand that if a man was poor he must work and earn money for himself. It was not right to ask for charity.

IV

When news came through of the assassination of Mahatma Gandhi, AB was to write as under to the Indians working for him:

Dear Patel and Staff,

No word can qualify such a crime. Though you and I follow different routes I wish you all to know that I sympathise from the depth of my heart and associate myself with your grief. Not India alone but the whole thinking world have lost a Saint. Selfless, his entire life devoted to lighten suffering, to right wrongs, completely detached he stood as a great and radiating light to guide us all. Should you agree with me I would like you to inform all the staff that tomorrow our office will be closed as a day of mourning during which, I am sure, you will all like to unite and pray.

A. Besse

Aden, 30th January, 1948.

16   Progress

The most important event of the middle thirties in AB's area was the growing Italo-Abyssinian tension, culminating in the Italian occupation which was to last until the spring of 1941. The Abyssinian War and its by-product, the private duel between AB and the Fascist Government, will be dealt with later in a separate chapter. Meanwhile so much else was happening in the firm of Besse that a complete account would fill several volumes. We can only give a few selected aspects and episodes, as illustrations of AB in action.

For twelve years after the Stoner settlement AB had his own office in Marseilles. The office had had an unhappy history. The managers successively in charge there had never lasted for more than a few months. Sometimes they failed to come up to AB's standards; sometimes they found AB impossible to work with. Not infrequently it was a combination of both. Things might go well for a few weeks, then would come friction; exasperation, explosion and a parting of the ways. In 1933 AB decided to have no more an office of his own but to appoint a local firm as agents on a commission basis. Meister & Co., of 6 rue Venture, were not a large firm, but Meister himself had excellent contacts and his partner, Di Domenico, was an acknowledged expert in the all-important field of hides and skins. The firm proposed and Besse accepted a gentlemen's agreement containing three points: (1) no written contract, (2) absolute mutual independence and, (3) no rude letters. There was cynical comment in the Marseilles business world, and bets were laid that the association would not last three months. It had in fact been going for less than that time when one of AB's more violent diatribes was delivered in the rue Venture. Di Domenico put it in an envelope and sent it back to Aden. 'Dear Mr Besse, This is against our agreement.' After more than thirty years Meister & Co. were still the Besse representatives in Marseilles.

AB from time to time considered the idea of making a similar arrangement in London. But the Halal Shipping Company was registered in London; and it would have been unwise to entrust outsiders with the all-important task of recruiting staff. So the London office was kept on and continued to feel the weight of AB's insistence on perfection. Typical is a letter of his to Davis of February 1934 beginning: 'There is not a line of the London mail this week that does not irritate me profoundly', and going on to six pages of single spaced typescript castigating instances of London's ignorance, gullibility, weakness, complacency, and misjudgement in a number of fields. His letters to Simpson, the London manager, were often of greater length, and, almost always, of equal severity. It may be felt that, in the circumstances, London was not doing so badly. Their turnover for 1933 amounted to over £360 000 and many of the very varied and highly responsible tasks Aden set them were not reflected in the turnover. They were housed, for economy's sake, in a shabby building in Weston Street, off the Surrey end of London Bridge. And the highest salary, that of Simpson the manager, was £500 a year with an extra £50 for looking after the Halal Shipping Co.

All the same it would be wrong to think of the London office as composed of cowed nonentities. They could, and sometimes did, answer back. AB was always working out private code groups to reduce the cost of inter-office cables. For use to London he devised a five-letter group to mean 'Do not be silly.' London was duly notified. Simpson and Fenn (then with him) were indignant, and tacked the group on to their next cable back to Aden. Nothing more was heard of it.

II

We have seen that it was the support of the National Bank of India that enabled AB to keep afloat after the Stoner crisis. AB then took the line that this was sound business judgement on their part, which in fact it undoubtedly was; and he was at no time prepared to see the Bank making what he considered to be undue profits at his expense. We have a letter of his to Davis in early 1935:

> To that Bank, between the years 1925 and 1934, we paid Rs 727 125 IN INTEREST ALONE. . . . If you add to that figure the commissions earned on London and other business, the profits made in discounting our bills, on telegraphic transfers, in other words, a sum which must amount to at least double the interest charges, you will

arrive at a total of two million rupees in ten years!!! Is it not enough to make anyone's blood boil?

Yet, no later than last year we had to transfer our money, to the last penny, against our bills for Sugar purchased. We were called upon to do the same a few weeks ago for Chrysler bills.... Two years ago Lawrence (NBI manager) was talking about 'fictitious profits' in our Balance Sheets...

Never having been able to see eye to eye with you concerning the attitude of the Bank towards us, it is possible that you may be able to preserve the sentiments of respect and loyalty you have always had for these people. But I have none. You may even allow Mr Lawrence to bang the table again in your presence. But not I. That is why I must ask you to adhere unswervingly to the instructions I have given Simpson to take advantage of the Trust Receipts up to the hilt, never paying a Bill until it is due, thus reducing our overdraft in London and enabling us to profit by the low discount rates charged on these bills, or, if you prefer to take the only attitude that *I* feel is compatible with our position, go to the managers, Munroe and Lawrence, and make it clear to them that we cannot and will not agree any longer to pay whenever the goods are disposed of. The choice rests with you...

III

It has been said that the spectacular growth of the firm of Besse was due not to long-term planning, but to AB's flair in seizing a chance opportunity and to his determination and drive in exploiting its potentialities. A case in point is the Soap Factory, which AB acquired in 1934 from a local Arab who had got into difficulties. It was a very small concern, housed in a dilapidated building in Crater, the machinery ancient and decrepit. AB engaged a technician. In 1935 he moved the factory to Ma'alla and bought new plant. There were plenty of growing pains; and plenty of indignant letters from AB on the shortcomings of successive managers. But soap was manufactured and began to be disposed of at a profit. In 1937 AB installed additional plant to produce his own coconut oil. In 1938, to obtain fuller value from the by-products, he set up a glycerine factory. It was in this year that a cargo ship heading north from Aden caught fire: the cargo of copra was jettisoned and washed up on the Arabian beaches. AB bought the lot for a song. There were the inevitable arguments with the various petty sheikhs who claimed to own the foreshore: but AB acquired a considerable quantity of copra at negligible cost. By 1939 the factory was making substantial profits. Not long after the outbreak of World War II no other soap was available in all the area, and the problem was to find the raw materials. In 1943 visitors to the house in the Aidrus Road were struck by the new and curious smell, emanating not least from the immaculate AB himself: it was due to the poor quality of the only ingredients that could be acquired for the soap.

IV

All this time AB and his office were gaining considerable expertise in the matter of shipping. This was to be put to good use from 1937 when the Halal Shipping Co. began to act as agent for other shipping lines using the port of Aden. Meanwhile, in late 1935, the Halal's own fleet consisted of the *El Amin* and the *El Hak*, two tugs, six dhows and sixteen lighters. On lighters we have a note from AB to the local manager of the NBI.

> It may also interest your Head Office to know that since last June we
> have added three wooden lighters (worth £1000 each) to our
> fleet and have timber for six more. The object of this building
> programme is clear from the Halal Shipping Co. Balance Sheet since
> it shows a profit of over Rs 15,000 under this head when we had only
> four lighters working.

AB was the first to equip an Aden dhow with a small diesel engine. In 1936 he had an important meat contract, and the problem was to bring in sheep from Berbera to Aden against the monsoon. But motorised dhows soon showed their worth on other routes. In the war years, with the acute shipping shortage, they were to prove invaluable. The RAF stations along the southern shore of the Arabian peninsular were all fuelled by AB's dhows.

There were technical problems. In the traditional Arab dhow:

> Owing to the method of construction the hull is very weak, both
> longitudinally and transversely. Very large planks, timbers, deck
> beams, keel, stem and stern section are used, in themselves these
> items are strong, but the method of connection is weak at several
> vital positions. This is why, when a dhow grounds on any type of

beach in a heavy sea she will start to break up almost at once.
Grounded on rocks under the same conditions she will disintegrate
in a matter of hours. ... If you wish to convert a sailing dhow to a
motor dhow considerable alterations are necessary to the stern
frame ...[1]

The working life of a motor dhow is shorter than that of a sailing dhow.
The motor dhow can be used in all seasons and can proceed against
wind and sea with all the wear and tear that this involves. But in spite of
its relatively shorter life it proved to be enormously more profitable. It
is remarkable that throughout AB's lifetime only one of his dhows
became a total loss.

At first the more old-fashioned *nakhudas* had misgivings, all the
more so because a motorised dhow had to carry an Indian 'driver' or
senior mechanic to look after the engine. But they soon realised the
advantages. Aden's instructions were that engines should only be used
when wind conditions prevented the use of sail. But in spite of Aden's
check on fuel consumption and weather reports, and in spite of the
introduction of fines for non-compliance, these instructions were
consistently ignored. 'I well understand,' AB was to note, 'and am
annoyed that our *nakhudas* with engines never use their sails, and,
without blinking an eyelid, invent all sorts of reasons for not going
where they do not want to go.' Arguments, when a motorised dhow
returned to port, were long and acrimonious.

V

The *El Amin* and the *El Hak* played a decisive role in the building up
of the Besse empire, and it is a pity we have so meagre a record of their
early years. Their history must have been one of trial and error. AB
was new to the business when he founded the Halal Shipping Company, and the local hazards, physical and psychological, were innumerable. It was his drive, his determination and his insistent attention to
the smallest detail that ultimately made for success. Though it is true
that profitability was helped by the fact that, in the Aden of that time,
the rules under the Merchant Shipping Acts were only sketchily
enforced, AB's ships were often (and sometimes considerably) overloaded. On the other hand, in the matter of ships' complement, the
Halal Shipping Company went further than the Board of Trade
required: The *El Hak* for instance carried a total of sixty-seven men,

including the captain, two deck officers, a chief engineer and a second
and third (all Europeans) and three Indian drivers. This wealth of
personnel was local practice, arising from local conditions. The crew
were used for coolie work, for loading and unloading; and the engineers and drivers undertook running repairs and adjustments – there
being no repair facilities at most of the ports of call. Even so the
engineers had plenty of time on their hands. But of course when the
ship was carrying the owner, occupying the captain's cabin and with an
eagle eye on all that was going on, every one took care to be seen to be
vigorously busy.

As already mentioned, the problem of officers and engineers for the
Halal ships was an ever recurring theme in AB's letters to his London
office. For instance, in January 1934:

> We require to know as exactly as possible what our obligations are
> towards our deck officers and engineers in accordance with BOT
> regulations, and a memorandum drawn up on this point by expert
> lawyers is essential. There must be *some* means of making it possible
> for us to get rid of any members of our ships' staffs who introduce an
> undesirable element on board or fail to give us satisfaction in their
> work, even if no tangible fault can be cited as an excuse for our desire
> to dismiss them. ... Another point which must be taken up is the
> possibility of extending the contract to three years. When they keep
> sober the life of these seafaring men is a very healthy one.

All his life AB was to fight against reluctance to serve in the Red Sea.
In the late forties a Mrs Hafter was, as an experiment, taken on by the
London office with the special task of recruiting officers for the Halal.
AB noted.

> I pointed out to her that living at sea, and particularly in the Red Sea,
> is most pleasant; and the fears which seem to be entertained by the
> candidates are entirely groundless. As a rule they will always find the
> work is relatively easy, the food on board could not be improved
> upon and the salaries are high. I went so far as instructing her to
> ignore doctor's advices if her own judgement did not concur.

Ships' captains, of course, were all important, and in view of their
responsibilities they had certain financial inducements. One was
'sheep money', with cargoes of livestock: the captain would receive
one rupee for each sheep landed alive and sound at the port of

destination. There was also commission, but of this little evidence is available. In the middle thirties one of AB's ships ran on a sandbank off Jedda. The Jedda authorities held an enquiry and the captain was exonerated. It was his last voyage for the firm, and we have a letter from AB telling the London office that he should be paid the balance of salary due. But, AB added, in spite of the findings of the enquiry he was convinced the captain had been at fault; he should therefore not be paid the one half per-cent commission on the profits of the voyage unless the lawyers felt the firm had no chance of avoiding the obligation. Apparently the lawyers, opinion was not as AB wished, for on a subsequent appointment AB wrote that a commission would be considered 'but in no circumstances should this be written into the contract'.

VI

In September 1937 Davis (at Aden) was able to write to AB in France:

Dear Mr Besse,
    Attached are rough calculations which I have asked Parekh to make out quickly in order to give you an idea of the earnings of EL HAK during the summer months. You will see that between the 1st June and the 31st August she earned approximately £8000. We estimate that during September her earnings will be about £3000, making a total of £11 000 for the four months – 1200 Rs per day – which is very satisfactory ...

VII

The Shell side of the business continued to expand. AB was never reconciled to the 'As Is' agreement, and over the years there were indignant letters to St Helen's Court or to Cairo complaining that the Standard Vacuum or (more often) the Texas local agents were exceeding their quotas, and asking for authority to take drastic counter-action. The replies received were always sympathetic; but it was clear Shell were not prepared to risk a major clash with the American companies over the issues raised. In the end AB came to his own conclusion, and we have a directive of his to the Aden office sent out from Le Paradou in the summer of 1937:

SHELL

As I have written about this time and time again without having
succeeded in making Aden understand, I feel at a loss as to how I
should express my thoughts. Still, I believe that when one writes to
somebody to take the law into his hands, to lead and put the
competitors, who will then be unable to countermove, in front of the
accomplished fact; and allow him to act according to the best of his
ability and the circumstances, it should be enough, not only to
enable him to maintain the percentage the firm is entitled to, but also
to exceed it. Aden is fully aware, as I have often said before, that
although Cairo may object officially to anything we do, they will in
their heart of hearts rejoice whenever it happens to be to their
advantage ...

VIII

The mounting tension over Abyssinia greatly increased the demand
for Shell products throughout AB's area. All parties directly or
indirectly involved were eager to build up their stocks of oil fuels. In
1935, apart from the substantial volume handled through the Besse
organisation, Shell (Cairo) were selling very large quantities in Egypt –
largely to the Italians who proceeded to ship to Massawa and Mogadiscio. Under the agreement the firm of Besse was entitled to commission
on these 'direct sales'. When no relevant statements were forthcoming
from Cairo, AB wrote, in early December 1935, to complain to St
Helen's Court. Rowbottom of Shell replied on 20 December; but his
letter did not satisfy AB, and in a further letter dated 6 January 1936
he reacted very sharply indeed. He was by now in an extremely strong
position. Parekh's Indian intelligence *réseau* had been at work, and
copies of the manifests of ships carrying Shell products to Italian East
African ports were in AB's private safe in Aden. This last letter of
AB's went up to the highest level in St Helen's Court, and the cable in
reply, dated 20 January, is signed Godber:

Have just seen your letter sixth to Rowbottom and assure you that
you have entirely misunderstood his letter twentieth December
which I saw before despatch – full stop – we telegraphing Cairo
to-day to enquire about amount commission owing you which you
state to be twenty thousand pounds as nothing is further from our
mind than hold up commission – full stop – quite clear from your

letter that misunderstanding exists which can be quite quickly removed by personal visit therefore am arranging Rowbottom continues to Aden...

Thereafter the matter was on the way to a satisfactory settlement. Shell (Cairo) produced the relevant statements and arranged for payment of the commission due. Nevertheless we have a memo from the Aden Accounts Department, dated as late as December 1937, prodding Cairo over certain direct sales to AGIP, to the Italian Air Force, and to the Djibouti representative of the French Air Ministry.

IX

Meanwhile a more serious storm was blowing up. Bunkering was excluded from AB's agreement with Shell. AB was, for the time being, more or less reconciled to bunkering in Aden remaining in the hands of the Anglo-Persian. But Djibouti was another matter. As Shell came nearer to the decision to start bunkering in that port, AB became increasingly restive lest this valuable agency be entrusted to another firm.

AB's enormous correspondence contains harsh words about all his competitors, but his most bitter hostility was reserved for the Compagnie Maritime d'Afrique Orientale. One factor may have been his dislike of Michel Cot. Cot, Chairman of the Banque de l'Indo-Chine, of the Chemin de Fer d'Ethiopie, and of many other concerns apart from the CMAO, was very much a *grand seigneur* of international big business. Tall, slender, impeccably elegant, with the highest social connection in every capital, his visits to the outposts of his financial empire were in the nature of a royal progress. On his first meeting with AB in Addis Abeba he had treated him with the studied affability he would naturally show to a successful local dealer in hides and skins. AB never forgave him.

It is possible that Shell had made their decision over the Djibouti bunkering before the flurry over commission on direct sales became acute. In any case they were taking a calculated risk. AB was certain to be upset by the decision. To lose his services could, at the moment, be extremely inconvenient. But they reckoned that in spite of his disappointment he would remain Shell agent.

On 22 January 1936 two days after Godber's telegram, Rowbottom wrote to AB from London to confirm his coming visit: 'It is quite obvious you are very cross with us about something or other, and we all agree that the matter can quite easily be explained to you in a personal conversation.' There was no mention of Djibouti bunkering.

On that same day AB wrote two letters. One was to Rowbottom: 'Unless I have the sensation that there is implicit mutual trust I find it exceedingly difficult to work with anyone. It is the nature of the beast and I am too old to mend my ways.' The other was to Davis. 'Rowbottom's visit will, I hope, clear the air, for I do not intend to let him go until I have obtained a definite answer to several questions. . . . I shall make it very clear to him that unless implicit trust prevails on both sides I prefer to give up working for Shell . . .'. It may well be that AB had a suspicion of what was to come.

As already mentioned mail between London and Aden took fourteen days en route; and at that moment another letter from St Helen's Court, dated 13 January and signed by Agnew, was on its way to AB:

> We have satisfied ourselves that our very good friends the Messageries Maritimes are largely interested in the Compagnie d'Afrique Orientale and that therefore it is essential that the Djibouti bunkering installation should be put up and worked through the medium of that firm.

Agnew's letter was delivered in Aden on 27 January. AB promptly cabled his resignation to London. How far he intended to maintain his decision may be open to doubt: the Shell agency was too integral a part of the firm that meant so much to him. But he was angry at the loss of this lucrative new opening and, even more so, at the blow to his pride on being passed over in favour of a firm for whom he had so long and so loudly expressed his contempt. He was determined that Shell should feel his anger.

Rowbottom and Charvet (Martin's successor in Cairo) landed at Steamer Point on 6 February. They were informed that AB was 'too busy' to see them, and spent the next forty-eight hours kicking their heels in the local hotel. When at last they were admitted the storm broke, and for two whole days the Shell executives were exposed to the full blast of AB's displeasure. And then, abruptly, the atmosphere changed; the clouds all seemed to roll away and AB's charm came out. The rest of the visit passed in cordial and constructive discussion. Once back in Cairo Charvet wrote enthusiastically to thank AB for 'those days spent with you in Aden – what a lesson they contain!' Agnew wrote from London to express the 'profound relief' at AB's withdrawal of his resignation. On a more tangible plane AB was invited to take on the valuable agency of the International Paint and Compositions Co. – a subsidiary of Shell; and on 6 March 1936 the interest on the debt to Anglo-Saxon in respect of AB's two ships was reduced from $4\frac{1}{2}$ per cent to 4 per cent. For the next five years there was to be no major flurry between St Helen's Court and Besse. All the same AB continued to keep a watchful eye on his firm's interests. There is a note of his to Davis in late 1937:

Another source of wonder to me was the discovery that for years past we have been keeping two of our iron lighters at the disposal of Shell for storage of Kerosene and Benzine for shipment to outside ports in order to avoid payments of tolls, landing charges etc. – a facility which, in spite of the great saving to Shell, we made them a present of. Henceforward Shell will be debited with the hire of these craft.

17   Achievement

The middle thirties were profitable years for the firm of Besse. Davis's repeated visits to the United States had resulted in good connections with important American tanners and glove makers: very substantial orders for skins were now coming in. There is a note from AB in late 1935 that a cargo of Polish sugar had been sold with good profit. A little later he was writing:

> Thanks to our purchase of Russian Sugar we can sell it at such a rate as to prevent others making anything but a heavy loss, whilst we ourselves make a profit.... As regard X's competition we have no alternative but to fight and fight and fight. Every time we hear of a sale we should warn the buyer that we mean to see to it that no profit for him results from the transaction. We did this a few years ago with Shell products, and the method proved effective.

But for the moment there is no trace in AB's letters of the satisfaction of achievement. It may be that he did not know how well the firm was doing. For all his flair and drive he was no accountant: it was said of him that he could not read a balance sheet. In any case the restless demon that drove him left no time for complacency. Early in 1934 he was writing to Davis:

> We shall never get out of this vicious circle, it is hopeless and I feel desperate. The longing for the day when, having squared with the Bank, I can leave this firm for good has now become so acute that it is positively aching. I cannot continue to waste my life as I am doing and it is high time I turned my eyes towards other aims than those I have been pursuing up to the present and which have proved such a failure. I have not the time, and besides, I feel you would not understand, to explain what all this means to me, but it is as well that you and the others should know my irrevocable decision to give up

the fight as soon as I have freed myself from my obligations towards both the Anglo-Saxon and the Bank.

His letters to HB give little glimpses of his day-to-day life. His music – 'the quartet and the sonata that we know so well'. His climbs, and the stray dog 'that delightful creature' that attached himself to him and followed him everywhere. The time that Mohamed Aly, for once, made a muddle of the picnic basket, having forgotten the tin opener, the wine and the butter. An evening with one of the most distinguished of the Aden administrators. 'X is good company if one can stop him drinking,' And his thanks to HB for her Christmas present:

> Your present is still packed up till next week. Why make excuses, my dearest, and to me of all people who can never choose a present to give? Every time I tried I could not get myself into the shop. I must have the very best, and my avarice makes me run away from the price of it. Dear wife and incomparable partner, you will get nothing from me; in a way I feel I have given you everything I have.

But mostly the mood is one of gloom. He was depressed at the way the world was shaping – dictatorships, nationalism, hate. 'What will our children have to face? As for the Laval–Mussolini Pact – *Pouah, quel dégoût!* And there was the pitiless pressure of work. 'The mail has just arrived', he wrote to HB at the end of 1934. 'Goodbye to music, reading, walks, letter-writing to my dearest. Goodbye to self-communion, to contemplation, to those blessed moments of repose when one's whole being blends into the Infinite. Where is the Man, where are the Men, who can take the torch from my falling hands?'

II

Abruptly the mood changed. It was in the winter of 1935–6, when HB was in Aden with her husband. On 2 December 1935 AB wrote to Davis:

> On Friday last, my dear Davis, Parekh rushed upstairs, almost crying with emotion, to announce the wonderful news that we no longer had an overdraft at the Bank here! As this happy state of affairs has been achieved not by any extraordinary turn of the wheel of fortune but by steady earnings, I think I should have little

difficulty henceforward in avoiding the onerous help of these confounded bankers of ours.

It is the first milestone, and two more only remain before we reach the goal of complete independence I have been striving so long to attain. The second one is the overdraft in London, which can be considerably reduced the very day the Trust Receipt principle is abandoned. . . . The third and last milestone will be the Anglo-Saxon – but it is one that I do not worry about for an instant. I feel that it will be passed without our noticing it by the monthly payments I intend to resume. I may be an optimist, but I do believe that before 1936 is out our independence will be complete!

Now that the great ship has reached harbour – and developed beautifully in the stormy process – profits will probably run into very large figures indeed, and I think it is high time we studied a scheme either of profit-sharing or a Provident Fund, which latter we might create, in its main lines, on the basis of that of the Shell. It would give the members of our staff, both europeans and native, a feeling of security and increase their attachment to the firm . . .

On 18 December AB again wrote to Davis:

I can imagine what your first reaction will be to the decision to build a third ship, larger than the two others and whose cost is certainly not likely to be less than £50 000; but I wish you to know that it was not taken lightly.

The reason is the following. Parekh is worried to death by the Income Tax Inspector – a new man who seems to take exception to our system of Bookkeeping. Apart from that, however, the fantastic profits our ships are making at present and the fact that by June *El Amin* will be completely written off in our books and *El Hak* reduced to a purely nominal value, points to earnings on such a scale that they will be absorbed almost in their entirety by the Excess Profits Tax. Rather than see such a thing happen Parekh suggests, not without reason, that the construction of a new unit would enable us to 'wangle' out of the exactions of the IT Authorities. His argument – to put it in a nutshell – is that the money would be better invested in a ship than poured into the coffers of the Government . . .

If I were a younger man than I am I should not hesitate, for it is clear that whatever the outcome of the present fray between Mussolini and the Emperor of Abyssinia, the doors of the latter country will be forced, and whatever the dominating influence in Abyssinia –

whether it be Italian or a League Mandate – the vast area between Kisimayu to the Sudan frontier is bound to be developed. It is likely, therefore, that we shall see a period of intense activity follow the present hostilities, lasting for several years, and so far as I can see, there is no shipping organisation in this part of the world capable of coping with it . . .

There is a further letter to Davis, dated 1 January 1936.

This week a fresh feather has been added to Parekh's cap. Our Accounts have been passed and we are let off very lightly indeed. But what it has cost our friend in anxiety, hard work, clever handling and strain generally only I know. . . . But we are playing with fire, and if we have succeeded in averting the danger on this occasion, thanks to Parekh's masterly handling of the affair, it would be folly to imagine that the same juggling can be repeated *ad vitam eternam*. . . . Our idea would be to form a limited company to take charge of Aden under a style in which my own name would be embodied, such as A. Besse Limited – A. Besse Incorporated – The Mercantile Company of A. Besse Ltd. etc. etc. resident in Aden or London, as the expert thinks best . . . . and another firm; under a totally different name, in which my own might not even figure, registered in Abyssinia . . .

III

It is clear from these letters that 1936 was to be an important milestone in the history of the firm of Besse. On the domestic front the Provident Fund was instituted – all members of the office staff, European, Indian and Arab, paying in one month's salary per annum to be matched by a similar contribution from the firm. If an employee had served for five years or more he would, on retirement, be entitled to the firm's contribution as well as his own. Very few of the Europeans lasted for as much as five years, but for the non-Europeans this was an important concession. 1936 also saw the start of the A. Besse & Co. Football Club with its red and green jerseys (the colours chosen for the Halal Shipping Company). The firm provided the jerseys and other equipment and the club – enthusiastically supported by the Arab staff – soon came to take its place among the leading clubs in Aden.

1936 also saw constitutional developments. For technical reasons the Halal Shipping Co. Ltd. had been registered in London in 1924.

Otherwise, hitherto, the firm had been just AB. But in 1936 A. Besse & Co. (Aden) Ltd. was registered in Aden, the Directors being AB, Davis and Parekh. In December of the same year A. Besse & Co. (London) Ltd. was formed in London. 1938 saw the establishment in Aden of Arabian Airways Ltd. which will be dealt with in a later chapter. It was not until 1950, the last year of AB's life, that two separate companies were formed for Ethiopia – A. Besse & Co. (Ethiopia) Ltd. and the A. Besse Trading Company (Diredawa) Ltd.

The formation of the Aden company helped the tax position. There was to be no trouble with the Aden Tax authorities for the rest of AB's life. AB of course was too jealously devoted to the interests of his firm to forego any viable means of tax avoidance; and he maintained that officials had no moral justification in attempting to levy tax on the profits of transactions where the goods concerned had not been actually landed in Aden. He also disliked any prying into his private affairs. As was explained to the Revenue authorities after his death 'Mr Besse never allowed anybody ... to visualise the extent of his wealth.' This held good of his own staff. Certain books were kept by Parekh personally; and issues arising from the ramifications of 'Head Office A/C', 'A. Besse Personal A/C' and 'A. Besse Red Sea A/C' were only discussed and settled at night or in the small hours by AB and Parekh in conditions of absolute secrecy. The good relations with the Aden tax officials were largely due to Parekh's diplomacy and skill.

IV

In the event the third ship was not to be built until after World War II. We do not have Davis's reply to AB's letter of 18 December, but Davis evidently considered the project to be too adventurous. AB was displeased. He wrote back on 14 January 1936:

I am quite prepared to let you argue and even be convinced that if I had stuck to Blackheads I might have been a richer man – a consideration that has no interest for me. But our firm would have been a very different thing from what it is. . . . Your motto is 'Safety First'. Risks, as far as I alone am concerned, are the element in which I thrive above all others . . .

On 20 January he wrote to explain the case to Simpson, the London manager, who was (for the moment) in his good books.

How many instances could I quote in condemnation of Davis' negative attitude to life since the outset of our relations? Hitherto I have always carried out my schemes regardless of his or, for that matter, anybody else's opinion. The result is there to-day for all to see and to prove whether I was right or wrong. But Time is relentless and I can no longer shut my eyes to the fact that the burden I have carried so lightly all these years is becoming heavier than my shoulders can bear and the day can no longer be distant when I shall be forced to lay it down. The young members of my staff are promising, it is true, but it is too early to judge whether they will be fit to take the torch out of my hands and continue my lifework in the spirit in which I created it.

I feel, therefore, that those whose life is wrapped up in this firm of mine have a right to express an opinion, and after Davis' yours, my dear Simpson, matters most. I must therefore ask you to give the matter deep and searching thought, turning the problem over and over in your mind and heart, weighing it in the light of your personal strength and moral fortitude, sizing up the difficulties that lie ahead – for difficulties there will always be despite the strength and privileges of our position to-day, and decide. ... I warn you, however, that this firm, with which you have been associated for so many years and which you have seen soaring upward and onward in spite of gigantic obstacles, and of which, alas! you know so little, was born to great achievements and must, in the nature of things, continue to grow and develop with accruing momentum. You and Davis may wish to stem the ever-rising tide, arrest the soaring flight – it was not created to become a grocer's shop, and if it is reduced to such it will atrophy and die ...

Simpson was in favour of the project, and made the suggestion, which appealed to AB, of having the new ship built in Germany. Davis, however, continued to oppose, and in the end AB, in a mood of depression following the loss of the Djibouti bunkering, allowed the matter to drop. In years to come, when it was obvious that a third ship would have been a gold mine, Davis was to be frequently and tartly reminded of the opportunity that his caution had caused the firm to miss.

V

It is difficult to know what to make of AB's constantly reiterated longing for retirement. It has been suggested that in his heart he had no

intention of finding an heir outside his own family, and that the quest
for messiahs was largely a device for stimulating the staff and keeping
up the standard of recruiting. There may be some truth in this. But, as
far as the family are concerned, André the eldest son, had, by 1936,
been working for the firm for some years and the experience had not
been a happy one. There was AB's chronic inability to make real
contact with the younger generation; and the gap between father and
son became unbridgeable. We have a sad letter from AB to Davis,
complaining bitterly of André's 'stubborn reserve'. HB's two boys
were still children back in France with their mother or the governess.
Writing to Petrouchka in 1935 AB wonders whether they will grow
into 'a Lone Wolf like their father, or will they just be sheep?' In a
letter to HB of about the same time he wrote:

> Real joy is only in creation. Why has fate made me now too old to
> lead my children along the trail that I have blazed? Show them what
> I have done – creation, living, supple, serene. Say to them 'This is as
> far as I could go. . . . here is the torch, take it, head high, strong in the
> power that I have left you . . .'

But in any case there is the question as to whether AB would have
found retirement from active management to be psychologically possible. His talk of advancing age and failing grasp is mere rhetoric. At
fifty-nine he could out-climb, out-swim and out-work most men of half
his age. His magnificent constitution was unimpaired as were his grasp
of detail and his urge for further adventure. Where, one wonders,
outside the firm that meant so much to him, could he have found the
essential outlet for his torrent of energy? In the event, this particular
resolution of his was never to be put to the test. He would retire, but
there was always one more obstacle to be surmounted first. There had
been the Stoner pyramid; the NBI overdraft; the debt to the Anglo-
Saxon for his ships. And now, in 1936, there were the problems facing
the firm as a result of the war in Abyssinia.

18 The Abyssinian War

It was AB's fate quite frequently to come into collision with Italians.
We have long and angry letters from him to Davis in early 1934
regarding the two Italian mechanics in charge of the garage in the
Aidrus Road;

> On Friday last I was informed by the faithful Ahmed Said that in
> flagrant contravention of their new contract, in accordance with
> which they were to pay for their own electric current, X and Y fixed
> up a contraption by which the current used by their Kelvinators was
> registered not in their own meters but in the firm's ...

In course of AB's vigorous investigation of 'this nauseating affair'
other facts came to light.

> In short, I do not think there is an Italian in the place, from the
> Consul himself (who has a battery belonging to us which he has
> never asked to pay for), down to the last Italian workman, who has
> not 'done' the firm, thanks to X's munificent treatment of his
> compatriots at our expense! ...

AB sent a sharp letter to the Italian Consul. The Consul took the line
that the whole affair was a storm in a tea-cup. AB, he suggested, could,
if he wished, take X to court; but if he failed to prove his case X would
be entitled to heavy damages for defamation. This was a snub that AB
could not forgive. His relations with the Italian Consulate became and
remained extremely unfriendly, In 1937 he was to conclude a letter:
'Kindly accept, *Monsieur le Consul*, the expression of my profound
contempt.'

More serious was the trouble that blew up at Mogadiscio. Leopard
skins from Italian Somaliland were of better quality and commanded a
higher price than those from Ethiopia. In the thirties the authorities at

Mogadiscio – presumably with the idea of keeping up the numbers of leopards – issued an order forbidding the export of these skins. But no effective measures were or could be taken to prevent the killing of leopards up country; and quantities of the skins were smuggled over the land frontier to Mombasa and exported from there. There was no Besse branch or agency to buy these skins in Kenya. However bales of other skins shipped to Aden by the Besse branch at Mogadiscio became apt to contain a small quantity of leopard skins discreetly packed between the layers. Nearly all firms operating along the Benadir and Red Sea Coasts were then in the habit of taking steps to make poorly paid customs officials well disposed. But on this occasion, at Mogadiscio, something went wrong. The bales were opened in the customs yard and the leopard skins discovered. It is possible that there was a deliberate intention to frame the firm of Besse. There is no firm evidence that the local manager was acting on AB's instructions, or even that AB was aware of what was happening. Nevertheless a criminal charge was brought against AB personally in the Mogadiscio courts, and after protracted legal and procedural delays, he was convicted *in absentia*.

The Besse manager in Mogadiscio had been dismissed not long after the affair first came to light, and it was his successor who had charge of the case. He had contacts in Rome, and, unknown to AB, he made use of them to arrange for lawyers there to apply for an amnesty. Rather surprisingly this was granted – to AB's extreme indignation. His own part throughout had been to write violent letters to all and sundry, denouncing Italian ineptitude and bad faith. Inevitably these letters became known to the Italians and their result was to make him *persona non grata* to Italian officials in East Africa and, in particular, to the very influential Quadrumvir de Vecchi de Val Cismondo, Governor of Italian Somaliland. Well before the Abyssinian War broke out AB was on the Fascist Black List.

II

As the clash in Abyssinia became more and more imminent most of the big foreign firms active in the area thought it prudent to reduce their operations to a minimum. AB took the opposite line. As we have seen from his letters on the proposed third ship, he was convinced that, whatever the outcome of the crisis, the new Ethiopia was ultimately bound to offer unlimited opportunities for intensive trading. His branches were instructed to step up their activities, to buy everything available at acceptable prices; and to put themselves in a position to dominate the market, both for export and import, as soon as a final settlement was reached. But meanwhile he was not prepared to agree to ill-considered investment. With the worsening of the political situation, far, sighted Ethiopians and their foreign sympathisers took the line that the greater the British stake in the Ethiopian economy, the better the chances of effective British backing. One scheme put up was extensive road development throughout the country – know-how, material and finance to be supplied by Shell. It was obvious that Shell would be influenced by the views of their local agent; and the British Minister in Addis Abeba, Sir Sidney Barton, who enthusiastically supported the proposal, came over to Aden to sell the idea to AB. There was an interview at which HB was present. Sir Sidney put up his case. AB replied that Shell would only lose their money and that he would strongly advise St Helen's Court to have nothing to do with the matter. The minister was disappointed. 'Mr Besse,' he said, 'your attitude is most un-British.'

III

On 3 October 1935 the Italian armies crossed the frontier. The nature of the terrain and the exceptionally heavy autumn rains held up their advance. As late as mid-November the war seemed to be making little difference to the day-to-day life of the Ethiopian capital. It was now that occurred one of the not infrequent upsets in the management of the Addis Abeba branch. Relations between the Belgian manager and his employer in Aden had never been happy, and another Belgian, Maurice Weerts, had been earmarked to go up from Djibouti, to act as Number Two. At the end of November AB received a letter from the Addis Abeba manager: 'It is inconsistent with my dignity to submit to the constant stream of insults in your correspondence and I proffer my resignation.' Weerts was told to leave for Addis Abeba at once, taking with him AB's reply which he was to hand over personally, and to be ready himself to assume charge. He arrived on 5 December and handed over the letter. It ran: 'I am gratified to note the first sign of dignity you have shown while in my employment and your resignation is accepted.' Weerts felt that his term as manager in Addis Abeba was likely to be an eventful one.

In mid-January AB prodded his Abyssinian branches: they were not buying anything like the quantities of hides and skins he was expecting. In February, in view of the Ethiopian censorship on letters, Weerts came down the line to Djibouti to report: the Italians were advancing from the south and there seemed to be nothing to stop them cutting the railway. AB was then chiefly preoccupied with the probable devaluation of the French franc:[1] his branches were instructed to arrange to owe to the Chemin de Fer d'Ethiopie and to the Djibouti Treasury as large a sum in francs as possible. In March Weerts reported that the atmosphere in Addis Abeba was extremely nervy. AB told him he should not take local panic too seriously. In due course things would return to normal. Meanwhile he (Weerts) should get on with his trading, and should have no qualms about accumulating large stocks of Maria Theresa dollars. In April came the first Italian air raids on Addis Abeba, and a collapse of morale and public order seemed imminent. It was then that AB took one of the biggest gambles of his whole career. He bought up, at a bargain price and for his own account, the whole stock of fuels and oil products in the Shell depots in Addis Abeba.

IV

April 1936 saw the hardest fighting of the war, and the Ethiopian army was decisively beaten. The Emperor returned to his capital and, on the late evening of 1 May, left with his suite by special train for Djibouti and for exile. News of his departure leaked out during the night, and the disorders began which lasted four days till the first Italian troops moved in. The authorities had left the military arms stores open for the population to help themselves. The motive, supposing there was one, may have been to encourage guerilla resistance. But, for the time being, there was no sign of any will to resist. The milling, leaderless mobs, swollen by deserters and stragglers from the defeated armies, surged along the streets, broke into the liquor stores, then into shops, warehouses and private houses. There was a wave of xenophobic fury against foreigners. There was arson, indiscriminate shooting and a number of senseless killings. Those who remained sober enough loaded caravans of loot to drive off to their villages up country.

On the morning of 2 May Weerts on arrival at his office in the vast and well-stocked Besse compound was faced with difficult decisions. The presence of Europeans was likely to provoke xenophobia: furthermore Madame Weerts was expecting a baby. So he took her off to the British Legation, considered for some reason or other to be more secure than the French. Davidson – his English Number Two – went off on a series of rescue operations, driving round the city in his car, picking up stranded foreigners and conveying them to their Legations. The organisation of the defence of the compound was largely left to one Rahmato, a senior Ethiopian employee. Unskilled labour at the compound included a group of Rahmato's fellow tribesmen, and these were considered the core of the defence. Military expertise, such as it was, came from an elderly Sikh night-watchman, who, many years before, had been a sergeant in the army in India.

The need was for arms. In view of the wild shooting in the streets a Besse lorry was lined with earth-filled coffee bags and in this improvised armoured vehicle the head chauffeur and two or three other stalwarts went off to the arsenal. All they could obtain on their first foray was 1000 rounds of small arms ammunition. A second expedition produced a dozen rifles which were distributed among Rahmato's tribesmen. The gateways to the compound were blocked, weak spots reinforced, sentries posted, and the garrison waited for the assault. But, perhaps luckily, an assault never came. The gangs of looters may have realised the place would be defended, and in any case there was easier game elsewhere. When the rioting subsided on the arrival of the Italians the rich Besse compound remained intact. At the outlying stores there had been some losses: sugar, soap and candles at the Customs Depot; stocks of coffee at the Besse coffee godown at the railway station; 100 cases of petrol and 200 cases of kerosene at the Shell depot in Addis Abeba; and there was some damage at the Shell Akaki depot outside the town, though this proved to be less extensive than at first was feared. By and large the firm of Besse had come out of it all very well.

V

AB at this time, in accordance with his normal routine, was about to embark for Europe. Just before leaving Aden, on 7 May, he telegraphed Weerts his delight at the news that all the staff were safe. Meanwhile the Italians were restoring order in Addis Abeba; and on 22 May Weerts was able to report that the railway once more was working normally, and that he had already loaded ten railway wagons of export goods, which was six times as much as the loadings of all the competition combined. This letter, many weeks en route, seemed to confirm AB's belief that the crisis was over and he sent off a general directive from Le Paradou on 1 July.

You must insist that Aden and Djibouti send you *everything* that you ask for – not only the usual import goods but cars, lorries, Shell products etc. I want us to intensify sales. While it is possible for us to get prices showing a good margin we must *not* be afraid of accumulating MT dollars. Moreover – this is most important – I do not mind you acquiring export goods (skins etc.) at higher prices than those prevailing in Europe provided the difference is less than our profit on our imports. this policy should allow you completely to monopolise the market, because our competitors will not follow us on to ground they think is dangerous. This buying will use up a very large quantity of dollars and you may even have to draw on Aden. You know my views on finance. So long as new regulations are not put into force and the money of the country remains – as it must – the MT dollar, this is the only currency we should recognise. If, to oblige the authorities, you should be forced from time to time to accept a sum in lire, this sum should never exceed the sum in lire you have to pay out in any one week for customs duties.

Mails between Ethiopia and Aden – let alone Le Paradou – were apt to be slow and uncertain in any case. War conditions and the Italian censorship meant further delays. In late June Weerts was complaining to Collins in Aden: 'I have heard nothing from Mr Besse for six weeks. A little note from him would do me a lot of good, I am sure it would encourage me to hold out.' He was having a difficult time. One of the first acts of the Italian military had been to requisition all the oil stocks in the former Shell depots. Order had been restored, more or less, in Addis Abeba, but up country there was banditry, sporadic guerrilla fighting and a break-down of transport owing to the heavy spring rains. More serious still were the stringent regulations issued by the Exchange Control Department of the Banca d'Italia. Any foreign currency acquired through exports must be surrendered against lire, and any goods imported might only be sold for lire. Weerts appealed to the French Legation, but the French (and other) Legations were preoccupied with the Italian insistence that they be withdrawn and consulates established in their place. The new regulations were such as completely to hamstring the activities of the firm of Besse. The only form of business that seemed to Weerts to be feasible was the import of Italian cotton piece goods that could be paid for in lire.

It was in the late summer, when AB was in London, that he fully realised what was happening. He went at once to the French Embassy and the Ambassador suggested he should call on the Foreign Minister on his way back through Paris. M de St Quentin received him amiably, and for the moment AB felt optimistic – '*Action imminente*' he wired out to his son André (then in charge in Djibouti) '*maintenir, résister*'. He had hopes of securing the good offices of Paul Reynaud: 'Reynaud', he wrote 'is a forceful personality, specially feared at the present juncture . . .'. He believed that the Italians would be forced to compromise: 'They are beginning to realise that their 'conquest' of Abyssinia is far from complete. . . . In Italy itself trouble is brewing everywhere.' But the weeks passed and nothing happened. He planned, as soon as he got back to Aden, to proceed to Addis Abeba and argue his case in person. But his application for an entry permit was refused. He was *persona non grata* in Italian East Africa.

Meanwhile Weerts had at last obtained some satisfaction over the requisitioned oil stocks. He had originally sent in an invoice in MT dollars. The Italians maintained that only lire were available. Argument went on for many weeks. 'Finally' (to quote Weerts) 'the deal was settled over a rather beautiful leopard skin, and I sent two trucks to Italian Headquarters to load many tons of silver dollars.' The firm now had the wherewithal to buy local produce if and when export again became feasible. But on the afternoon of the first Sunday of January 1937 Weerts was having tea in his garden when there appeared two carabinieri and four armed members of the Guardia di Finanza. They presented a formal document headed '*D'Ordine del Capo del Governo*'. The content was that the firm of Besse were forbidden to trade on Ethiopian territory. There was no motivation given. It was an order from the Head of the Government, i.e. Mussolini himself, and that was sufficient. The motives behind the order are fairly obvious. AB was listed as an enemy of Fascism. It was unthinkable that he would cooperate in Italian plans for the economic development of their new Empire. His share of the Ethiopian trade was far too large. And there were now a number of firms and institutions who had their eye on that share of the trade and who were eager to provide appropriate motivation to the Italian authorities.

VI

Early in 1937, when AB was still in Aden, some persons started a smear campaign in Rome. We have a vigorous letter of protest from AB to *Le Journal* following an article in late March from their Rome correspondent, implying that AB had been guilty of smuggling, gunrunning, drug traffic and other misdemeanours. Six weeks later, as he was returning to Europe for the summer, there was a curious incident. HB had left Aden for Le Paradou a few days previously. She went to Marseilles airport to meet her husband who was due to arrive on a British plane. The plane landed without AB; the pilot explained that he had been taken off at Brindisi by the Italian police. From the airport HB phoned to Paris to Marius Moutet, Minister of Colonies, who, of all his colleagues, had shown most sympathetic interest in AB's affairs. Moutet acted at once. Twenty-four hours later AB flew in to Marseilles, having travelled via Amsterdam and Paris. He never gave anybody any details of what had happened to him.

All that summer he went on with his exasperated attempts to goad the French Government into action. His lobbying might have been more effective had it been more restrained: he may well have antagonised a number of those concerned. We find him bitterly complaining of 'endless waits in ministerial ante-rooms, lying promises, unacknowledged letters, passive resistance as a cloak for impotence, politeness and petty deceptions by our Great Men – Illustrissimus Sanctus Quentinus Cunctator – indepartmental muddles, terror of responsibility ...'. In the autumn he wrote, perhaps not entirely sincerely, to Moutet: 'If I did not keep telling myself that my experiences, once generally known, would be of use to French businessmen established abroad, I would throw in my hand completely.'

Meanwhile in Addis Abeba Weerts was fighting his lonely battle with considerable resource. To quote his own words:

Our argument to the Fascist Authorities was that we had not been at war with them and that we had not been defeated, therefore we should be paid before leaving the country. They agreed and offered lire, which could not be accepted because we were forbidden to exist in Italian territories; the Italians had no foreign currency for such a purpose, may be they tried to tire us out, but I declared my willingness to stay until they had the required foreign currency. Later on, when Rome was asking why we were still there, or perhaps when Italian Services wanted our premises, the best of all in Addis Abeba, I suggested to transform our assets into hides and skins and to export them without surrendering the foreign currency of the proceeds. Much to my surprise, this was accepted, and the Italian did not take the trouble to check on how much money was involved. So I found a door open for keeping some commercial activity, and in order to confuse the Italian Guardia di Finanza on duty, we put all our stocks at the entrance of the compound where there was a window on the street, and we provided the guards with comfortable seats inside the compound, the window being not under their eyes so they could not see what was coming in. The result was that we bought and brought in regularly the most profitable commodity at the time, sheepskins, not only with our own money but also with money given to us by trustworthy persons who wanted to export their lire illegally. This went on for very many months and the Italians never got suspicious, they merely marvelled at the size of our investment in Ethiopia. . . . Incredible as it is, our books or our Bank account was never checked; otherwise I would have been punished very seriously for an offence against control regulations.

In late June 1937 Aden were able to report to AB in Le Paradou that Weerts had secured permission for certain exports without the surrender of currency. By now it was possible to avoid the Italian postal censorship; friendly officials in Djibouti were allowing André to use the diplomatic bag to the French Consul General in Addis Abeba.[2] In August Aden reported that forty tons of skins were on their way from Addis Abeba; moreover Weerts had used his surplus lire to buy Italian piece goods which he was selling at a substantial profit. AB was very sparing in his praise of his employees but he now noted of Weerts: 'I approve every step he has taken. In fact I wonder if I could have done so well myself.'

The summer of 1937 brought plenty of problems for Weerts. There was a move by the Italian military to requisition the firm's offices and compound. There was trouble over Besse property at Dessie and at Jimma, all the more difficult to deal with as Weerts himself was not allowed to leave the capital. He was offered a substantial bribe to desert Besse and join a newly established Italian firm. There was an elaborate plot to trick him into signing a power of attorney in favour of a lawyer, who, it turned out, was in fact employed by the Italian secret police. But these storms were weathered and the flow of goods continued down the railway to Djibouti.

In September AB wrote to Davis: 'Once we have removed all we can from Addis Abeba we will leave a guardian there till things get better.' None the less he continued his bombardment of the Paris ministries. He urged reprisals at Djibouti. There was Italian property there that might be sequestered, and all manner of restrictions that might be placed on Italian use of the Chemin de Fer d'Ethiopie till full satisfaction had been given to the house of Besse. But, in spite of Moutet, the

French Cabinet had no wish for drastic action. The one point gained was that the Ministry of Foreign Affairs secured Italian consent for AB to visit Addis Abeba to put his case to the Viceroy.

AB was back in Aden in October 1937 and, the following month, went up to the Ethiopian capital for his interview with Marshal Graziani. Sitting in the Viceroy's ante-room beforehand he told Weerts that if he was kept waiting he would walk out. But he was admitted on the stroke of eleven, the hour prescribed. AB stated his case. Graziani replied that the decision had been made in Rome; all he could do was to put an enquiry to Rome as to whether the matter might be reconsidered. As things turned out, shortly after AB's visit Graziani was seriously wounded in a terrorist attack by Ethiopian patriots on his official residence. He was recalled to Italy, and the Duke of Aosta took his place. Feelers were put out in the hope of arranging a second visit by AB. The new Viceroy replied that Rome's decision was final and that no useful purpose would be served by a further interview. An idea was then mooted that AB should apply for an audience with Mussolini in Rome. But discreet enquiries made it clear that there was no prospect of the application being granted, and the idea was dropped.

By the spring of 1938 Weerts had completed his task of disposing of the stocks. He himself was exhausted after the efforts of the past thirty months. In May he was recalled to Aden and was replaced at Addis Abeba by one of the staff from Mogadiscio. But, as AB had foreseen, the newcomer's role was in effect only that of caretaker for the Besse premises.

VII

There is an epilogue to AB's visit to Addis Abeba. Soon after his return to Aden he wrote confidentially to Sir Stewart Syme, Governor of the Sudan. Sir Stewart as we have seen had served in Aden, and had retained AB's respect. In his letter of 14 December 1937 AB informed him that he had, following his visit to Abyssinia, compiled a report for the information of the French Government which he had passed to M. Marius Moutet, Minister of Colonies. The report was *sous une forme romancée*, as AB had important interests and staff in the country and he did not wish to endanger them. The substance of the report was that the Italian position was untenable. It was unthinkable that they could maintain their position in Ethiopia. 'But even if the fruit is ripe one has to shake the tree to make it drop.' The solution to the problem, AB continued, could be found in the person of an Ethiopian ex-diplomat,

Ato Tekle Hawariat. He knew him personally, had had several talks with him. His prestige was such that he could rally support all over Abyssinia.

> With a modicum of aid from your Government or from mine, and with financial support to which I am ready to contribute substantially, he is prepared to undertake the venture. . . . It is for you to judge. It is no business of mine to express an opinion on what could or should be done . . .

AB's report *sous forme romancée* has not survived, and we have no information as to British or French official reactions. However, later in 1938, Weerts (back in Aden) was instructed by AB to pass 20 000 MT dollars to Tekle Hawariat. The money was to be used for sabotage of communications inside Abyssinia and for the purchase of arms for anti-Fascist partisans. It was made clear that if worthwhile results were obtained very substantial further sums would be made available. It appears that Tekle Hawariat took the dollars to Djibouti and arranged to send them inland, by couriers, to a certain Nagash in the Danakil country. But the couriers were caught and killed by Italian frontier guards and irregulars near the French Somaliland border.

19   Maria Theresa Dollars

I

A by-product of the Abyssinian War was to enable AB to make substantial profits out of deals in Maria Theresa dollars. These dollars or thalers, minted in Vienna, had for generations been the traditional currency of Ethiopia. But they were also in use in wide adjacent areas on either side of the Red Sea and the narrows where the natives were unwilling to accept paper money. An MT dollar, of about the size of an English five-shilling piece, had a silver content of slightly more than three-quarters of a fine ounce. Its value could thus be assessed in terms of the current price of silver. But its local value in terms of other currencies was apt to depend on supply and demand, and there were times when the margins gave opportunities for profitable trading. Thus if silver was high and the local MT dollar rate was low, it might pay to buy up the dollars available locally and ship them as bullion to London or other centres. If the rates were the other way, then it would pay to order new silver dollars from the Vienna Mint and dispose of them locally. There had for years been intermittent trading along these lines, in which AB had sometimes taken part. But it was the Abssinian War and its aftermath that made it big business.

It is unfortunate that the surviving records of AB's deals in MT dollars are so few and so scrappy. But we have a letter of his from Aden to Davis written in December 1935, when the Italians were advancing in Abyssinia but were still some months away from their occupation of the capital:

A time is almost certain to come when we shall find it advisable, if not absolutely necessary, to resume our importation from Vienna of MT dollars. A fact which shows which way the wind is blowing is that with silver at about 20d an oz., thus making the dollar work out at Rs 1.10, the rate here is notwithstanding maintained at Rs 1.30, the demand which keeps it so high emanating from Port Sudan, whence the thalers find their way to the Italians in Eritrea, where they are

120

exchanged for lire, which, in their turn, find a ready market in Aden. The profits realized on this traffic are so enormous that the risks it entails – of depreciation of the dollar and of being caught – are cheerfully run. Besides the demand for Port Sudan there is a scarcity of thalers in the Hadhramaut, as well as at Hodeida . . .

AB went on to give instructions to Davis to line up the Austrian Mint so that, on receipt of a telegram from Aden, Vienna could quote a price for immediate delivery of an initial order for two hundred thousand thalers. He was then unaware of a recent agreement between the Italian and Austrian governments under which the Vienna Mint was no longer to mint MT dollars and was to hand over the dies to the Italians. As soon as he heard of this he decided to arrange for the minting in London. In late January 1936 he was writing to Davis:

> You will be surprised to hear that X (of the London Office) mentions not a word in his letter about MT dollars. The fact that the Austrian Government had handed over dies to the Italians cannot but signify that no more of these thalers will be minted for any other than Italian Government account! Why, therefore, have no offers been forthcoming? Is X asleep, or is it a fresh proof that, knowing and understanding nothing about the activities of this firm of ours beyond the immediate precincts of the London office, he is incapable of realising what his silence means to us? . . .

In due course the London office approached the Royal Mint. AB's impatience is understandable in view of the potential profitability of the business. One MT dollar weighed 0·902368 troy ounces. As the dollar contained 83·333 per cent of fine silver, its silver content was 0·751672 fine ounces. Assuming the price of silver to be 20·3125 pence per standard ounce – the equivalent of 21·975 pence per fine ounce – and allowing 1·38 pence for minting and alloy, and rather more than 0·2 pence for freight, insurance and interest on outlay, the cost of each dollar c.i.f. Aden would work out at a small fraction over 18d. And in Aden the dollar was fetching more than 24d.

Negotiations with the Royal Mint took far longer than AB had expected. The dies had to be produced and perfected. The approval of the Treasury was required. It was the firm that had to provide the silver, and the acquisition of silver involved various technicalities. As the London office reported:

Should we require to buy silver we would have to place our order
with a broker (giving limits) before we know the price: this price is
fixed by the silver brokers at two p.m. each day, and the previous
twenty four hours business is booked at this price.

Furthermore there were the traditional relationships between the big
bullion brokers, the Mint and the Treasury which provoked AB's
indignation. He noted when visiting London in the summer of 1937:

In this country, which is supposed to be free, there are sharks, as
large as those in the Red Sea, and furthermore graft which is
considered to be a monopoly of the US and a subject of derision in
England is common here also.

He went so far as to ask his lawyer's advice on legality of existing
arrangements between the Royal Mint and the brokers; but he was
evidently advised not to institute proceedings.

AB's impatience was all the more natural because, by early 1937,
the Royal Mint was already supplying other customers; and the trade
in dollars, as AB noted, was 'no longer a business, but a fortune falling
from the skies'. The reasons for this state of affairs were simple. These
dollars were the only currency that the Ethiopian villagers would
accept. The Italian authorities needed vast quantities to buy local
produce in order to feed their armies. But the villagers, once they had
the dollars, could find nothing to buy with them; so the coins were
buried or hidden, and passed out of circulation. The Italians' decision
to maintain an exchange rate, in Ethiopia, of 13·50 lire per MT dollar
gave opportunities for local ingenuity and resource. Dollars were
smuggled into Ethiopia where they were exchanged for lire and the lire
smuggled out and conveyed by various and devious routes back to
Italy. But of course what ultimately happened to the newly minted
dollars was no concern of the house of Besse. The firm was merely
concerned with the perfectly legitimate business of satisfying the big
demand of brokers throughout the Red Sea area.

AB was eager to find alternative sources of supply. Enquiries as to
the possibility of minting in Brussels came to nothing. But in early
1937 one Grapin, who acted as AB's agent in Paris, was negotiating
with the French Monnaie. In June the Monnaie was working on an
initial order for $600 000. AB of course was well aware that the going
was too good to last. 'The profit', he noted, 'that we are likely to make
at the beginning should be enormous, but we must set aside something

in prevision of a loss later on.' In spite of all attempts at secrecy more and more concerns were certain to take an interest. In September 1937 it was learned that the Banque de l'Indo-Chine intended to place an order for minting. Keen as was the demand, some time or other saturation point was bound to be reached. The attitude of the firm of Besse was summed up in a memo by the London office: 'What we would like would be to make a big profit out of it for ourselves, and smash the market for all these sharks who are speculating in an article which is no concern of theirs whatever.'

II

By January 1938 full agreement with the Royal Mint had at last been reached, and work was in hand on an initial order for 250 000 MT dollars. A further 200 000 were ordered in February, and 500 000 in April. Orders placed in May totalled 1 650 000. The dollars in their leaden packing (whether from London or Paris) were consigned to Aden. Some of the heavy cases were here trans-shipped for other destinations. The remainder were carted to the Aidrus Road and stored on the ground floor of the main Besse building, pending disposal to Indian and Arab brokers. As already noted, the physical weight of the coins serves as insurance against theft. During the whole period we know only of one instance where a case was broken into; and all the thieves succeeded in taking away was $50.

AB's policy is illustrated in a long directive he wrote in early August 1938:

> We shall have willy nilly to buy extensively from the Monnaie in order to prevent them selling elsewhere. Grapin is keeping a close watch in order to prevent new contracts being entered into with anybody but ourselves. It is reasonable to expect that we may be caught with a certain amount of MT dollars in hand when the tide turns. However, the loss we would have to face should not be considerable in view of the fact that we buy these dollars at the price of the silver plus the minting cost. But to be absolutely sure, a close coordination of London's and Paris' watchfulness over the work and output of the Mints will be necessary. I believe that we can rely on Grapin who is, after all, keenly interested in the welfare of this new venture; I cannot, however, in my heart of hearts, believe for a moment that Mr Simpson will be at the height of this task, so new to

him, as it will mean a close and constant contact with the Treasury, the Mint, the Silver Brokers etc. . . . It will be up to Aden not to let a week pass without calling his attention to the necessity of keeping them fully acquainted with whatever takes place in London. He must continue to give the Treasury the impression that we are still very keen buyers, as in fact we are since London's conditions are better than Paris. But should he learn that London is prepared to mint on a larger scale, Aden will then have to be doubly cautious and see to it that all the dollars we have contracted for are resold, or instruct Grapin to cancel our contracts if this can be done within reasonable terms . . .

London should also see to it, from now onwards, that these shipments of specie are made at as low a cost as possible and I advise them to see personally (not by correspondence) the heads of the departments concerned of the P&O, BI, Orient Line, Scandinavian Coy., Strick Line, Messageries Maritimes, Union Castle, etc., in fact all the companies who have regular and direct sailings from Marseilles to Aden. They will also have to take into account the frequency of the sailings and the speed of the steamers.

As regards Aden, I suggest that we make as little noise as possible about this affair. In fact, I would prefer to earn less and have the best part of our dollars shipped to Hodeida where, in ordinary circumstances, Sheikh Omar can easily absorb 100 000 monthly, even if it meant a slight loss on the rates obtainable in Aden. It is quite possible that these Dollars could be sold in large quantities in Jedda especially when one considers the magnitude of the smuggling which is being carried out at present between the Saudi ports and Massawa. It is also conceivable that Dollars could be absorbed in the Hadhramaut coast, at Djibouti, at Berberah and a special organisation should be created from now on to cope with the huge sums we may be obliged to buy from the Monnaie . . .

The logical conclusion of what is likely to take place is a steady depreciation in the rates for these Dollars, and Aden should see to it that we have no balance in cash of that currency and, as far as can be controlled, no outstandings . . .

III

A total of $1 725 000 were supplied by the Royal Mint up to early November 1938, when AB took advantage of the clause in the contract enabling him to cancel the balance of his orders. In April 1940 the position once again appeared to be favourable, and he ordered a further 550 000. Of these, 250 000 were shipped during May. But by that time AB himself was out of action following his plane crash and had left for France; and the Aden office found it prudent to cancel the $300 000 outstanding.

20   Arabian Airways

I

In the early thirties a journey from Aden to the Hadhramaut was quite an undertaking. The first stage was to get to Mukalla. Those reluctant to face the discomfort and uncertainties of travel by dhow must wait for one of the rare steamers. The voyage by steamer, in the most favourable weather conditions, took over thirty hours. From Mukalla on to Shibam, Seiyun or Tarim the journey was by mule or camel. Travel to other destinations was also time-consuming. The passage from Aden to Hodeida by steamer (if and when available) was also over thirty hours. Cowasjee Dinshaw ran a biweekly service Aden to Djibouti with two small and ancient steamers, taking (wind and weather permitting) fourteen hours for the trip of 109 miles. There were occasional Italian steamers for the far more distant Mogadiscio and Massawa. Such were communications when AB first considered the possibilities of air transport.

Facilities for aircraft in South West Arabia were limited. In Aden the RAF had their airstrip at Khormaksar. By arrangement with the Protectorate Administration the RAF had established airstrips at Mukalla, Mukeiris, Dhala and in the Hadhramaut. Pilots had to contend with high temperatures, high winds, poor weather forecasting, and, over most of the Protectorate, high altitudes. Few charts of any accuracy were available. Airstrip markings were mostly non-existent and ground maintenance very poor. Windsocks were only rarely available: smoke flares would be fired on the first run over the course. Refuelling had to be carried out by the pilot himself, with the precarious assistance of local bedouin. The fuel was stored in four-gallon tins and, inevitably, many of these were often found to be empty. RAF ground radio equipment was available on the better airstrips, but servicing was difficult, and it was apt to happen that the radio was not working.

II

We do not know when the idea of buying a plane first occurred to AB. He must long have resented the waste of time involved in getting round his branches and agencies with existing communications; and his habit of looking ahead must have assured him of the big future for air transport throughout his area. In 1934 and 1935 he was asking his contacts in Shell and elsewhere for advice on the technical aspects and instructing his London office to make detailed enquiries. During 1935 the pressure on London was stepped up and early in 1936 the decision was taken. In due course an ex-RAF pilot was engaged and a machine purchased. It was a four-seater Monospar, G-AEJB, with two Pobjoy engines totalling 190 h.p.

The maiden flight was fixed for 31 July 1936, from Croydon to Cannes (the nearest airfield to AB at Le Paradou). Passengers were HB and three of her children – Ariane, Joy and Peter. A disaster would have made a considerable gap in the Besse family: but AB was not easily deterred by physical risk whether to himself or to his dearest. As things turned out this particular flight was to give him many hours of anxious waiting.

After crossing the channel the pilot lost his bearings and there was a forced landing at Rouen. The party accordingly were very late in arriving at Le Bourget, from where they could phone news of their progress to Le Paradou. (The Monospar had no W/T, so there were no means of communication when in flight.) Departure next morning from Le Bourget was delayed because of starter trouble, so they were late landing at Lyons, and later still setting off again south, where they ran into a strong mistral. The route laid down had entailed turning east at Avignon; but the pilot missed Avignon and went straight on. Some time later HB recognised the Marignane airport, north-west of Marseilles. She knew the coast well and thenceforward directed the unhappy pilot to Cannes. A week late the plane (with Meryem as passenger) took off for the return to Croydon. Once more there was navigational trouble. It took the aircraft nearly six hours to reach Le Bourget. On the final lap it ran into bad weather and had to land for the night at Abbeville. AB was so disgusted that he felt inclined to sell back the plane to the suppliers – emphasising that it had only done fifteen hours actual flying – and to terminate the agreement with the pilot.

But he had second thoughts. There is a gap in the surviving correspondence but in April 1937 he wrote to Simpson:

I am finding it exceedingly difficult to take a final decision regarding buying a second plane or even keeping the Monospar... Once this nauseating affair of Abyssinia is over and normality prevails again I shall feel that my task is finished.... I would therefore prefer Davis to take the decision.... If the concerted opinion is against developing this air venture nothing will be left except to dismiss the pilot and sell the Monospar. I confess it would not be altogether without regret that I should do so, but I shall almost certainly abide by the decision the three of you take – Davis, yourself and Collins.

There followed detailed instructions about enquiries that Simpson was to make regarding the Air Navigation Act – one point uppermost in AB's mind being whether it would be possible for planes to be inspected by the RAF at Aden rather than have to send them periodically to Cairo.

It was quite obvious that, whatever he may have written, AB had made his mind up, and Simpson, Davis and Collins tactfully acquiesced. During the summer of 1937 (with AB at Le Paradou) the London office was kept very busy. The choice was eventually made of a Short Scion (G-AEJL) – with a Pobjoy engine like that of the Monospar – as a second machine. It turned out that the venture was to cost more than had been envisaged. The experts were insistent that in Aden conditions a pilot should not be asked to fly more than 400 hours a year, so that, with two planes, a second pilot must be engaged. Then each machine should have a spare engine.[1] Finally the only suitable ground engineer available made it a condition that his wife should follow him to Aden. On this last AB wrote to Simpson on 2 July:

When the time comes for his wife to join him I shall not feel inclined to give him any more than the living allowance for a single man – it would create a very undesirable precedent if I started making allowances for wives.... It seems unwarranted to have to pay such a large salary for a ground engineer – £450 per annum. It must be clearly laid down in the contract that when not working on the planes he must be available for work elsewhere.

On the ultimate outlook AB was optimistic. 'It can only be a matter of time before an air service pays in our part of the world where communications are slow, difficult and a strain on one's powers of endurance.' He envisaged a weekly service Aden – Mukalla – Shibam (a three-hour flight), and, as soon as the French agreed, a weekly service to Djibouti (105 minutes). When and if Italian permission was forthcoming there should be services Aden – Djibouti – Mogadiscio, and Aden – Djibouti – Addis Abeba; and, once the Imam was squared, Aden – Hodeida – Sanaa.

Meanwhile the Monospar and the original pilot had been operating at Aden since early 1937. Permission for passenger flights (as opposed to private trips with members of the staff) to and from Djibouti had not yet been obtained, but attempts were being made at a passenger service to the Hadhramaut. There were still navigational difficulties. One morning in May (when AB was back in France and Davis in charge in Aden) the Monospar took off for Djibouti, and completely disappeared for several hours. It later transpired she had gone off course and been forced to land at Obok. Davis pleaded for the plane to be fitted with W/T: the cost of installation would be well repaid with the saving in anxiety. On the Arabian side of the narrows there were the inevitable local hazards. Bedouin, in the neighbourhood of the airstrips, would not leave the plane alone. There were minor breakages and a good deal of pilfering. The pilot, who spoke not a word of Arabic, was continually struggling to prevent last-minute loading by native passengers of bulky, heavy and unexpected packages. In June there was a case when a party who had booked to Shibam backed out at the last minute because 'one of them weighed 200 lbs, which meant that we could not take the whole party'. Davis suggested that cheaper fares might stimulate Arab air-mindedness. AB (at Le Paradou) disagreed. The fare Aden – Mukalla, he felt, should stay at 100 Rs, and Mukalla – Seiyum 50 Rs: an appropriate fare for Aden – Djibouti would need 90 Rs, as against the 50 Rs for a passage in the Cowasjee steamers. At the end of June Davis reported that the running expenses of the Monospar to date were 12 234 Rs, as against earnings of 1873 Rs.

III

By the end of the summer of 1937 some definite progress seemed to have been made. The purchase of the Short Scion had been completed. The ground engineer had been engaged. The lawyers had finalised the wording to be printed on the passenger tickets and had arranged for the registration, in Aden, of Arabian Airways Ltd. A point to which AB attached importance was, that 'our liabilities, whatever may happen, must be limited to the extent of the company's capital'. This capital was fixed at £5000 – in five hundred shares of ten pounds each.

Three hundred and fifty shares were in AB's name, one hundred in HB's, and the remaining fifty reserved for Davis and/or such other employee of the firm who might be appointed a director.

When AB returned to Aden in the autumn of 1937, Arabian Airways, with its two small planes and its two pilots, was operating a service between Aden and the Hadhramaut. But the volume of traffic was meagre – nothing like what could be reasonably expected from the Djibouti run. AB now conceived the idea of extending the Djibouti service to Khartoum. Mails between London and Aden took a fortnight. But a link with Imperial Airways at Khartoum would enable airmail letters to arrive in four days; and the subsidy involved would make all the difference to the profitability of Arabian Airways. The London office was instructed to discuss the project with the Air Ministry.

IV

In late November or early December 1937 there were major setbacks. The Scion crashed. We have no details, but in a letter to Simpson AB refers to it as 'smashed to matchwood'. And both the pilots were out of action; one was unable to fly because of eye trouble, and the other had had his licence cancelled on medical grounds. Simpson was told to find two more pilots and purchase a new plane. In early January 1938 he cabled he had purchased a reconditioned Short Scion for £2 000. AB answered rather tartly. A plane was no good without a pilot to fly it, in any case there was the Monospar still intact; Simpson should learn not to put the cart before the horse. Luckily within a month Simpson was able to report that he had found the pilots.

In mid-February AB noted:

> During the period of inactivity I have been thinking very deeply about this venture and have reluctantly come to the conclusion it is not viable unless we can extend it to Djibouti and Khartoum and may be later on to Jedda. If that condition cannot be fulfilled it is useless to hope that we shall ever make it pay.

At the same time he took Simpson to task for agreeing that the ground engineer's wife should come out with the pilots in the new plane:

> ... In the first place it would add to the danger of the journey by lessening the pay load which would have been so useful for extra

petrol, and in the second I happen to know she is a chain smoker, a type of woman I have met often enough to know that she will never make a good housewife. . . . It now remains for you to continue your negotiations with the Air Ministry to get the Djibouti affair settled without further delay. I take it X is bringing out all the data to enable me to take a decision as regards Khartoum.

The new Scion, with the pilots, took off from Rochester on 10 March, and within a week landed safely at Khormaksar. Later in the month it carried AB and HB on a successful trip to Mukalla and the Hadhramaut. But official approval of the proposed extensions seemed fated to become involved in the interdepartmental tangles that AB found so extremely exasperating. Simpson and Davis (now in London) kept calling at the Air Ministry. They were told that the approval of the project was by no means ruled out; but it was a pre-condition of any subsidy that the Governments of Aden and of British Somaliland should also agree to contribute. And of course other departments must be consulted. As for Djibouti, the matter had been put to the French authorities, but no answer had so far been received. AB made enquiries in Paris and learned that the dossier had gone astray between the various ministries involved: he sent off an urgent plea to his friend Moutet. Meanwhile Government House at Khartoum acknowledged receipt of the proposals from Messrs A Besse & Co. But the matter could not be considered in the absence of Mr Muchmore, the Finance Officer, who was away in hospital. It was not known when he was likely to be back.

On 30 March AB noted:

Between Djibouti and Aden the number of passengers is so considerable that we could probably charge no more than what Cowasjee demands for a passage on his miserable little ships, which means the entire passenger traffic as well as the mails will fall into our hands. The matter is pressing in the extreme for it is galling beyond words to have two planes, two pilots and a ground engineer on the spot twiddling their thumbs and costing a small fortune when there is such a large traffic to be done.

In late April AB went back to Le Paradou. There was still no news from either London or Paris. A month later Davis wrote from Aden that it would be a pity to close down, but he could not see any alternative. His next letter was concerned with a violent personal quarrel (all too apt to happen in an Aden summer) between the ground engineer and one of the pilots: it seemed inevitable that one or other would have to be replaced. On 23 June London reported there was no prospect of a subsidy being approved in the foreseeable future for a link with Imperial Airways. In early August Davis sent in the Arabian Airways accounts for the previous twelve months. AB wrote back on 28 August:

> I am sorry to see that the cost of the Arabian Airways venture is so high. I was fully prepared to suffer a loss, but I must admit that I did not think that it would prove to be so great. It is, of course, quite possible that this fresh undertaking will never pay, yet, experience remains to show us that every Air Line had had to surmount tremendous difficulties at the outset, and to-day, not only are they doing well, but in many cases they are flourishing. The advantages which air travel affords are so great that those people who have sampled this means of transport will most certainly return to it, more especially so in our part of the world, when it is compared with land or sea routes. All things considered I feel quite sure that in due course this venture should prove fruitful. However, as I have told you so often, I feel that the time has come for me to withdraw from the colossal work of steering the firm I have built, and if you arrive at the conclusion that the whole matter should be shelved, I shall agree with you, and shall call off the search for an efficient Ground Engineer. Our planes can then be sold for whatever price they can fetch.

We do not know what Davis replied on this occasion. He had, as we have seen, given his opinion in May. In the event the two little planes continued, for another year, to carry their trickle of passengers to and from the Hadhramaut. In September 1939 both pilots and the ground engineer were called up for service with the RAF; and Arabian Airways Ltd. came to an end. Factors largely outside AB's control had made it the one major venture of his to end in failure. But it is of interest to note that ten years later, when Aden Airways Ltd. was formed as a subsidiary of BOAC to cover the area on either side of the Bab el Mandab, it was AB who was invited to become its first chairman.

21 Staff Again

I

At the end of April 1937, as AB was about to leave Aden for France, there was an unfortunate incident at Djibouti with the customs authorities, resulting in the firm being fined 74 000 frs[1]: it was a blow to the firm's prestige, which AB felt keenly. Soon after his arrival at Le Paradou there was a sharp exchange with Davis over the perennial problem of recruiting officers and engineers for the two ships. Davis sent in a note comparing rates and conditions in the Halal Shipping Co. with those in the Anglo-Saxon fleet; and suggested that, as an inducement, future agreements should provide for five months' leave following twenty-five months' service. AB considered the idea 'preposterous'. 'I do not believe for a moment that terms have anything to do with the difficulty you experience in finding men. The conditions we offer are fair enough; the root of the trouble lies in the lack of influence of our London office...'.

But in spite of these minor difficulties and in spite of the unresolved problems in Italian East Africa, the years 1937 and 1938 were the most prosperous that the firm of Besse had ever experienced. AB's bold policy was being justified. Demand, and prices, were rising. He was convinced they would rise still further. In his general directive to the Aden office of 8 July 1937 he wrote: 'Put as much pressure as you can everywhere to keep down prices, but continue to buy.' In the twelve months to 30 June of all the skins exported from British Somaliland 60 per cent had been shipped by the firm of Besse. The growth and complexity of the business, and AB's insistence on being kept informed in minutest detail, made the compilation of the weekly mail from Aden to Le Paradou a serious operation. Even the assembly of the papers had its problems. 'I want to know,' AB wrote out on 15 June 'who was responsible for the packing of the mail sent to me last week. I counted seventy-four clips, three-quarters of which were quite necessary.'

AB returned to Aden in the autumn of 1937. In November, as we have seen, he went up to Addis Abeba for his interview with Graziani. In February or March 1938 he had a confidential letter from a friend of his in Djibouti, Commandant de Jonquières, asking him if he would be willing to accept an appointment as Honorary French Consul in Aden. This letter has not survived, and we have no information as to its background. Moutet, the Minister of Colonies, may or may not have been involved; but it would be rather surprising if the idea found favour with the Ministry of Foreign Affairs.

In any case AB considered the proposal unacceptable. In his reply, dated 22 March, he gave two reasons for finding it was out of the question – his advancing age, and the fact that for five months every year he was away from Aden. There are some characteristic comments on the world of diplomacy – '*Ces plumitifs, ces diplomates, et toute cette pègre parisienne* ...'. Equally characteristic is his reaction to the tributes to himself which must have formed part of de Jonquières' original letter:

> But let me tell you that I am in no way worthy of admiration. Those born with the creative spirit are bound, in spite of themselves, to create. If they succeed, if they possess that mixture of audacity and good sense that enables them to carry through a venture, it is not a matter of merit. The one essential is to create, causing the least possible harm to others, in a spirit of complete self abnegation, and holding out, when opportunity allows, a helping hand to the weak.

II

Back in Le Paradou, in May 1938, his mood was one of depression. He had, as always, been overworking and his eyes were troubling him again. We have a manuscript letter to Davis in Aden of 3 May:

> Were I not haunted with the idea of the international political situation I would relax entirely and rebuild my whole life. Please, please take things easily. Worry will not help. We are today like a squirrel in a revolving cage, and tomorrow will be worse than today...

The letter goes on in four foolscap pages of AB's spidery little handwriting, largely concerned with the latest unpleasantness at the ill-starred Djibouti branch. A check on the stores in the godowns there had revealed that large quantities of goods were missing, and it was difficult to find out exactly what had happened. The employee primarily responsible for the stocks in the store was Parekh's brother; but as soon as the deficiencies came to light he went sick and produced a doctor's certificate that he was suffering from nervous breakdown. Parekh himself came over from Aden to make a thorough investigation: but AB found his report unsatisfactory – all the more so because it turned out that the brother had been shipped back to Bombay before the enquiry was completed.[2] Other incidents came to AB's mind, and he began to wonder whether perhaps his absolute confidence in Parekh had not been misplaced. But the letter to Davis ends with a repetition of the very uncharacteristic injunction 'please, please take things as they come along'.

Ten days later he wrote 'there cannot be anything radically wrong with my eyes, for the moment I cease to use them they cease to pain me'. The old voracity for work came back to him. He was not, he complained, sufficiently kept in the picture by Aden. What he required, *inter alia*, were:

> a bi-monthly report from Grady on the construction of the dhows, and the motors destined to be put into them; from Coleman likewise on aerodrome construction, roads, in fact anything that concerns asphalt; from the Mechanical Section a statement of stocks, goods on order and sales; from the Gums Department a list of stocks, purchases and shipments (like the one the Soap Factory sends me weekly); from the Halal Shipping Company an idea of the movements of our ships . . .

Finally, a personal note: 'When in Aden I had a perfect gallery of ties, of which only a bare dozen could be found on my arrival here.'

The problem of the missing ties was cleared up. In early June he noted that his 'eyesight was better, general health not much'. A few days later he was bombarding Simpson in London and Davis in Aden on the ever recurrent problem of staff recruitment. 'What, I ask you, does the selling of a few hides and skins matter beside the crying need of the firm for Men?'

As we have seen AB placed the main responsibility for recruitment on the London office. That office had a number of handicaps. The premises were dingy and uninviting, as was their setting in Weston Street, SE1. The salaries that could be offered were not tempting, and nothing precise could be said about future prospects. And then of course there were the stories put about by disgruntled ex-employees. But the main difficulty, for the London managers, lay in AB's unpredictability. As Shell had found over secondments, it was impossible to foretell who would and who would not be found to be acceptable; or indeed, in the rare cases of a favourable first impression, for how many weeks that favour was likely to last.

In the third week of June AB sent Simpson a formidable indictment of London's recruiting failures. Simpson's reply has not survived, but we have a further letter from AB dated 27 June:

Your letter does not state whether or not you admit failure. In the negative, (sic) I would like you to comply with the instructions contained in my previous letter to let me have a list of the men you have engaged in the past who have subsequently proved to be a success. If, on the other hand, you realise how utterly you have failed in this matter of primordial importance, and admit that you are unable to do better, you must understand all that your admission means, and the measure in which it will affect the future of our London organisation . . .

On 10 July he wrote to Davis.

You will see that Simpson is impervious to all that I can write or say. His callousness indeed is unbelievable, despite the fact that it is this matter of Staff which alone has prevented me from closing our office in London. . . . I am at an utter loss how to tackle this problem.

A few days later AB went to London and spent some time in Weston Street. On 1 August he wrote again to Davis.

I discussed this question of Staff with them, using all the driving power at my command as well as all the arguments my mind could conceive, but I knew only too well when I left the office that it was just so much water on a duck's back – nothing had penetrated. . . . My failure was emphasized by your answer to my letter on the subject. All your present collaborators in Aden, according to you, are perfect, and whenever they fail it is not their fault but yours! . . . As though you were responsible for their shortcomings!! This attitude of yours shows the nobility of your soul, but, believe me, my dear Davis, it is not conducive to the attainment of the result I have in view or the aim I am pursuing. . . According to my view, we must continue our search tirelessly, ceaselessly, until we have eliminated all the duds. All the As, the Bs, the Cs, the Ds, the Es, as well as others we have in Aden and London who will never attain our standard must go, and be replaced by men and women with initiative, enthusiasm and a high sense of duty, men and women proud to belong to a firm like ours . . .

III

Meanwhile there had been what AB in a letter to Davis described as 'a very painful occurrence'. A newly engaged secretary, after three months in the London office, was due to sail for Aden in July. AB and HB, with their usual hospitality, invited her to break her journey at Le Paradou before embarking at Marseilles. A few hours after she had left the house AB came across some papers. They turned out to be carbons of private letters to two other girls in the London office. We do not know what she had written, but, to quote AB:

they throw such an ugly light upon her character and mentality that I could scarcely believe my eyes, and if, at that eleventh hour, I could have prevented her leaving I should have telephoned Marseilles without a moment's delay. But alas, it was already too late. I am writing her this week, for she must know what I think of her, and have no idea how she will take my indictment. . . . Although she has forfeited my confidence this need not affect the programme I had laid down for her if she rises above her meaner self and takes my letter in a noble spirit . . .

Before the indictment could reach Aden the girl had written a chatty letter of thanks to her host at Le Paradou. It was all very interesting at Aden, she told him. But perhaps the curtains in her room could be changed, as they were getting very shabby. And 'I am perfectly sure Mohamed Aly thinks women indecent creatures . . . he is rather inclined to confuse a sense of responsibility with tyranny . . .'. In due course Davis reported that the new secretary seemed to be a good worker. AB replied. 'I am glad you are finding her of use. As, however, it is beyond my power to work with anybody for whom I have lost respect, the idea of collaboration between us must be dismissed forever.' She did not stay with the firm very long.

22 World War II

At the time of Munich AB was in London with HB. They dined at Frascati's and went to Studio One. There was a newsreel of the return of Mr Chamberlain from Germany and some members of the audience hissed. AB, strongly opposed to the Munich agreement, was gratified at what he felt to be the healthy state of public opinion in Great Britain. A few weeks later he was back in Aden. For the firm of Besse the year between Munich and the beginning of World War II was an uneventful one, or rather as uneventful as was possible with AB in command. It was an extremely prosperous year; and there were more digs at Davis for having opposed the acquisition of a third ship.

> Not only would we have been in a position to-day to crush Cowasjee, but the larger vessel I had in mind would undoubtedly have rendered us the greatest of service in connection with the transport of Java sugar, Rangoon rice and Bombay seeds.... At the price at which we could have acquired such a unit at that time, it could have been re-sold, even before it was finished, at double the cost. With Parekh, too, who joined me in approving the scheme, this matter must be a sore point...'

AB was of course in Europe again for the summer of 1939, and was at Le Paradou at the outbreak of World War II. He left for Aden almost immediately. HB stayed on in France to make arrangements for the children, but came out to join her husband before Christmas.

The phoney war seemed to make little difference to everyday life in Aden. As far as the firm was concerned the pilots and the ground engineer were called up, and the Scion and the Monospar were grounded. One by one the younger Englishmen and Frenchmen went off to join the services. There could be no question of new recruits from London, and the quest for Men was in abeyance. But there remained the Indian staff, with their high standard of competence and high morale, who were fully to justify AB's faith. Prabhulal Mehta, for instance, assumed charge of the vitally important and ever more complicated Shell Department, and was to remain in charge till some years after the war. Furthermore it was still possible to bring in young Indians from Bombay. Indeed, war conditions were to show the strength of the organisation that AB had built up. Trade with Europe inevitably became more difficult. But, up to late 1941, the war was confined to Europe, and AB had established firm connections with important manufacturers and traders in America, in India and the Far East. Among the agencies he held were those of the American Export Lines, the President Lines and the Holland–Oost Azie Lijn. The firm of Besse continued to prosper.

II

In early April came the German moves on Denmark and Norway: all this was remote from the little world of Aden. One of the problems exercising AB and HB was how to give their staff some respite from the summer heat. The RAF were planning a rest camp at Mukeiris, seven thousand feet up in the hills of the Protectorate: it might be possible also to establish there a rest camp for the firm, but the first step was to have a look at the place. AB still had his two small aircraft. One of the young men on the RAF ground staff had flying qualifications, and permission was obtained for him to make the trip. Early in the morning of 26 April they took off in the Scion – AB, HB and the temporary pilot. They landed safely, saw what they wanted, and boarded the plane for the return journey.

But the Scion crashed on taking off. HB and the pilot, severely shaken, managed to make their way out. AB was seriously, almost certainly dangerously, injured. With extreme difficulty he was extricated from the wreckage – the Scion had to be completely written off – and laid on a stretcher. Luckily the local RAF W/T was functioning and an urgent message tapped out to Aden. Three hours later a plane arrived with an RAF doctor. Again with great difficulty AB was loaded on board. He was taken first to the RAF Hospital then, that same night, transferred to the Aden Civilian Hospital. X-rays showed the vertebrae to have been telescoped. He was encased in plaster-of-Paris.

Unceasing pain was aggravated by the intense summer heat, which that year in Aden had set in earlier than usual. Periodically the plaster-of-Paris had to be ripped open. AB in any case was a difficult patient and refused to submit to any form of discipline. After forty-eight hours the doctor in charge of the hospital was demanding that he should be removed. So he was carried up the stairs to his penthouse in the Aidrus Road and HB found a Danish nurse to help look after him.

It was essential that he should leave for Europe, where he could find more elaborate medical facilities and, especially, where he could escape the Aden heat. It was found possible to book passages to Marseilles on the P & O SS *Narkunda*. A rumour came round that because of the way the war was going in Europe the ship might be diverted: but HB was confidentially informed by a naval friend that she was carrying important stores for Malta, and so was bound to go on to Marseilles. An urgent cable had already been sent to Davis in America to make his way back to Aden as soon as possible.

The doctors were unable to make any forecast as to the probabilities of recovery. On 4 May AB, still in great pain, dictated a few lines for Parekh. Of his son André, he wrote:

> He would be able to live a life of leisure should he wish to relinquish his connection with the firm. If on the other hand he felt the time had come to show he was a Man – the son of a Man – and was prepared to put on his shoulders the mantle his father had tried to wear with dignity and with honour throughout the whole of his life . . .

Of HB he noted:

> Not only has she been my companion through every crisis of my life, but also has helped materially, in fact on all planes, in winning the success we have achieved. Our wills are of a different nature, but they are equally strong, equally supple, hers will react better than mine in case of emergency, but, probably, mine can see further ahead. Our ideals have been the same and in many instances she has rectified my errors of judgement regarding men and women, being more indulgent than I am.

On the following day, 5 March, he wrote a letter to be handed to Davis on arrival:

> The notes and letter addressed to Parekh should have been addressed to you. I am deeply sorry to have to place such an enormous burden on your shoulders; but there is only one attitude in life for a man like myself – namely to give the task in hand every ounce of

strength and will available and leave the rest to Destiny. I am convinced that you cherish and obey the same ideal and I entreat you, whatever happens, never worry about material things.

On 6 May AB was taken on board the *Narkunda*. Four days later as the ship was entering the Suez Canal came the first broadcasts of the great German offensive in the West. On the day the *Narkunda* reached Marseilles the German Army entered Amiens. A fellow passenger was J. R. Kynaston of the British American Tobacco Company – later to be appointed Director of Economic Control at Aden. He remembers that while awaiting disembarkation AB was turning over in his mind the line that he should take in the event of France being knocked out of the war. AB was carried on shore on a stretcher and spent two nights in a clinic at Marseilles. Then HB moved him to their house in Toulon. News from the battle fronts grew grimmer. On 28 May AB telegraphed to Weerts (in charge at Aden pending the arrival of Davis) 'Tell GED (i.e. Davis) that to lose business or even to see the firm collapse are matters of complete indifference. To-day we have all more serious things to think about.' A few days later he was moved on to Le Paradou and from there, on 5 June, he wrote to Weerts:

The order of the day for all of us now is fortitude. The ordeals already undergone have been terrible, and I fear we have now to face trials more terrible still. To lose heart would be pointless – and could lead only to so appalling an outcome that (quite apart from our loyalty and our self-respect) we have now no choice. I am enraged to feel I can make no contribution to the common cause.

On 10 June Italy entered the war. On 21 June the armistice was signed at Compiègne. It was then that AB sent his telegram instructing Davis to inform the Governor of Aden that all the assets of the firm of Besse were to be placed at the disposal of the British Government, provided that Great Britain remained at war. Davis, after consultation with Weerts and with some misgivings, passed on the message to Government House, where legalistic minds in the Secretariat were concerned about the validity of instructions emanating from a French citizen domiciled in Vichy territory.

AB's injuries were to have a permanent effect. The more arduous physical exertions that had long been so dear to him, the marathon swims and the climbs up the stiffest of the cliffs round Crater, were no longer to be possible. But the speed of his return to active life was remarkable. This was due to physical resilience and determination rather than to any medical treatment. The doctors could only prescribe complete rest and at least six months in the plaster-of-Paris casing. AB discarded it after three months. But of course manual labour, like clearing the woods round Le Paradou (one of his favourite outlets), were, for the moment, out of the question. He could only potter about. He spent his days, as he afterwards wrote 'fretting myself into a state bordering on frenzy'.

Late one evening in the autumn two men turned up at Le Paradou. They were Marius Moutet, ex-Minister of Colonies and AB's old ally, and his son: the Vichy police were on their trail. They were taken in for the night. Early next morning the son was sent off in one direction, escorted by the young Besse family: it was thought that a party of children would allay police suspicions. Moutet was despatched in another direction in AB's car. By that time no petrol for private purposes was available in France; but AB had a small supply still left and the chauffeur was instructed to take his passenger as far as the fuel would last,leaving just enough to bring the car back. That night a squad of police arrived at Le Paradou and searched the house – luckily missing a suitcase of documents that Moutet had left behind. Later on HB had a long and far from risk-free journey to deposit the suitcase at a safe address indicated by Moutet. In due course news came through that the fugitives were safe in Switzerland.

As soon as he had discarded his plaster-of-Paris casing AB's over-whelming desire was to get back to Aden. Once out of France the passage onward should not be too difficult; after all the firm were agents for important neutral shipping lines. The problem was the Vichy exit permit. As soon as AB was fit enough to make the journey he went to Vichy to present his application in person. He met with a blank refusal. The authorities must have been aware of his telegram to Davis on the collapse of France, and may well have had strong suspicions with regard to Moutet's escape. They had every reason to look on AB with disfavour. The outlook was very gloomy.

That AB was eventually able to leave was a matter of pure good fortune. One morning as HB was in the garden of Le Paradou, a surprisingly elegant private car drew up, with an extremely elegant couple on board. They were interested in a ruined cottage on the slopes above the house; and wished to know whether it and the land around it were by any chance for sale. There was, of course, no question of selling any of the Le Paradou property, but HB, looking for some distraction in the monotony of AB's life, invited them in to lunch. The couple, it appeared, were hoping to find a site in the neighbourhood to build a house for their holidays. The husband was a steel magnate from Lorraine. Convinced that Germany had won the war, he was now involved with collaborationist and German interests in schemes for the industrial development of the New Europe. But political differences were not allowed to disturb the harmony of the lunch. The visitor expressed sympathy with AB's plight, and offered to use his influence in Vichy to secure an exit permit. The offer was gratefully accepted. There were of course further delays but, in late January 1941, the exit permit was granted.

There was no possibility of taking out the children. AB was still far from recovered, and HB had no choice but to go with him. Hurried arrangements had to be made for the children to stay on at Le Paradou with their governess Miss Ogilvie in charge.[1] On 4 February 1941 AB and HB crossed the frontier into Spain. In Lisbon the local agent of the American Export Lines found them a passage to New York. Here they had a long wait for an opportunity to proceed further. It was bitterly cold in New York and AB had no overcoat – all spare clothing had been left behind for the family at Le Paradou. There was a visit to a store in Fifth Avenue where AB was much taken with a camel hair coat. He was so disgusted on hearing the price that he walked out of the shop. But HB was skilfully persistent and in the end the coat was purchased and destined to become a cherished possession in Europe up to his death.

There was a chance of leaving for Mombasa on a small Egyptian steamer, the SS *Zam Zam*. This was turned down, luckily as it proved, for the *Zam Zam* was torpedoed in the Atlantic. Finally it was once more the American Export Lines who provided the solution by offering two berths on a fast cargo steamer to Colombo. From Colombo AB and HB flew in a single-engined plane to Bombay; and completed their journey in a little ship of the Khedivial Mail. They reached Aden in early May 1941, almost exactly a year after their departure in the SS *Narkunda*.

23 Aden in War-Time

It was a profound relief to AB to be back in Aden, with day-to-day life once more in the familiar rhythm; though his swims and his climbs were necessarily less strenuous than before his accident. There is an elegant reference in Freya Stark's memoirs:

> ... Hilda Besse and Anton, sparkling with gaiety and malice. King of the Red Sea coasts and their commerce, and living – as befitted the manipulator of so many of its complicated strings – a little and not uncritically apart, he would take me climbing over the dead crags of Aden ...[1]

But as far as the firm was concerned the impact of war conditions was heavy. We have a letter from AB to one of his Shell friends, written in the early summer of 1941:

> As soon as France collapsed and I saw the awful trend the policy of her so-called leaders was taking, I cabled Davis to put everything I possessed at the disposal of the Government here. And sure enough, when I arrived I found practically all my instruments of work, both material and human, working for the common cause. My two ships, of which I was so proud, have been driven almost to death and have not seen a dry dock for eight months. Not only are they filthy both inside and out and in dire need of an overhaul, but some officers and men, feeling they are beyond the control we constantly exercised over them, have gone to seed, I am told that even X is invariably drunk. ... All our stocks of Iron, Steel, Wood, Cement etc. were requisitioned, thus preventing the completion of a large workshop we were building opposite your godowns at Ma'alla. The rump staff left is at the beck and call, day and night, of the various Administrations.

Long before AB's return official controls had been clamped down on the Aden economy. The new regulations had been hastily drafted, and had, perforce, often to be administered by men with little knowledge of local conditions and little experience of the infinite ingenuity of Arabs and others in finding ways round. A few years later AB was to write:

> We had, in Aden, Government Control of trade in all its branches and that most pernicious of war-time organizations, the United Kingdom Commercial Corporation. The need of goods of every kind was so urgent in all the surrounding countries and prices were so high that the temptation to mislead the Control, or to evade it, was overwhelming. From important firms, down to undisguised scally-wags, every body dabbled in everything ...

> Men who had previously had no standing whatsoever, became immensely wealthy through the smuggling trade, a new word being introduced into the Arabic vocabulary to denote it – Parachute. ... The smugglers soon realized that they were immune from punishment. Y, Z and others were caught red-handed more than once but mere reprimands could not be expected to deter them. In the Government files there must undoubtedly be records of enormous quantities of goods which found their way to Sheikh Othman where at 300 yards distance in Dar el Amir (just inside the Sultanate of Lahej) they could be disposed of freely at five, ten and twenty times the price they had been bought at through the Control. These goods found their way to places such as Fukum, Ras Imran etc. where dhows picked them up. Others were shipped from little creeks like Fisherman's Bay, where they would be ferried out to the waiting dhows ...

AB's indignation at the state of business in the Colony may have one of his incentives to write his 'Qualities of a Merchant' in the course of the summer of 1941[2]. But competition, whether from the government sponsored UKCC or from the mushroom profiteers, had by no means impaired the fortunes of *La Maison Besse*. Davis, as always, had been an extremely competent general manager. Parekh and his Indian collaborators had found scope for their remarkable flexibility and resource. During AB's absence the firm had been making substantial profits.

II

Within a few weeks of AB's return to Aden there came a major flurry involving Government House and Shell. It arose from a decision by the Aden authorities that deliveries of oil products to the Protectorate and to the Yemen should be made only against official permits issued in Aden. The motive was a political one, to ensure that these supplies should go only to those in whom the British authorities had confidence. AB found himself confronted with a *fait accompli*. His reaction comes out in a letter he wrote some years later:

> The Governor of Aden ... had the impudence to interfere in our affairs, dictating certain deliveries to be made through the nefarious medium of A (a senior Government House official). When I refused to obey his instructions he sent a long cable to Charvet (Shell's Representative in Cairo) and complained of non-cooperation on my part ...

The cable from the Governor, Sir John Hathorn-Hall, reached Cairo in mid-July. Charvet, beset by a spate of other war-time problems, sent off a diplomatic reply to the Governor and on the same day, 18 July, cabled direct to AB:

> Much concerned at receiving communication from Governor suggesting in very moderate terms your attitude not conducive cooperation with Government. .... Fully understand your difficulties which Governor's letter shows he also fully appreciates and anxious remedy, but no solution can be reached without Government's good will. Present situation most unfortunate and particularly undesirable your own interest owing possible effect on discussions with view obtaining HMG's confirmation your appointment as our representative Ethiopia.

The inclusion of the final paragraph was a serious psychological error. It was a suggestion that AB should pocket his pride and his dignity in the hope of a material reward, i.e. the Shell agency in the newly liberated Ethiopia. Meanwhile, though Charvet's reply to the Governor had not been repeated to AB, he had, by some means or other, come to know the contents and found it to include the words 'much regret the attitude of our representative'. To apologise was not part of AB's nature, and he bitterly resented apologies being offered by third parties on his behalf. He telegraphed his resignation to London.

What followed was to some extent a repetition of the Djibouti bunkering crisis of 1936. Charvet with other high executives arrived by air, and, for days, were made to wilt under the force of AB's displeasure. Finally, and abruptly, his resignation was withdrawn. A working arrangement was reached on the question of oil permits; and in due course AB was confirmed as Shell agent in Ethiopia. But the warmth of the former reconciliation was lacking; Charvet was never fully forgiven. And when, in late August, the Shell Head Office expressed the hope of future friendly relations between their Red Sea agent and Government House, AB replied: 'I wish your General Manager in Cairo to understand that under no consideration whatever am I prepared to have "friendly relations" with people I despise.'

III

AB in one of his letters of June, 1941, refers to 'the ill natured gossip of certain officials and competitors who, less successful than ourselves because less competent and less far-seeing, try to take their revenge by backbiting'. As we have seen, AB had never been on friendly terms with Union Club circles. His capacity for contempt, which he made no attempt to hide, and the ruthlessness of some of his methods, naturally added to his enemies. There were plenty of people in Aden ready to believe, or at least to pass on, any story to his disadvantage. AB's loyalty to the Allied cause should have been obvious enough. There was his cult for Churchill (whom, one feels, he must have regarded as a kindred spirit); the help he rendered certain services on intelligence matters; his support of the Free French.[3] Nevertheless he was a Frenchman with a Vichy domicile, and certain members of the hastily expanded local security service felt it their duty to make sure. There is a story, possibly apocryphal, of two of them calling on him to find out whether he was pro-Laval or pro-de Gaulle; and AB, very bored with the interview, telling them he was pro-Besse.

Then there was the case of the powdered milk. On the fall of France the British Navy imposed a blockade on French Somaliland. With the Italian capitulation in East Africa, Djibouti and its hinterland became completely isolated and remained so till the colony rallied to de Gaulle in December 1942. With no resources of its own the tiny area was reduced to near starvation. André Besse had remained there in charge of the branch, his family with him. The Aden Free French had an outpost in Zeila, in clandestine touch with sympathisers in Djibouti. HB arranged with a French officer friend to smuggle in some tins of powdered milk for André's baby. An official got to hear of this, and an attempt was made to build up a charge of blockade running against the firm of Besse. But HB called on the Admiral, and the affair was dismissed as a storm in a tea cup.

More serious was the censorship incident. On the liberation of Ethiopia in May 1941, Weerts made his way to Addis Abeba to open up. The firm's activities there will be dealt with in a later chapter. Meanwhile, for the time being, all outgoing mails from Aden were subject to military censorship. AB disliked having his letters read by officials, and resented the delay involved. Moreover it was an old tradition of the firm that mail for the outlying branches should whenever possible be carried by hand. When Weerts was established in Addis Abeba, his wife (in Aden) made ready to join him. Once again suspicions were aroused. Madame Weerts when about to embark was stopped by the police and searched. Sewn up in the lining of her coat was the firm's mail to Addis Abeba. AB was summoned to the Governor. According to one who was present at the interview AB remained silent, the blood visibly mounting. Suddenly he burst into an angry roar, marched out of the room and went home. A small police squad was detailed to the Aidrus Road, and for the next twelve hours AB was nominally under house arrest. Then, wisely, the matter was allowed to drop. One aftermath was discreet work by the firm's most trusted Arab carpenter, preparing safe hiding places on some of the dhows.

IV

The trouble over permits for Shell products meant that AB's relations with Sir John Hathorn-Hall got off to a bad start. In any case he disliked any form of official control, and the friendly relations so desired by Shell were slow in coming. Matters came to a head in late October 1941 when Sir John wrote to AB:

> Of the many letters that you have seen fit to address to this Government most have contained matter calculated to give offence and several have contained baseless imputations against public officers, some of a most serious character. These communications have naturally caused resentment ...

AB replied:

I am perfectly prepared to concede that my letters are forceful, but, hating waste – whether of time, effort or money – as much as I do ambiguity, I strive to make my correspondence as concise and clear as possible.

Inconclusive as this exchange may seem it helped to clear the air. It was not to be expected that the two men could ever become friends, but there emerged a certain mutual respect. From now on co-operation was possible, to the advantage to all concerned. The importance of the firm of Besse very soon became apparent when Aden town and Aden garrison ran short of sugar. The UKCC had none. AB had. He flatly refused to negotiate with or through the UKCC; the authorities must deal direct with him. As soon as the deals were completed the town was full of rumours of Besse profiteering. AB put up a notice on his office door giving the cost of the sugar c.i.f. Aden; the proceeds of the sales; the profit on the transactions; and the donation of the firm to the Spitfire fund, being exactly the amount of the profit.

In late 1941 the Australian authorities gave notice that they would no longer be able to supply Aden with cereals. UKCC were unable to suggest an alternative source. Kynaston, now Director of Civil Supplies, took the line that only the firm of Besse could provide the necessary know-how, organisation and drive. There was much argument in official circles, but in the end AB was appointed Buying Agent for the Government of Aden. By this time Weerts had opened up branches and agencies throughout Ethiopia: and it was largely from there that the cereals (and other commodities) were obtained. The arrangement worked so successfully that, in spite of protests from rival firms, it was continued till 1948. This mark of official confidence afforded AB much satisfaction, and, as Shell had found many years before, when he felt he was trusted he gave of his best. The prices he charged were scrupulously reasonable; but, as he insisted on all deals being at replacement cost, the firm ran no risk of loss. In the event the accumulated earnings on freight, lighterage, storage and the rest added up to a very substantial profit. It was an advantage that throughout liaison with the various Aden authorities was canalised through Kynaston, who, as a businessman, could see AB's point of view even though instructions from London were apt to be rigid. There were flurries of course, and a good deal of plain speaking. But by and large the association was friendly, even cordial. It is significant that Kynaston was the only visitor ever to call in the Aidrus Road whose appearance prompted Mohamed Aly to produce, unbidden, a box of cigarettes.

We have mentioned the donation to the Spitfire fund. In April 1942 Sir John Hathorn-Hall wrote to thank AB for a 'princely gift' to War Charities. Later in the war when there was a food shortage in certain areas, AB financed, and, with HB, in face of official scepticism, set up and carried through a famine relief operation in Sheikh Othman: and then arranged for something similar in the Hadhramaut. There may well have been other instances. It is typical of AB that no list of his benefactions was ever compiled.

But in spite of the improved relations, there seems to have lingered the feeling that certain matters could be dealt with more smoothly if AB were out of the way. In the spring of 1942 the Governor wrote to ask him if he would care to consider taking up some important post in England. AB, wisely, refused. Aden was his home ground: he had no desire to leave it for the unfamiliar and certainly uncongenial world of inter-departmental committees. In October 1943 there came a more specific offer from Sir Edward Spears. AB should come to Beirut and work on Anglo-French co-operation. AB again refused: 'I am no diplomat. I know of one way only of negotiation – the direct one.'

V

In 1942 AB spent an immensely busy summer, mostly in Ethiopia. A year later his business was working smoothly enough to allow him to take a holiday – an extended tour of the Lebanon with HB. The local Shell representatives made much of him, and there were good concerts in Beirut; altogether the interlude was a happy one. Back in Aden in 1944 we hear something of him from the then American Consul, William Sands.

One of Sands' first official tasks had been to investigate the credit-worthiness of A. Besse & Co. The NBI informed him that the firm was good for a million pounds. Shortly afterwards he called in the Aidrus Road. Sands himself is six foot three and at first glance AB seemed short, stocky, and unimpressive except for his curiously penetrating eyes. Later the impact of the man's personality was such that Sands' other Aden memories are dim and blurred. AB, for his part, found that his visitor spoke excellent French, was a keen Arabist, loved music and, in addition, was a good listener. A few days later he called at the US Consulate in Steamer Point and accepted a very small whisky filled up to the brim with soda. Sands had already heard enough of him to realise that a call like this was an event that was almost unheard of.

A friendship developed. Sands was a frequent dinner guest on AB's veranda. There was music, and much talk. AB once suggested that Sands must have come across a number of stories about him and he was quite ready, if Sands so wished, to tell him the truth. Sands in fact had heard a great many stories, but felt it tactful to explain that he never listened to gossip.[4] Time and again AB would return to the théme of his longed – for retirement. Business had become a disagreeable chore – and had reached the point where he could run his firm with his left hand. As soon as the war was over he would leave it all, get right away, devote his life to art, to music and to philosophy: he could happily spend months – years even – in contemplation of the stained glass in Chartres Cathedral. Sands was convinced he meant what he said. But then there was the utter impossibility of such a man ever taking to an inactive life.

VI

The war years had been a grim and anxious period for Miss Ogilvie and the five Besses left at Le Paradou in January 1941. News reaching Aden had been scrappy, and on the liberation of Provence the first thought of AB and HB was a visit home. Luckily their help to the Free French in the Red Sea area had brought excellent relations with Gaston Palewski; they were allotted berths on a Free French warship, and landed at Toulon in December 1944. House and family at Le Paradou were found intact, and they went on to Paris and London. In London they found Meryem, whom they had not seen for ten years, and two small grandchildren. Jeff Collins, still unforgiven, was overseas with the Army.

The cold, shabby, tired and hungry Europe of the last winter of the war was a shock to AB. The children came on board to greet him at Toulon, and he was indignant at their exuberant excitement on seeing butter on the table; they of course had not seen butter for three years. In London, refusing Meryem's offer to come with him, he set out alone to walk to his office. Three hours later he came back, exhausted and for once acknowledging defeat; he had lost his way in the bombed ruins south of London Bridge. He and HB went on to Edinburgh, less battered than London, to find a boarding school for Monna and to arrange for Ariane to be accepted as probationer nurse in an Edinburgh hospital. Then back to Le Paradou, to await the first available passage from Marseilles to Aden.

There seems to have been no discussion of future plans with any of the family. The boys, AB decided, should come out with him to Aden and start work in the firm on the bottom rung of the ladder. (André by now had resigned and was with a rival concern in Addis Abeba.) Joy too should come out to Aden and live and work in the Aidrus Road. But Joy revolted. She had made friends with some American officers and found herself a congenial job with a Military Mission in Toulon. She flatly refused to leave France.

24   The Firm in Ethiopia

I

Perhaps the outstanding development of the firm of Besse was in post-liberation Ethiopia, and it will be convenient to deal with this in a separate chapter, even though this means going a few years ahead. For AB it was a matter of extreme urgency to start up again in Abyssinia. Thanks, in part, to Kynaston's influence with the various authorities, Maurice Weerts was allowed to leave for Berbera in good time; after an adventurous journey he reached Addis Abeba in mid-May 1941, a few days after the arrival of the first British troops. He took possession of the Besse offices and compound which he found intact, and set to work to re-establish the agencies up country. There were three facts that made for the firm's rapid success. The first was the remarkable Italian achievement in road building during their occupation: by 1941 the almost roadless empire had acquired a network of four thousand miles of good metalled roads. With the muddles and uncertainties of the post-liberation period the roads rapidly deteriorated, but they were there. Indeed the war-time revictualment of Aden, the supplies coming from Northern Ethiopia, can be said to have been made possible by the Italian road engineers. Secondly AB as agent for Dodge, had the lorries; and thanks to the failure of the attempt by the British Military to expel the Italian civilians it was possible to find skilled drivers and mechanics. Thirdly, AB as Shell agent had the fuel.

Road transport was more than ever essential. So long as French Somaliland remained loyal to Vichy, Addis Abeba was cut off from its port and railhead, Djibouti. Attempts were made by the military to work the long section of the Chemin de Fer d'Ethiopie in Abyssinian territory for what it was worth. But locomotives and rolling stock were in poor condition, as was also the permanent way. The railway workshops at DireDawa had been looted and were barely starting to function again. In December 1942 Djibouti rallied to de Gaulle, but the working of the line as a whole was bedevilled by friction between the British Military, the Occupied Territory Administration, UKCC,

the CFE management, the emerging Ethiopian Government and the
Free French administration in Djibouti, who were all in some way or
other involved.[1] In any case the capacity of the line was at first
extremely limited. There were no tank wagons: oil products had to be
carried in drums. Home-made tank wagons were improvised in the
Besse workshops and were used, albeit with some misgivings on the
part of the railway management. Later, tank wagons were imported
from America. In 1946 the line was handed back to its French owners
and the CFE acquired tank wagons of its own. Very shortly afterwards
tariffs were raised to a level that AB considered quite unjustified, and
he decided to fight the railway; of which more later. Meanwhile, in the
early years, goods in either direction were mostly moved by road.
Massawa, the best equipped port, is 750 miles from Addis Abeba.
With Berbera, Assab and Zeila the road-haul is shorter by some 200
miles, but port facilities were very primitive. And the roads, now that
the Italians were gone, were deteriorating rapidly.

II

War conditions made for a keen demand for all the traditional Besse
exports from Ethiopia – hides, skins, coffee, gums – and now, with the
provisioning of Aden, cereals. With imports as with exports, the
problem was not now to sell the goods, but how to acquire and
transport them. Cotton yarns and piece goods came from the USA and
India; building materials and ironmongery from a number of sources.
The I. G. Farben and Agfa agencies had of course come to an end with
the outbreak of war; but in their place the Besse letter-heading carried
a number of equally familiar names – ICI, CIBA, Kodak, Philips,
Underwood.

The end of the Ethiopian Salt Monopoly provided a new opening for
the firm of Besse. There are salt deposits in Aden, French Somaliland
near Djibouti, and in the neighbourhood of Assab in Eritrea. Up to
1936 the Djibouti Salines (French-owned and French-managed) held
the monopoly throughout Ethiopia. During the Italian occupation
agreement was reached for Italian participation in the Salines and the
monopoly was continued. On liberation, in May 1941 the monopoly
was abolished and the import and sale of salt became free. For the next
eighteen months salt reached Ethiopia from Assab and to some extent
from Aden. The firm of Besse took part in the trade and most of the
Aden salt came across the narrows in AB's dhows. At the end of 1942

French Somaliland rallied to the Free French, and the Djibouti Salines once more came into the picture. In 1944 there was talk of a renewal of the monopoly. AB told Weerts that this idea must be scotched; Weerts successfully lobbied certain members of the Ethiopian Parliament, and the proposal was dropped for the time being. Meanwhile negotiations were on foot, under the aegis of the Banque de l'Indo-Chine, which culminated in the purchase of the Assab salt works by the Djibouti Salines. The next development was for AB to secure the exclusive agency in Ethiopia for Djibouti and Assab salt. At first, to the indignation of Djibouti, he brought over occasional consignments from Aden,[2] but later found it more profitable to obtain all his supplies from the African deposits. There is a note of his dated February 1948.

> Our Association with the Banque de l'Indo-Chine has procured for us a monopoly, on a commission basis, of the sale of salt throughout Abyssinia. Salt can be sent up to Addis Abeba from Djibouti by the CFE or from Assab by lorry. From Addis Abeba we send it on by lorry to our branches and agencies up country, thus procuring valuable outward cargo. The lorries come back to Addis with skins, coffee etc.

In the last year of AB's life commission on salt came to 660 000 East African shillings.[3] In addition there were the substantial earnings on handling, transport and storage.

III

The story of AB's part in the re-establishment of Shell in Ethiopia would fill a volume. There was the matter of Akaki. During the Italian occupation the Italian AGIP had constructed an elaborate system of oil depots at Akaki, outside Addis Abeba. When the British troops arrived in May 1941 they naturally took it over. The following month AB got the military authorities to agree to his use of the installations for Shell. In February 1942 the Ethiopian Government assumed legal possession of all Italian assets. The firm of Besse continued to use Akaki for Shell products. But AB realised it was a permanent asset of enormous value, and was confident he could buy it outright from the Ethiopian Government at a bargain price. Shell had misgivings as to the possible repercussions of the proposed purchase on their various properties in Italy; for the moment they were inclined to prefer a short-term lease. AB was insistent. In late 1942 he wrote to the Shell head office 'I have been dinning into Cairo's ears for months the vital importance of the Akaki installation.' He was told the matter was under careful consideration.

As Shell were well aware, one could never count on the passive acquiescence of their Red Sea agent. We have a letter from AB (mid-1942) to Davis on the matter of commission:

> This is a very thorny subject, and Shell have a way to put things in a manner which is not satisfactory. At times we have seen a different interpretation being put to what we took it to mean in the first instance. . . . They propose to pay the commission at the full rate on the wholesale price less transport etc. Such has never been the case in the past. It must be pointed out that to run an organisation today is much more costly than ever before. Addis Abeba is going to be exceptionally costly. . . . It is advisable therefore that if we accept the rate they quote we do it as a temporary measure. . . . Regarding Army business Shell stipulate they will pay us $2\frac{1}{2}\%$ on quantities handled by our firm. This is a very clever remark. They want to have the depot under their control and their remarks seem to suggest that for such deliveries there will be no commission to us!!

Then there was the question of local management. In February 1942 AB (from Aden) wrote to Mackintosh who had succeeded Charvet in Cairo: 'I wish you to know that unless you yourself wish to send some one out to inspect stocks books etc. . . . I refuse to have any member of your staff managing the Shell Department.' However the technical problems involved in starting up again in Ethiopia were such that the secondment of someone from Shell proved to be essential, and in the early summer of 1942 David Barran arrived in Addis Abeba. AB remained determined to put a strict limit to his activities.

> We must instruct Weerts to avoid any interference of Barran in market matters. . . . As for supplies to the forces there is no reason why Barran's interference should be necessary. . . . As a matter of fact it should be our policy in Addis Abeba to do away with any help from any member of the Shell staff.

As it turned out, Barran's work in Ethiopia was so successful that for a time he stood high in AB's good books. But, as so often happened there was a sudden and violent revulsion of feeling and Barran was abruptly recalled in March 1943.[4] It was not long afterwards that serious trouble arose with the Ethiopian administration. Years later, in a letter to Godber, AB wrote of:

> my battle with the Ethiopian officials – ministries of finance, trade and communications – who were issuing requisition orders for quantities large enough to absorb the whole of the limited supplies we were able to obtain during the war, and reselling the black oils at 300 per cent profit and the white at 150 per cent. I stopped all deliveries, refused to honour the requisition orders, and it would not be too much to say that for a short period my life was in danger for I was in Addis Abeba at the time ...

The first result of all this was to convince certain individuals in Addis Abeba that life would be both easier and more profitable if AB were out of the way. They accordingly briefed their authorities to the effect that AB's 'insulting and threatening behaviour' to Ethiopian Government organs made him unfit to hold the Shell agency. And in the early summer of 1943 the Ethiopian Chargé d'Affaires in Cairo called on Mackintosh with an official memorandum requesting AB's replacement. Mackintosh, backed by his superiors in London, on due consideration took the line that 'the Oil Companies must resist the attempt by the Ethiopian Government to dictate their methods and choice of organisation as this would represent a restraint on liberty of action and freedom of trade, both of which are objectives for which the present war is being fought ...'. AB had a number of audiences with the Emperor. There were ministers and senior officials to be interviewed. In the end the storm blew over.

But AB felt strongly that Shell should have backed him more promptly and more forcefully. He wrote to Mackintosh:

> Had you reacted to the trumped up grievances as I had every right to expect you would and replied to the Ethiopian Chargé d'Affaires who brought you the famous letter that I have been, am and will remain your trusted agent, whose decisions you were prepared to endorse without question, the whole affair would have been settled by now and in all probability the culprits punished, for the emperor was simply waiting for a statement of the kind from you in order to take action.

He concluded:

I must admit that if we were face to face, my dear Mackintosh, in spite of the deep affection I have for you, I would use even more forcible language that I have in this letter, for my sense of outrage is very acute.

Meanwhile someone in Shell seems to have felt that AB's methods with the Ethiopian ministries were too brusque and too forceful, and that things would go more smoothly if Bedwell (Barran's successor) were to act as intermediary. The idea was put to AB, and, as one would expect, was flatly turned down. 'You know me very little if you think I could accept such a solution. Let me hasten to add this is no reflection upon Bedwell who is certainly animated by the best possible spirit . . .'. (As it turned out Bedwell, like Barran before him, enjoyed only a brief period of favour. AB came to suspect him too of unwarranted curiosity regarding the Besse accounts, and he had also to be abruptly recalled.)

IV

In due course Shell came round to the idea of an outright purchase or a long-term lease of the Akaki installations, but it was years before the matter was finally settled. A formal inventory of all the various items involved was not drawn up till 1944. The lawyers continued to argue. All manner of considerations were put up by the Ethiopian government departments concerned, and by the declared and undeclared allies of rival oil companies. There were moves to short-circuit Besse and deal direct with St Helen's Court or Cairo. There is a letter from AB to Mackintosh dated March 1946: 'What an amount of correspondence has been exchanged about this Akaki affair, whereas it would have been so easy had we only had your proper support at the outset.' He was especially indignant at attempts at direct exchanges between Ethiopian officials and Shell. 'Anything that can create in the mind of an Ethiopian official the idea that he can discuss matters direct with you causes untold harm.' And later: 'Under no consideration will I ever agree to work with scoundrels whose sole aim is to force you to give them a share in the distributions of your products.'

In April 1946 AB was suggesting that, in order to bring the other parties to their senses, negotiations should be broken off and an application made for a new site on which to build a Shell depot. But three months later agreement seemed to be imminent. In September 1946 a draft contract was drawn up under which Shell should acquire the installations outright and a ninety-nine year lease of the site (at double the price that could originally have been negotiated). Some of the lawyers were still unhappy and there was more argument and the inevitable last-minute hitches. But the contract was signed on 29 November 1946. Four days later AB wrote to St Helen's Court:

I wish to state that thanks to your Cairo office this Akaki affair has been the most depressing, the most heart-rending and the most nauseating one that I have ever had to tackle – and the most costly too. Will it be a lesson to you and will you henceforward . . . leave me free to act as I think best? I doubt it. But if I am ever again confronted with such difficulties and receive from you, instead of the support I am entitled to, systematic obstructionism I shall give up the battle before it is joined.

V

A few months after the signature of the Akaki contract came the repercussions of the temporary world shortage of oil products. There had been a spectacular rise in consumption. Consumption in the USA rose from 147 million tons in 1937 to 254 million tons in 1947. In the UK the rise was from 11 million to 16 million.[5] For the oil companies the resultant problem was not so much one of production as of distribution. There was a world shortage of tankers. Shell were thus forced to limit their deliveries to Ethiopia, and became, in consequence, target for a whole spate of angry letters from AB.

By mid-1947 AB was already preparing for his battle with the Chemin de Fer d'Ethiopie. As early as 1944 he was thinking of substantially increasing his fleet of lorries. In late 1946 the CFE put up their tariffs, and the matter became more urgent. But by this time Ethiopian and Eritrean roads had deteriorated to such an extent that a standard lorry was unlikely to make the 550-mile haul from Assab to Addis Abeba, up the steep gradients to the plateau. AB approached a leading British manufacturer, but the firm was unwilling to make the adjustments he wanted. He then tried the Italian Lancia who showed no such reluctance. A sample consignment stood up well to stringent tests on the spot, and AB placed a large order.

There were two abandoned Italian oil tanks at Assab. In 1947 AB bought them. His manager at Assab was one Capetini, an Italian, with some knowledge of engineering and a remarkable talent for improvisation. Capetini put the tanks in order and started work on a jetty made out of oil drums. The idea was that tankers should discharge into a pipeline laid along the jetty to the tanks on shore. Shell at first were sceptical about the whole scheme, but they did provide some of the material for the pipeline. More was obtained from surplus war stocks in Egypt. All this of course took time. In late 1948 Shell sent out an expert to examine the work. His report, while not wholly unfavourable, contained a number of reservations (the truth being that Shell were reluctant to risk their precious tankers alongside a somewhat amateurish jetty). A copy was sent to AB, and provoked a caustic reply from him on 3 February 1949.

The technical difficulties mentioned in the report of your expert simply do not exist.... Information varies according to the nature of the man who supplies it and also according to his angle of vision. I have never seen a scheme as it actually stands when under examination, and I hope I never shall; I invariably see it from the point of view of its potentialities when fully developed. I am so conscious of all the advantages of Assab that if you do not agree I will myself buy a tanker to keep the port supplied...

In the next few months the position became easier, and Shell agreed to use Assab. One of AB's marathon letters to St Helen's Court (early autumn 1949) contains the following passage:

...Thanks to our Akaki installation, to our new depot at Dire-Dawa, to our branches all over the territory, to the tanks I bought at Assab and have had fully repaired, to our fleet of Lancia lorries (incomparable vehicles), to our workshops, whose expert mechanics are fully aware of the importance of maintaining each machine in perfect condition, and to our three ships and fleet of dhows, we are in a position to supply entirely the eastern and northern parts of Ethiopia. Pumps have been erected at all the vital points, and our organisation there is growing at such a pace that before the end of the year, when Assab is in working order and able to receive tankers carrying white oil, I hope to be able to turn to you and say: 'Gentlemen, Ethiopia is yours.'

VI

The Besse lorry fleet for the Assab – Dessie – Addis Abeba run consisted of one hundred and four large Lancias, with Goodyear tyres. Drivers and mechanics were nearly all Italians. The journey, when all went well, took three days. As a safeguard against breakdown or attack by bandits the vehicles moved in small convoys, stopping for the night, when the drivers (who were armed) slept in their cabs. The road surface was such that a set of tyres seldom lasted for more than one round trip. The fleet comprised both tank lorries and goods lorries. Salt could be economically conveyed to the capital from Assab for 8 MT dollars per 100 kilograms, whereas the corresponding CFE rate from Djibouti was 14 dollars. Besse could convey cotton goods for $12 per 100 kilograms: the CFE rate might be anything up to $50. On the return journey the goods lorries carried hides, skins and other export goods. As to the tankers, Weerts, in face of initial scepticism, devised means of cleaning them so that they returned to Assab full of coffee. When the service got into its stride, some two-thirds of its capacity was taken up by the firm's own products – leaving one-third available for outside customers.[6]

The Chemin de Fer d'Ethiopie became seriously concerned at this competition, and made a number of attempts to come to some arrangement with AB. Details are no longer available. But we have a undated note by AB to one of his staff:

I would like to know the reason which incited Leclerc du Sablon (a CFE director) to offer us £60 000 a year on condition we confined our transport activities between Assab and Addis Abeba to petroleum products; and, when that offer was refused by us, to reduce the railway tariffs at a single stroke by 60% ...

And on 8 March 1951 AB wrote to a friend in Shell:

Two days' discussion with Leclerc du Sablon have led to nothing. We have agreed to disagree ... on our part at the cost of several hundred thousand pounds we have built up an organisation second to none which has proved to be a most valuable asset and is working perfectly well ... to hand it over to the railway without adequate compensation is impossible.

25 Post-War

On VE Day AB and HB were in Aden, and spent the rest of the year
1945 between Aden and Ethiopia. That winter HB fell ill; and AB,
perhaps remembering the state of France as he had last seen it, decided
to take her for a cure to the Lebanon, where they spent the summer of
1946. The cure was successful; and in the spring of 1947 it was decided
to go all the way to France in *El Hak*. They disembarked at St Raphael.
The port had been badly damaged during the war and repairs had
hardly been started. But local good will made up for the lack of port
facilities. AB, with memories of the Europe of 1944, had brought with
him a number of crates of foodstuffs; thanks to his largesse the
unloading and the twenty-five mile journey on to Le Paradou were in
the nature of a triumphal progress.

It was now that AB made his first move in the matter of education.
The needs of the age, he was convinced, were initiative and independence: and he was now prepared to put up the money for a school or
college where these qualities could be fostered. In the summer of 1947
he arranged an appointment with the Ministry of Education in Paris,
and called there with HB. The official reaction to his idea of a 'Collège
de Rebelles' was unsympathetic. There were, he was told, two main
difficulties. One was financial: the French Inland Revenue would have
to be satisfied as to the tax position of the funds involved – whether or
not they came from outside France. Secondly, it was out of the
question that the Ministry could recognise diplomas or degrees
awarded by an independent institution as suggested by AB; consequently holders would not be eligible for any posts in France requiring
educational qualifications, and no parents would take the risk of
allowing their sons to enter. AB was dissatisfied with this ruling and
wished to take the matter to a higher level. He appealed to Palewski,
and Palewski promised to arrange an interview with General de
Gaulle. AB waited on in Paris. A week passed and nothing happened.
AB lost patience and left. A few days later he was instructing his

London solicitor, R. A. H. Clyde, to investigate the possibilities of founding an institution in Great Britain.[1]

In the autumn AB was back in Aden. At the beginning of December came the rioting following the announcement of the partition of Palestine. A very short time afterwards there was a family incident. Peter and Tony were unhappy in Aden: it was not so much the menial jobs, long hours and meagre pay packet as the ever present surveillance of Parekh and Mohamed Aly. In due course Peter was to persuade his father to let him leave for an engineering course in London. Tony stayed on, working in the godowns. Friends of the family used to say 'there was a lot of the old man in Tony'. Tension mounted. At the end of 1947, following a serious clash with his father Tony left the Aidrus Road house and disappeared. In due course it transpired he had gone to Steamer Point and embarked on a cargo ship bound for New York. He was not to see AB again for over a year.

II

On leaving the firm Petrouchka had settled in Switzerland. Once the war was over she wrote to AB, and the intermittent exchange went on until nearly the end of his life. AB enjoyed this correspondence; and we see a number of facets of his varying moods. There is the ageing man of the world as Mentor to an attractive younger woman. Her wording, he tells her, is not as it should be: she means no harm – it is merely a feminine kink – and when they are next together he will dictate her some letters to show how letters should be phrased. He shows interest in her self-analysis: he would like to think that she has benefited from his advice and his example. There is the philosopher: 'The life of every intelligent man takes place on various planes.' 'An intelligent man is always complex. His superiority shows itself when his complexities harmonise into simplicities and form one whole.' 'As you grow old, like me, you will grow out of all passion, become humble.' A little later he was writing: 'I would like to attain a happy state of *ataraxia*. But I have always been, and, alas, alas, alas, I remain a creature of passion, impatient, ever ready, like Don Quixote, to tilt my lance at Evil.' Again and again he complains of overwork. 'I have let my business grow and it has become a little world. It hangs round my neck like a millstone. Where is the man who can take over my burden?' 'I have become a machine, working without respite, without distraction. Our business has become gigantic.' We have his concern at the state of France: ' "Victory", "Peace", Words, words, words, as Hamlet says. My compatriots have their judgements warped, and their rulers do not know what they are doing. We are far from peace either at home or abroad.' And, in late June 1947: 'I am impatient to be back in Aden – I would rather the intense heat there than to suffer in every fibre of my being at the chaos that is France today.' One project that never materialised was a visit to the Soviet Union with Petrouchka as interpreter.

> ... When we go together to Russia – that mysterious, terrifying Russia in which I can hardly believe. There is something inhuman about Russia: I cannot think the present state of things will last. But I do ardently wish to see it with my own eyes, provided of course I can go about in complete freedom.[2]

Much of the correspondence with Petrouchka was taken up with staff recruiting which, now that the war was over, was once more very much in AB's mind. Simpson, the London Manager, was no longer with the firm (the parting had been abrupt and uncordial), but his successor was finding equal difficulty in the quest for Men. As AB noted,

> I have written uncounted letters to London on this all important subject of Staff, our office there being the only instrument that has been available to us for the search, engagement and initial testing of the men and women without whom no progress can be made. Alas!, London has failed us consistently and at times the would-be collaborators they have sent us have proved not only useless but actually harmful; they appear to have been drawn almost exclusively from that horrible suburban element peculiar to England which, for all the wishful thinking in the world, can never produce the type of individual we need so direly ...

AB, determined to leave no stone unturned, now asked Petrouchka to find recruits.

Petrouchka got busy. Names were submitted, qualifications weighed, family backgrounds investigated. She was instructed to warn candidates to be modest over salary claims: they must have confidence in AB's generosity once they had proved their worth. Finally two young Swiss were approved and went out to Aden. Soon after their arrival Petrouchka was asked to find out what they were writing home to their families. As so often happened, neither of them lasted for more than a few months with the firm. But both made successful careers in other fields on their return to Europe.

III

On 29 November 1947 the United Nations approved by a majority vote the partition of Palestine. The immediate reaction of the Aden Arab leaders was to order a three-day strike, culminating in mob violence and attacks on the Jewish quarter. This quarter is in Crater just off the Aidrus Road, and AB from his roof could see much that was happening. During a lull he walked round the quarter with Tony, later remarking it would have been nice to have met there some senior British officials. On 9 December he sent off a six-page letter to Government House, describing what he had seen, diagnosing the roots of the trouble, and making his recommendations for the future. He begins:

> The first day the crowds were in a holiday mood and although we had a big demonstration in front of our house and several leaders entered our office in an attempt to induce our Arab staff to cease work, with a few jokes and the help of Captain Bruce (whose behaviour was absolutely admirable) the crowd was dispersed without incident. Towards evening the mood obviously changed and the first signs of violence appeared. Cars were attacked and set fire to in many parts of Crater. With the necessary show of force the situation could nevertheless still have been got under control. But the Arabs had had too clear a proof of the timidity of the local authorities ...
>
> Matters quickly became so serious that a curfew was decreed in Crater – decreed – but certainly not imposed, since it was left to the Aden Police Levies to enforce it, and in order to realise how they performed their duty it was necessary to be in the thick of things, as we are in our house, and watch the uninterrupted stream of looters passing from a part of the Jewish quarter where the mob had broken into godowns and houses, crossing the road under the rifles of the supposed guards and, most wonderful of all, see the APL armoured cars stop every few yards to let men staggering under their loads of loot (cotton goods building material, carpets, radios, etc.) proceed on their way! ...
>
> After the looting came its inevitable successor, Arson, and very

soon Crater looked as if it had sustained an aerial bombardment.
The largest Jewish houses have been gutted and we are informed by
eye-witnesses that, as the Jews tried to escape from the flames, they
were slaughtered in cold blood . . .

Yesterday afternoon the connivance of the Levies not only in the
looting but the arson was clearly visible from our verandah. We
watched Arabs with great flaming torches passing freely amongst
the guards posted round the Jewish quarter.

Quite apart from the hideous mob violence that was allowed to
develop in a town where the arrest and punishment in public of the
ringleaders at the outset would have sufficed to nip the horror in the
bud, by far the largest part of the population being peacefully
inclined, I would like the Government to realize that the whole of
Aden has been paralysed, including the port where we are unable to
attend to a large number of ships consigned to us. Moreover after a
48 hours curfew imposed strictly enough on the innocent, hunger is
becoming general. The loss of British prestige in the eyes of the very
mixed population of Aden, where most European countries are
represented as well as America, to say nothing of Indians and Arabs,
can better be imagined than described. . . .

In his diagnosis AB barely touches on the Palestine issue. He finds
the root of the trouble to be the general moral deterioration, for which,
characteristically, he considers the war-time economic controls to be
largely responsible. He cites a number of instances of unscrupulous
Arabs who found they could evade them with impunity. If trickery can
go unpunished, so can violence. He lists recent attacks on Europeans
and points out that the perpetrators when caught and convicted were
given quite inadequate sentences, while the instigators who had organised and financed the attacks had never even been charged although
their identities were common knowledge.

AB's recommendations for the future come under five headings: (1)
Deportation from Aden of all those persons, numbering perhaps
20 000, whether Arab or Jew, who cannot produce a paper justifying
their presence; (2) Disbandment of the Levies, and their replacement
by a British garrison; (3) Complete reorganisation of the local police;
(4) Instructions to magistrates to act with utmost speed and severity;
and (5) Segregation of the Aden Jews in a separate quarter on the
outskirts of Crater.

AB's letter concludes:

If the measures suggested are taken, or others equally efficacious which have not occurred to me, and a permanent British Garrison is maintained here which can be relied upon to quell disorders at the outset and defend the minorities in the population, we may hope to see Aden become once again the haven of peace and order that it has been for over a century, in spite of the currents of hatred and violence which eddy all round the world elsewhere.

This letter was passed up to the Governor, and Sir Reginald Champion's reply is dated 18 December:

... It is no excuse for us, but it is no less true, that Aden is not alone in the world in its fruiting of thugs and crooks and profiteers as the result of conditions during recent past years. It is also true that what may be generally known or believed about bad-hats is only too often not enough for prosecution and retribution, with the consequence that – as in all history and in all lands – the crooks of to-day become the aristocrats of to-morrow. Nobody deplores these matters more than I, but I assure you from my pretty long experience as an administrator that it is not so easy as you may imagine to take drastic short-cuts to their cure ...

The Governor goes through the various matters raised by AB, which were all, he assures him, under urgent official consideration. The long and courteous reply closes on a note of cautious optimism:

I think that if the partition of Palestine had not been decided upon the late disturbances might not have occurred: that sooner or later the Palestine problem will be settled with some degree of finality and that thereafter there will be a general decrease of Arab – Jewish feeling in these regions; and that in the meantime a short-range policy of security for the Jewish community in Aden will suffice ...

We have no record of AB's carrying the correspondence any further.

IV

All this time the firm continued to grow. In 1937 the Aden staff had been eight Europeans, twenty Indians and twenty Arabs, with some

400 manual labourers. By 1948 in Aden alone there were 43 Europeans, 69 Indians and 81 Arabs in managerial and clerical posts. The manual labour force had risen to 2171. The Halal fleet consisted of *El Hak* and *El Amin* with two larger motor vessels on order in Scotland. There were fifteen dhows ranging up to 400 tons – the larger dhows all fitted with diesel engines. There were four tugs, four motor launches, and six iron and eighteen wooden lighters. Three of the dhows were en route for Calicut to bring timber for the new building programme (eight lighters and six motor launches).

New ventures in Aden were the Crescent Hotel at Steamer Point, acquired (as the Soap Factory had been) by a chance opportunity; and the floating dock. This last had originally been brought to Massawa by the Italians, and sunk there on the collapse of their East African Empire. The British Navy raised it, took it over, and early in 1947 AB bought it from the Admiralty for £30 000. His idea was to use it for his own little fleet, in particular to save the time and expense involved in sending *El Hak* and *El Amin* to Suez or Mombasa to be docked. (In the thirties AB had tried having underwater work done by divers in Aden, but the experiment had not been a success.) The dock was duly used for AB's ships, and, since plant and labour must not be allowed to stand idle, outside work was also accepted.

This outside ship work increased rapidly with the growth of the agency work of the Halal Shipping Company. It was natural for the Halal to pass to the Marine Workshop any work required on the ships they were handling. And one of the problems facing Hugh Millar (ex-Burma Marine Service, who arrived in late 1947 to take charge) was the acquisition of more plant and more skilled labour to meet the ever-increasing calls. The purchase of a new machine tool or the recruitment of a technician from Europe needed AB's explicit approval, and AB's reluctance to spend money was here intensified by the fact that he could not (and knew that he could not) appreciate the technical issues involved. He was apt to be suspicious when he felt he was out of his depth; and to get him to agree to buy a new machine might take months. But at one stage old Wilhelm Wilhelmsen of the Wilhelmsen Line told AB he wished all work at Aden on any of his ships to be undertaken by the Besse Marine Workshop. Thereafter things became easier.

Not that the life of the manager could ever be an easy one. There were all the difficulties – physical, climatic and psychological – endemic in precision work under Aden conditions. There was the impact of AB himself, liable to turn up without warning at any hour of the day or night, and to make trouble if he found or suspected anyone not to be working their hardest. There was the perennial shortage of skilled labour. The Marine Workshop was the first concern in Aden to start a system of indentured apprenticeship, in conjunction with the Aden Technical College founded and financed by AB. There was a fair supply of boys who wished to become apprentices; but as soon as they had learned enough to command better wages elsewhere they were apt to melt away. But by and large the Marine Workshop successfully tackled its difficulties and earned good money.

Another and extremely important source of income, thanks largely to the flair and ingenuity of Parekh and his Indian collaborators, was in the post-war currency situation – particularly after the introduction of the Marshall Plan and the consequent flow of US dollars. We have a letter from Davis to one of his Cairo Shell contacts dated early January 1949:

> In this part of the world the free dollar and the official dollar have existed side by side for some time, and by reason of the fact that certain of our branches are not British Companies and are not subject to British law, we ourselves, through these branches, are able to enjoy the plus value of the free dollar. Frankly, trade otherwise would be impracticable. ... We understand that Shell, being entirely British, cannot agree to deal in free dollars ...

There is a private letter from AB (also to a Shell friend) of about the same date. 'My last sale of dollars amounted at a single stroke to one million, which were sold at 79 pence per dollar instead of the official rate of 60d.'

V

The post-war years show a number of instances of AB's philanthropy. The Besse Dispensary was opened in 1948 under an Indian doctor who was a full-time employee of the firm, The object was to afford a free medical service to all the office staff and workers. Serious cases were of course passed to hospital, but minor surgical work was undertaken at the Dispensary. In the first year of its existence the Dispensary dealt with nearly two thousand surgical cases – minor accidents and ulcers – and well over two thousand medical cases – chest, throat and gastric troubles. The great majority of patients were manual workers. The doctor also travelled on the firm's ships when carrying pilgrims to and from the Hejaz; and was available to attend ships in Aden harbour for whom the Halal Shipping Company were agents.

But most of AB's benefactions were quite outside the firm. There was the School for Girls at Sheikh Othman – he attached great importance to the education of Arab women; the Women's Centre in Crater (established by AB on the closing down of the previous centre run by the British Council); the Aden Technical College for Boys (already mentioned); a similar school in Djibouti. In due course there were to be substantial contributions to the University of Addis Abeba. In spite of his own determined atheism he was always willing to help on the philanthropic work of religious bodies such as the Church of Scotland Mission in Sheikh Othman, and the Catholic Mission in Crater. One feature is constant in all AB's good works – his insistence on remaining completely in the background, and his obstinate refusal to be thanked. We have no records available to draw up even an approximate list of his benefactions.

VI

In the spring of 1948 AB and HB once more came back to France in *El Hak*. The ship, on this occasion overloaded, was hit by a violent storm in the Gulf of Lyons, and for some hours those on board her seemed on the brink of catastrophe. The storm passed, and they made port; but a few days later, in Le Paradou, AB suffered a severe stroke. The effects were to last for the three remaining years of his life. The indomitable will stayed unimpaired. It was in the summer of 1948 that he paid his incognito visit to Oxford that assured the foundation of St Antony's College. There were big decisions still to be taken, and flashes of the old fire and vigour. But these were against a background of ever-increasing physical discomfort and ever more frequent fits of depression.

AB's main concern was, inevitably, for the future of the firm. It was in the late summer that he composed his mammoth review of the firm's activities, summarised in Appendix B on page 214 to serve as guide to his successors. Meanwhile HB had written to Tony in America. Letters were exchanged, and it was agreed that Tony would return (a decision made easier by the retirement of Parekh). The reconciliation meant more to AB than perhaps he was willing to admit. We have a letter to his youngest son dated 1 September 1948:

GED [i.e. Davis] does not realise that I am today at the end of my tether, and the few months still left me necessitate, for the sake of the firm, that I give you every moment of my time. In my present mood I feel this is the last year I shall spend in Aden, and as I have already written I wish for your return in February.

And later:

For a long time now I have known that I am condemned to hard labour for life. I even believe I have carried my cross with a song in my heart. But now . . .

26 St Antony's I

There are difficulties over compiling the full story of the inception of St Antony's. AB's correspondence with R. A. H. Clyde, his emissary in the UK, has been lost. There is, for some reason, a ban on the inspection of the early records in the Oxford University Registry. AB's letters, over thirty years, had repeatedly emphasised his wish to retire from business and devote himself to culture and the arts; but give no hint of any idea of founding a college. However there is no doubt as to the actual course of events. For AB's motives we depend on such evidence as we have of the lines on which his mind was working.

Bernard, his friend and mentor in his army days, had watched his career with interest. In a conversation with his daughter Germaine not long before his death in 1935, he wondered what AB was going to do with all his money. He must have known his former protégé far too well to suppose he would spend it on himself. Indeed one of AB's outstanding traits was the modesty of his way of life. In Aden and at Le Paradou he lived in comfort, but simple comfort. He had his little extravagances – stockings specially made for him in Bombay, and shoes from London and New York bespoke bootmakers.[1] But it took all HB's diplomacy, persistence and guile to make him patronise a West End tailor or shirtmaker. When in London he stayed not at the Savoy or Claridges but at the St Ermin's Hotel in Caxton Street. When he entertained it was at Frascati's; he would walk there and back and be displeased if a lady guest suggested a taxi. From Paris he would take a night train to Toulon, second class without sleeper. His frugality extended to his family. The idea that his children – or indeed anyone else – should have money to spend that they had not earned was abhorrent to him. His sons' allowances were very meagre. He was shocked when, after their reconciliation, his daughter Meryem told him that half a crown was not enough for a visit to her hairdresser.

All along we must never forget the intensity of his dedication to his idea of his firm. Expenditure, for however worthy a cause, could not be

172

justified if it in any way hindered or handicapped the firm's activities and growth. In the short-lived boom following World War I we find him subscribing to the good works run by Madame de Coppet and Madame Siegfried. Then came the shock of the Stoner crash; and thereafter, for some years, every spare penny had to be devoted to the firm's rehabilitation. In the middle twenties he was, laboriously, approaching the top step of the Stoner 'pyramid', but there remained the huge overdraft with the National Bank of India and the debt to the Anglo-Saxon on his ships. He still owed a great deal of money when he was caught by the 1930 slump; as the slump receded and business picked up there came the complications and uncertainties of the Abyssinian War and then of World War II.

By 1942 it was clear that A. Besse & Co. Ltd. was not only going to weather the storm but was likely to emerge considerably larger and more prosperous than it had ever been before. It was now that AB made a number of benefactions, mostly to local good causes. But these benefactions, substantial though some of them were, were not on a scale in any way to inhibit the firm's further expansion. By the middle forties a new situation had arisen. The firm was enormous. AB was beginning to feel his age. He no longer envisaged business developments beyond those which the firm could easily finance out of income. Huge credit balances were piling up in various parts of the world. The time was ripe for a supreme gesture. It was at this period that he remarked to Germaine Bernard: 'To build up a business on the scale of mine one has to be hard. Sometimes very hard. I would like now to make some recompense.'

As we have seen 'the making of Men' had been very much on AB's mind during almost the whole of his career. Originally this was bound up with the needs of his firm. It would be too much to expect that AB should realise the part played by the exuberance of his own ego in his difficulties over European staff. He blamed the ineptitude of those in charge of his London office. But as time went on he blamed also the spirit of the age, with its apathy, its cynicism, its urge for levelling down, its flabbiness – giving rise to a whole new generation 'with appetites of wolves and jaws of sheep'. What he saw of the state of his much loved France in his post-war visits appalled him. The rot, he felt, had set in. The only chance that he could see for the salvation of French youth lay in a new approach to education. For the French State system, as he had known it in his school days he had neither sympathy nor respect. As an atheist and anti-cleric, Catholic teaching could not be considered. The new approach, to build character, not to cram facts, must be on the lines he firmly believed to be the true ones.[2] And so he conceived his idea of the Collège de Rebelles and, when rebuffed by the French Ministry of Education, he turned to England.

In his oration of 8 October 1948 the Oxford Vice-Chancellor was to state 'our benefactor believes that no education so strengthens the moral qualities of students or is so productive of initiative and "grit" as that to be found in England and in particular in the College system'. We have no other record of AB's talks with Vice-Chancellor Stallybrass during his confidential visit in the summer of 1948. Of course AB knew very little of the English College system. But it is true that, in spite of his countless clashes with British officialdom (not to mention his undying hostility to that very British institution, the Union Club at Steamer Point), AB had a real affection and regard for England and English ways. In this his cult of Kipling must certainly have played a part, as did no doubt his cult of Churchill. But there were also a large number of British officials and officers who came to win his friendship and respect. Then there was Shell, the quality of whose senior British executives had made a lasting impression on him. All the same it would be wrong to assume from the Vice-Chancellor's words that AB was complacent about the state of England. We have ample evidence of his misgivings. England too was becoming affected by the spirit of the age. The object of his benefaction was to help prevent her following in the wake of France.

II

In late 1947 AB arranged that R. A. H. Clyde should be his emissary to investigate the possibilities of a new educational foundation in Great Britain. Clyde had, for some years, acted as solicitor to AB's London office; and had successfully tackled some tricky problems involving the Halal Shipping Company. His speciality was shipping rather than education, but he was a man of wide contacts and considerable resource. His brief was to travel round, enquire, discuss and report back to AB. In due course he started his quest. The first idea was an ambitious one, the establishment of a new university. But, in the winter of 1947–8, it did not seem that this suggestion was practicable. Clyde was assured by the headmasters of two famous public schools that it was unthinkable that a new university (if and when one could be founded) could attract a teaching staff of any calibre; and consequently no young man of any promise would risk the future by applying for admission. In the circumstances it seemed desirable to devise some means of linking the new foundation with an established university. Clyde himself had been to Oxford, but his memories were not particularly happy, and in the early summer of 1948 a confidential feeler was put to certain distinguished members of the Cambridge hierarchy. The proposal was that AB should fund an Anglo-French college in Jersey whose pupils should be eligible to sit for Cambridge degrees. This of course was unacceptable and the matter was allowed to drop. 'Three months later', to quote one of those approached, 'we heard that Oxford had got it.'

What had happened was that Clyde, in the end, went down to Oxford and called on the Registrar, Douglas Veale. A stately home in Wiltshire was then on the market and the suggestion was by this time that AB should buy the place and establish a college whose members could sit for Oxford degrees.

'If', Veale answered, 'your client wishes to found a college, why not found one here in Oxford?'

III

Clyde reported to AB at Le Paradou, and AB decided to come to Oxford. All precautions were taken to ensure secrecy. As already mentioned, we have no record of the conversations during his visit, which must, for him, have been a unique experience. For most of his life he had been used to dominate any company in which he found himself. Here he was on entirely unfamiliar ground, dealing with men whose quality he was quick to recognise. It is of interest that Sir Maurice Bowra's memory of him is of 'a quiet man'. What is important is the impression made upon him by the Vice-Chancellor, Dr William Stallybrass and the confidence that Stallybrass's personality inspired. Things moved quickly. The offer was formally notified to the University on 26 August 1948 and was accepted unanimously by a crowded Congregation on 15 September.

On 8 October, in his oration already quoted, the Vice-Chancellor also said:

The proposal put forward was one for a postgraduate College, one-third of the members of which were to be Frenchmen, and of a gift to enable existing Colleges to increase their accommodation with a similar provision as to the proportion of Frenchmen to be admitted amongst the additional students. The proffered gift, which proved to be one and a half million pounds, was of a magnitude almost unparalleled, and its acceptance involved such big issues and so wide a departure from precedent.... that it was clear that the ultimate decision as to acceptance must be taken by the whole University in Congregation. Therefore, though it was in the dead of the Long Vacation, Council was immediately summoned.

Council approached its consideration of the problem on the basis that one and a half million is worth no more than £5 if that for which the millions are given is something which is not wanted. Did this offer, therefore, give us something which was in line with what we envisaged as the proper future development of the University? The examination of the proposals was critical, but the more they were examined the more clearly it appeared that they gave us that which we most desired.... When later our benefactor, entirely as a result of his own further consideration and on his own initiative, said that he would prefer that there should be no rigid number of Frenchmen for whom a place was to be found, and that he would like it left to the University to determine whether the College should be limited to postgraduate members, the proposed College fell completely into the pattern marked out by our traditions.... With remarkable self-denial and wise prevision our benefactor has given the University a completely free choice ... and the College itself, once its character has been determined ... will be as autonomous as any of the ancient Foundations.... Our benefactor wishes men of all nationalities, and in particular of his own France, to have the benefits of such an education. For he believes that the future prospects for Europe and the world depend upon international understanding and upon international rather than national action. He has provided, therefore, that admission to the College shall be subject to no test of a religious, political, or racial character. The University by accepting the gift has bound itself to give effect both in the letter and in the spirit to the donor's wishes (which are its own). The donor wishes his name to remain unknown as he shuns publicity,[3] but it would be wrong not to put on record the deep appreciation which we have for a man with this Vision Splendid, who wishes the fruit of his life's work to be consecrated in St Antony's ...

Perhaps the most significant aspect of AB's benefaction was not the actual amount of the gift. He could part with a million and a half pounds without impairing the strength of the firm of Besse. It would in no way affect his own manner of living, nor embarrass the prospects of his children – not that this last was ever likely to weigh with him. But to withdraw his conditions, to hand over, unreservedly, to others the conduct of a project so near to his heart[4] was, for one of AB's temperament, an immense gesture. It was a supreme act of faith; and a remarkable tribute to the confidence that Stallybrass had inspired.

IV

The idea of the gift to existing colleges had arisen during the discussions between Veale and Clyde. AB was eager for young Frenchmen to benefit from his endowment, but it was obvious that some time must elapse before the new College was open and ready to take them. Accordingly the 'memorandum on a proposed college agreed with an anonymous benefactor's solicitor' (made public on 21 September) provides for a total sum of not less than £250 000 being available to certain of the poorer colleges to enable them to build new living accommodation, engage more teaching staff and establish new scholarships – on condition that preference be given to Frenchmen in the admissions thus increased.[5] The idea had been agreed by AB before his return to France, but there was an unfortunate misunderstanding over the financial aspect. AB assumed that his gift for St Antony's was to be cut to £1 250 000, thus leaving a quarter of a million for the existing colleges. But it was apparently hoped in some quarters in Oxford or London that he would be willing to put up an additional quarter million. In any case back in Le Paradou he received through the post a long legal document which he was to sign and return. He disliked such documents and passed it to HB. She pointed out that to sign would commit him to £1 750 000. AB was indignant.

Meanwhile Clyde had been considering the risk of eventual demands by the Inland Revenue. AB was now seventy-one. He had recently suffered a stroke. Should he die within three years of the gift being made irrevocable there would be substantial death duties. The solution seemed to lie in the gift being at once made irrevocable, and in the funds being deposited not only outside the jurisdiction but outside the sphere of influence of the British Authorities. AB was not happy at being pressed on this particular issue. It was not only that the insistence on speed seemed to imply an expectation of his early death. He had little confidence in lawyers and he mistrusted the elaborate network of committees that the proposed arrangements entailed. He felt the lawyers were making complications for motives of their own, and, incidentally, were cutting him off all the more completely from the project so near to his heart. He acquiesced; but this was one more of the factors that led to the break of his relations with Clyde.

There were of course technical problems involved in the transfer of so large a sum as a million and a half pounds. We are told that during his visit to England that summer AB arranged for an interview with Lord Halifax (Chancellor of Oxford University) to secure his good offices for the clearance of a huge cheque on a Beirut bank. Lord Halifax, the story goes on, was rather bewildered and the matter was not pursued. In the event the arrangements were worked out by AB's Indian experts in the Aden office. The funds, drawn from transferable credit balances in New York and elsewhere, were deposited in the Westminster Bank in Jersey and thence transferred by telegram to Dublin where Clyde had arranged for three Dublin residents to act as Trustees. The funds were invested in a special issue of 3 per cent Irish Exchequer Bonds 1965–70. Meanwhile the St Antony's Foundation Ltd. had been incorporated under the Companies Act in London. The foundation had a Council of Management, with Sir David Maxwell-Fyfe (later Lord Kilmuir) as Chairman, R. A. H. Clyde as Secretary, and the Vice-Chancellor of Oxford University as ex-officio member. At the same time the Hebdomadal Council in Oxford appointed a 'Committee on the Affairs of St Antony's' with the Vice-Chancellor in the chair. The creation of the new college was to be the joint task of the Committee in Oxford and the Council of Management in London.

On 28 October 1948 Vice-Chancellor Stallybrass fell from a London–Oxford train and died of his injuries.

27   St Antony's II

For the rest of 1948 the affairs of St Antony's seemed to be marking time. AB by now had broken off relations with Clyde, and there was a temporary coolness in his relationship with the University Registrar. Dean Lowe, the new Vice-Chancellor, had no developments to report to him. But before leaving Le Paradou for Aden in the autumn AB had established a new and very fruitful friendship.

Dr Kurt Hahn, headmaster of Gordonstoun, was on close terms with Sir Henry Willink, the Master of Magdalene. Shortly after Clyde's abortive approach to Cambridge Sir Henry informed Hahn of the existence of a mysterious Frenchman who was prepared to donate a very large sum to education. Hahn made discreet enquiries. Commander Christopher Arnold-Forster, a former Chairman of the Gordonstoun Board, happened to be a neighbour of AB's in Provence. A selection of Gordonstoun literature was sent out to Arnold-Forster who passed the papers to AB. AB was profoundly impressed at finding ideals so akin to his own. He was particularly struck by the form of the *Final Report to Parents*.[1] In the late summer Kurt Hahn came out to stay with Arnold-Forster who took him over to Le Paradou. Almost at once it transpired that both Hahn and AB had, in their early youth, been passionate protagonists of the innocence of Dreyfus: this first meeting was taken up with an eager discussion of the Dreyfus case. But the more AB learned about Gordonstoun the more the ideas behind the school appealed to him. Having made his irrevocable gift to Oxford he felt unable to consider handing over a capital sum; instead he arranged for a substantial annual subsidy.

During 1949, when things in Oxford seemed to be hanging fire, some of those close to AB were inclined to feel that the million and a half might more profitably have been donated to Gordonstoun.

By the winter of 1948–9 AB's health was causing concern to those
around him. He was overweight. As ever, he refused to submit to
discipline imposed from outside; and, in spite of all HB's efforts and
persuasion, his doctor's advice on diet was stubbornly disregarded. On
10 January 1949 he wrote to Petrouchka from Aden:

> Never more than now have I understood the supreme importance of
> health, because now I am at an age when, without being specifically
> ill, one can no longer rely on one's nerves, muscles, physical reac-
> tions, or, on another level on memory or power of concentration.
> One has a feeling of disintegration. . . . Luckily my wife has abound-
> ing energy, and if she is ever tired she does not let anyone know it.

In that same letter he wrote 'I have to write a paper on Education,
for which retirement and solitude are essential.' We do not know
whether the idea of this paper was AB's own or whether someone had
proposed his writing a brief for his new foundation. In due course the
paper was completed;[2] but when, later on, a copy was handed to the
Warden of St Antony's it was passed simply as an expression of AB's
private views, with no suggestion that it should influence policy.

In the spring of 1949 AB and HB returned to France. In the early
summer they came to Britain, visited Gordonstoun where they were
delighted with what they saw; and while in Scotland called on St
Andrew's University with a view to finding suitable graduates to join
the firm. A visit to Oxford was envisaged for the autumn, when, it was
hoped, there would be something tangible to discuss.

Back at Le Paradou AB corresponded with the Oxford Vice-Chancellor whose replies were courteous, but inconclusive. There was no
lack of good will among the distinguished men in Oxford and London
who were concerned with the project. But all were heavily preoccupied with other commitments, and no one could put the creation
of the new college as a top priority. As Vice-Chancellor Lowe was later
to write to the Provost of Worcester: 'One cause of the delay in the last
couple of months had been that Maxwell-Fyfe and I (the only two
effective members of the Council to date) could not find a date on
which to meet'. AB became increasingly impatient, and was determined that his Oxford visit should jolt the various committees into
action. But, later in the summer, his health took a turn for the worse.
There was talk of an operation, and it was doubtful whether he would

be fit enough to make the journey. The one encouraging development was the arrival of J. C. Masterman, Provost of Worcester College, who came out to France to stay with Arnold-Forster during the Long Vacation. AB took to him at once; and Masterman agreed to serve on the Council of Management and do what he could to speed up progress.

III

In his oration at the beginning of the new academic year, in early October 1949, the Vice-Chancellor referred at some length to the St Antony's project.

There is no denying that we have made a disappointing lack of progress – disappointing both to the donor and to ourselves. The first task of the University is to find a site, and it is this which has caused the delay... Twice already we had hoped that a reasonably satisfactory answer has been found, but each time, after protracted negotiations, our hopes were frustrated. The committee which we charged with this duty is continuing its work with other possibilities in mind. Of course the matter of the site is not the only aspect of St Antony's which demands consideration; important questions about its composition and policy have so far been left undecided. Earlier in the year there was an inclination deliberately to leave them undecided for two reasons. It was felt that the all-important thing at the moment was to press on with the search for a site. There was also a reluctance to tie the hands of the future College by making decisions in advance.... I cannot believe that this general attitude was wrong, and its motives were certainly irreproachable; but I am prepared to believe that our timing was wrong and that it might have been better to engage on the two kinds of preparatory task simultaneously.... The initiative lies not with the University as such, but with the Council of the St Antony's Foundation of which the Vice-Chancellor is a member, and a member, I should say, whose advice has constantly been sought and accepted. However that may be, I have been persuaded that now at any rate it is high time to grapple with the issues of policy involved. For that purpose the Council of the Foundation is now being strengthened by the addition of certain persons known to be acceptable to the Founder and in sympathy with his aims, and a meeting of this body will be held shortly...

Masterman sent a report of what was happening to Arnold-Forster, and expressed the hope that when AB came to Oxford he would stay with him in the Provost's lodgings. On 24 October AB wrote back:

Dear Mr Masterman,

Our mutual friend, Arnold-Forster, has sent me your memo to him dated 11th October. It was at my request that he asked you whether you could put me up during the short visit I intended paying to Oxford where a procrastination, a passive resistance and a lack of enthusiasm seem to prevail which I find it very hard to accept. I asked Dr Lowe to enlarge the St Antony Committee in order to admit certain men whom I felt would be more active and energetic than the present members, but he answered me somewhat evasively. [There follow some outspoken remarks about some of the persons concerned].... The death of Dr Stallybrass has proved to be a catastrophe for my scheme; whereas I was prepared to give to it the few years of life that remain to me and to put my heart and soul into its realisation, I have only one desire to-day, and that is to forget all about it. The very large sum of money I donated seems to have been rendered useless.... Arnold-Forster will doubtless have informed you that although the specialist I went to see at Lyons decided against the operation, many conditions were attached, and to cut a long story short, I am unable to leave this part of the world until I return to Aden on the 18th November. I have therefore had to abandon all idea of proceeding to England for the moment, which means that I have to forego the great pleasure it would have given me to spend 24 hours with you in Oxford. I would like to think that this is only a pleasure deferred and that you will welcome me next year when I return. In the meantime, please accept my grateful thanks for the hospitality you were prepared to offer me...

The wheels began to turn, though rather slowly. On 15 November, the Vice-Chancellor was writing to the Provost of Worcester: 'Of the four men whom Besse wanted, you have accepted, Arnold-Forster has refused (again), Ifor Evans is in the United States and Sir Walter Moberly has not replied...'. However on 24 November Masterman was elected to the Council of Management,[3] and became the Council's representative on the Committee on the Affairs of St Antony's at Oxford. On 5 December he wrote to AB to tell him what was happening, and on 16 December AB replied from Aden:

Dear Mr Masterman,

Thank you very much for your kind and most welcome letter dated the 5th December, which was forwarded on to me here. The news it contains is heartening and gives me the impression that at last some progress is being made after a most discouraging period of waiting. I agree entirely with all you write and look forward to hearing shortly that a Warden possessing all the qualities indicated by you has been found and is devoting all his enthusiasm and energies to my foundation. I am very happy to hear that you have received and accepted an invitation to join the enlarged Council and hope that in the near future you will be able to give me some more heartening news as a result of the first meeting. Needless to say, it will interest me also greatly to receive copies of the plans drawn up for additions to Worcester College. May I state my special satisfaction that part of my donation, to be devoted to the improvement of existing colleges, has been allocated to yours? . . .

IV

After Christmas the Committee got busy. As comes out in the above correspondence, it had been decided to appoint a Warden before proceeding to 'grapple with the issues of policy involved'. Meanwhile there was still the urgent problem of premises. Over this had been the disappointments to which the Vice-Chancellor had referred. Negotiations had been started for the purchase of Manchester College. At one stage it had been hoped that an immediate offer of £30 000 would induce the trustees to sell, and AB was asked if he would be willing to put up this additional sum. But it was at the time when he was extremely dissatisfied at the way things were shaping in Oxford and he flatly refused. There were negotiations for Bagley Wood, three miles out of Oxford on the way to Abingdon. Then there were two houses in South Parks Road. It was not till February 1950 that the solution was found in the shape of Halifax House at 62 Woodstock Road. This massive piece of Victorian gothic had been erected in the 1860s as a convent for the Anglican Order of the Holy and Undivided Trinity. By World War II it was too large for the sisters to keep up. The Order accordingly moved to South Leigh, a few miles out of Oxford (and later to a house near Malvern); and the building was taken over as a hostel for graduates under the name of Halifax House. It was now agreed that

Halifax House should move to South Parks Road and that 62 Woodstock Road should become St Antony's College.

Meanwhile on 9 February the Committee decided to offer the post of Warden to the Vice-Chancellor of a redbrick University. The offer was declined on 17 February and a further meeting was called. On this occasion it was unanimously agreed to offer the post to F. W. Deakin, Fellow of Wadham. Deakin was invited to call on the Vice-Chancellor and the offer was put to him. He was given a week to make his mind up. He decided to accept. On 14 March 1950 the Vice-Chancellor was able to inform the Chairman of the Council of Management that the problems as to Warden and premises had both been solved. At the same time the good news was sent out to AB. It was felt desirable that the new Warden and the benefactor should meet as soon as possible.

V

On the eve of his departure from Aden, 8 April 1950, AB wrote to Deakin:

> As soon as I arrive at Marseille my car will be waiting to take me to my property at Le Paradou, par Cavalaire (Var), where I hope it will be possible for me to receive you before I go on to Oxford. There, in the peace and beauty of that unique corner of France, we should have the time and the tranquillity to discuss present and future problems.

The visit was fixed for the last week in April. Deakin was allotted second class return railway fare (without sleeper) to Toulon. He arrived with his wife at 9 a.m. They were met by Miss Ogilvie, the former governess, who drove them to Le Paradou, where AB at once went into action. Deakin writes:

> I remember having received no briefing from the Vice-Chancellor, and was totally unaware of the background of differences with Clyde which played a large part in my first talk with AB. He produced a number of symbolic skeletons on the table, and I remember having to say 'yes' or 'no' to each of his grouses, knowing nothing whatever of the history of his relations with the University or with the Council of Management. I was struck at once by his directness in negotiation, and after having made up his mind very rapidly that I would 'do', he

listened to my plans for the new college. .... I realised by the time I left Le Paradou that AB was content to allow me to take over and had no intention of interfering in any way with the direction of the new institution. This attitude he consistently maintained until his death. ... It is true AB had a very nebulous idea about university activities, but there was nothing pretentious about him; and in his patriarchal background at Le Paradou he held his own very quietly in conversation on intellectual subjects. I remember being impressed from the beginning by the extent of his reading...

In according, unreservedly, his complete confidence to the new Warden AB had once more made a supreme gesture.[4]

VI

On 8 May AB wrote to Deakin in Oxford: 'I am still here in the flesh, but my mind is already in Oxford, building castles there.' A week later he wrote: 'In answer to your remark that you will need my fullest support in the accomplishment of your task, I can only repeat that you will find me ready to respond to any call at any time, up to the utmost limit of the strength that is left to me.'

There was correspondence as to the exact date of AB's Oxford visit. AB wished to accept Masterman's offer of hospitality at Worcester College, but the timing had to be fitted in with the Provost's existing commitments. HB was concerned over AB's health, and was anxious that he should not be overstrained. In the end they arrived at the Provost's lodgings on 18 June.

AB was highly gratified by his reception.

On 26 June he wrote to Davis from London:

I arrived back yesterday from Oxford, after a hectic, but at the same time very inspiring, week during which we were asked to visit all the Colleges which have benefited from our donation; and we were also present at the great ceremony of the 'Encaenia' – in which, as you know, I was made to participate. It was heart-warming to meet the spirit of co-operation and the enthusiasm of all the Heads of the different Colleges – and the solicitude of the Chancellor, Lord Halifax, and the Vice-Chancellor, John Lowe. Matters had not been arranged as I should have liked, and though we were living in a

College in an atmosphere certainly incomparable to anything I have experienced before, I had to leave it on Friday, as other arrangements had been made before we arrived. ... The Warden of the College, Bill Deakin, is altogether a superior man, who enjoys the respect and affection of everybody in Oxford. He has in him a spark of adventurous spirit which endears him to me, and he has a wife who – the same as mine – collaborates closely with him. Coming back to London I find all the correspondence exchanged about indigo ...

A fortnight later AB was writing to Deakin from Le Paradou:

For the first time in my life I have had to admit defeat. My brain refused to function any longer and I decided to leave London on Sunday. We arrived here the same day, only to find a temperature I have seldom experienced even in Aden. I am confronted on my arrival by an accumulation of letters, which, alas, demand an immediate reply. But my first duty is towards you, my dear Deakin, and our College (I should in fact say your College for the part I can play in it or can ever hope to play in it is insignificant) ...

AB goes on to refer to certain earlier difficulties over the project's implementation. But he adds:

... you may regard this letter as an attempt on my part to interfere. Indeed it is nothing of the kind, and if you interpret it as such I will be careful in future to avoid expressing any sentiment which could be taken, even from afar, as criticism of your actions. I am sure you must realise that nothing could be further from my mind.

A further letter is dated 20 August:

We all realise the magnitude and difficulty of your task and shall not be surprised if on occasion you give way to a feeling of discouragement. This must be fought against however, as you have already accomplished so much that it is impossible to believe for a moment that you will not triumph over all the other difficulties that beset your path. Need I repeat yet again that if there is *anything* any of us can do to help in big or small matters we shall be only too happy to do the little we can ....

In mid-September AB left France for Aden. Meanwhile in Oxford a Sub-Warden, a Bursar and two Fellows had been appointed; and at the start of the Michaelmas Term, on 8 October 1950, St Antony's College opened its doors with seven students. On that day the Warden received a telegram from AB in Aden: 'Deep sympathy complete trust surround you go ahead fearlessly all efforts regardless success find in themselves reward.'

To which the Warden replied: 'Deeply touched your kind message we are open and will strive to achieve our ends warmest greetings from us all at St Antony's.'

28   1949 – 50

All this time, in spite of ill health, in spite of the new horizons at Oxford and at Gordonstoun, there was no relaxation of AB's intense concentration on his business. There was no further launching out into new ventures: the formation, in 1950, of A. Besse & Co. (Ethiopia) Ltd. and of A. Besse Trading Co. (Diredawa) Ltd. was merely for administrative convenience. But there was ever-growing activity in all departments and all branches; and once again an international crisis – this time the war in Korea – stimulated demand and put up the prices of the goods that Besse could provide.

André had now come back to join the firm. But it was obvious that of the three brothers it was Tony who stood nearest to his father and on whom AB set his highest hopes; and AB's letters to his youngest son are often revealing. There are his schemes for the future – the creation of an organisation in Aden which can repair the largest ship. There are general principles: 'the firm's wealth has been built on purchases effected during those lull periods when all the competitors withdrew from the market, and one can pick and choose and at a low level of prices'. There are references to Davis: 'From our General Manager there is never a word about any of the staff that is not dithyrambic.' And again: 'the weekly report has for me one definite object – to know what is happening in those departments where GED never sticks his nose'. There are staff matters: 'the boss is often faced with delicate problems regarding the private life of a senior member of the staff. Read the enclosed letter, seal it up again and when quite dry pass it on to the addressee who must not suspect that you know the contents'.

Tony of course was also in receipt of advice from Davis, whose approach and whose wording were sometimes in contrast with those of AB. Of X, for instance (an American customer for skins), Davis wrote:

If letters from Aden to X appear severe this is absolutely essential, as despite my great friendship ... there is no doubt that the ups and downs of his business make him over-critical at times, and we adopt a strong attitude from Aden in order to keep our tight grip on the trade.' AB put it otherwise: 'X, judged by moral standards – those that really matter – is despicable.

II

Highlights of the post-war period included the completion of AB's two new (and larger) ships built for him at Ardrossan – *El Halae II* launched by his daughter Ariane early in 1949, and *El Kerim* launched by Meryem a year later. *El Halal II*, like her original namesake, was unlucky. Things kept on going wrong. It may have been that too many cooks had been called in for her design and for the supervision of her construction; there were the modifications demanded by AB himself; and in any case the London office was hardly equipped to co-ordinate and control the numerous experts involved. Nevertheless AB, as so often, laid the blame on London. On 6 August 1949 he wrote from Le Paradou to his London manager:

I cannot help feeling that in all this tragic affair of the ship London bears a heavy responsibility. . . . When one thinks of those monstrous cranes and unwieldy, heavy lifeboats – items which made the ship so unstable that an enormous amount of ballast had to be added at the expense of her carrying capacity; when one learns, moreover, that one of the cranes has already broken down, that the bilge pumps do not work, not to mention countless other hitches, one's feelings defy adequate expression. All this does not seem to worry you very much, however, whereas it keeps me awake at night. . . . It is so clear in my mind that I asked from the very beginning for a larger version of *El Hak*, as much larger as our floating dock could accommodate, that I am at a loss to understand how *El Halal* can be so different. If I were not a man I would surely weep over such a caricature of my wishes. To me it is a terrible condemnation of our London office which may lead me to take very far-reaching decisions.

The hard-pressed manager's reply is dated 10 August:

I must make the strongest protest to your remarks. You claim that none of the countless problems connected with *El Halal* seem to have worried me, which does not speak well for your judgement of human nature. The fact is that I have not had a proper night's sleep for the best part of three months, and my health has suffered to such a degree that I am now on the verge of collapse, and your remarks may well prove the last straw. . . . It is clear that you asked for a larger version of *El Hak*. Is it possible that you never read the correspondence in which it was shown that this could not be done? I cannot believe it; but if you wish, I will send you copies. In any case, I must have some complete rest, and I propose to absent myself from the office for some weeks – possibly in a sanatorium – so that I can build up my health again, and endeavour to disperse this state of complete despondency into which your remarks have thrown me . . .

AB's answer went back by return of post:

Your outburst dated 10th instant would tend to show me that you are satisfied with the achievements, with the staff situation and with the prestige of our London office, as also with the influence it wields. Unfortunately for you, I could write volumes on its deficiences, and on my sorrow at the opportunities lost; on what it could be in my eyes, and on what help it should be to Aden. If you believe, as your letter seems to show, that your judgement of human nature is sound, then there can be no doubt that our standards are altogether different. I am sorry that the bad state of your health prevents me from going further in my criticism, and nothing remains but for me to wish that your stay in a sanatorium will be long enough to procure for you the rest which you obviously so greatly need. . . . Let me point out, however, that I read in your correspondence to Aden that, contrary to my instructions, . . . [there follow complaints on another matter] . . . In fact, I have been wondering if it would not be better for everybody concerned for the firm to shut up shop. That would at least give you the rest you require . . . .

El Halal II remained a problem child. One of her main defects (as AB had noted) was a list – necessitating two hundred tons of permanent ballast and a corresponding loss of earning power. Nevertheless she paid her way. We have a note of the Aden office dated June 1950:

The gross earnings of *El Halal* for a period of 151 days, i.e. for the complete season when she first went to India until she returned to Aden were 589 526 Rs or 3 904.2.0 Rs per day. During this period disbursements were 305 650 Rs leaving a balance of 283 876 Rs.

Against the surplus of approximately £21 000, however, one has to take into account depreciation and interest on capital, and ... one has to bear in mind, that as she gets older one has to reckon on considerably more repairs. However, all told, we would state that she has slightly made better than make both ends meet. ...."

Moreover the shortcomings of *El Halal II* enabled AB to demand, and, through the efforts of the London office obtain, a substantial rebate on the cost of building *El Kerim*. And *El Kerim* was entirely satisfactory.

III

In the early winter of 1949 there was a curious incident in the Marine Workshop at Ma'alla. One morning the men refused to work. There was no explanation, and there had been no sign of impending trouble. Millar, the manager, who spoke no Arabic, was completely baffled. He could only report to head office and was informed that AB would come down in person next morning. Work was due to start at 7 a.m. Millar arrived at 6.59 to find a crowd of workers in the street outside, also AB who had been there for ten minutes and was restive at being kept waiting. The men were informed that those who wished to work should come in. The doors were opened and most of the men came in; those few who remained in the street had their names taken and were told they were dismissed. The doors were closed. Inside AB made a fifteen-minute speech in his forceful and individual Arabic. Work started. AB went round the shops and spoke again, individually, to the various groups at work. Then, without a word to Millar, he went back to his car and returned to Crater. The Marine Workshop resumed its normal rhythm. It was weeks later that Millar learned the explanation from an English-speaking Arab foreman. The men had been making their protest at the donation to England of so large a sum of the firm's money.

IV

Again and again AB came back to the question of staff. In February 1948 he was writing:

So long as we breathe the torpid stifling atmosphere of suburbia, all the aristocrats will leave us and we shall have to continue to limp with plebeians. The world has always been led and will continue to be led by aristocrats, no matter what social changes take place.... In all humility I state with conviction that if London had been moved by a different ideal and had known how to select staff, our firm would today be double its size. The only unsurmountable obstacle I have found in my path has been lack of men.

In the summer of that year, on his first visit to Oxford, he arranged for the firm to be on the books of the Oxford University Appointments Board. This AB regarded as a 'great trump card'.

From the testimony of one of these early Oxford recruits his beginnings with the firm were not encouraging. Joining the dingy London office in January 1949, WM was passed round the various sections, never staying anywhere long enough to get a grip on what was happening. He was called in for a short and formal interview in the early summer when AB arrived in London. Asked if he had learned much he replied, frankly, no. AB made no comment.

In due course he embarked on *El Hak* on her maiden voyage to Aden. Here he was put to work in the cereals department. He knew nothing about cereals, and the Indian clerks made clear he was wasting their time. Hours were long, pay was meagre; the staff mess was dull, Mohamed Aly authoritarian and the summer heat oppressive. AB's return to Aden in the autumn made little difference. The firm was now so large that there was little opportunity for a junior to experience the stimulating, if hazardous, close contact with his employer. One by one the trainees were summoned to dine in the penthouse. The newcomer had a few words with his host, but initiative in conversation was not encouraged, and AB did not deploy his charm. After dinner there were a few gramophone records, and at half-past nine it was time to say good-night.

Then one morning AB, walking through the office, beckoned to WM and told him he was to go to Dessie. It was some weeks before he actually left, but in the meantime he was put to work in the godowns, sorting and grading skins. AB always maintained that this was an essential stage of apprenticeship; and WM felt that at least he was really learning something. One Saturday afternoon he was called to AB and told to embark on a dhow leaving for Assab at 6 a.m. next morning. He packed his things, was given some sandwiches by Mohamed Aly, and very early on the Sunday morning was on board the dhow. From Assab he travelled on to Dessie with the convoy of Lancia lorries. In the next mail to reach Dessie was an enquiry from AB as to why he had not called to say goodbye. WM wrote back to explain he had not wished to disturb his chief at 5 a.m. AB replied that he was always accessible at any time.

V

Apart from learners fresh from school or university AB was keenly looking out for a young man of sufficient calibre and achievement to be placed at once in a responsible post; and he believed he had found what he wanted in the person of a young Frenchman working for Shell in one of their Middle Eastern companies. In the autumn of 1949 AB wrote a marathon letter to St Helen's Court asking Shell to agree to his release. Shell replied that they had their own plans for the man's future; these they would explain to him and leave him entirely free to make his choice. In due course he decided to stay with Shell. AB was ruffled and wondered, acidly, what his motives might be. A simple answer to this could be the certainty of a distinguished career with Shell; but it is also possible the young Frenchman may have heard of the unpredictability of AB's personal relationships.

A striking example of this, in the early post-war years, was when AB, for reasons that are still a mystery, turned against Maurice Weerts. In spite of all the latter's achievements on the firm's behalf AB decided to dismiss him. At this point Davis took a firm line: if Weerts went he would resign himself – and AB reluctantly agreed that he should stay. But AB's letters to Tony for some time to come, contain derogatory references to Weerts. As to the attitude of Davis, it was a question of conception of life. 'Stoic, Heroic, Nietzschean as my conception is, it differs almost to the point of being diametrically opposed to his [i.e. Davis'] which is that of a saint.'

VI

In the summer of 1950 AB had another of his clashes with officialdom. It concerned the Sudan, where the firm had been trading for some years and where AB saw the possibility of very considerable expansion. Unfortunately his local representatives had been caught out in a breach of the import/export regulations, since when the firm's operations had been restricted, and subjected to the strict scrutiny of the Sudan Government officials. AB was naturally anxious to clear the matter up. It turned out that one of his secretaries was a friend of the wife of the Director of Economics and Trade at Khartoum; and on 19 June he wrote him a personal letter from the lodgings of the Provost of Worcester.

Dear Mr Disney,

I am writing to you from Oxford, where I am surrounded by so much respect, understanding and affection and by men whose moral and intellectual level is so high that it seems nothing less than a sacrilege to occupy oneself with business – and what business, alas! But it is a sacrilege also to prevent a firm like mine, which enjoys the trust of all who have ever had dealings with it from pursuing its natural course.... Your predecessor left no stone unturned to hamper our development in your territory.... The dislike of this official pursued us at every turn ... whether his actions were dictated by friendship for other firms operating in his territory or merely by dislike of myself or my Port Sudan managers, I cannot say: but the fact remains that every possible obstacle was placed in our path. Possibly you may be in a position to enlighten me as to his motives.... When I return to London in a few days' time it is my intention to consult a friend, Sir David Maxwell-Fyfe – as well as Lord Halifax – and seek their advice as to the best means to be adopted in order to ensure that fair treatment be meted out to us.... It is my intention, on my way back to Aden, to call at Port Sudan for the express purpose of meeting you and clearing up the present highly unpleasant situation ...

Disney replied by return that he would be pleased to see AB if he came to Khartoum. But:

I should perhaps add that, before discussing – or authorising my deputy to discuss – the other matter, I shall expect to receive an unqualified apology for – and unreserved withdrawal of – your strictures on my predecessor. You will, perhaps, on reflection, agree that this must be the inevitable preliminary to an interview which otherwise could hardly avoid being both brief and unpleasant for both of us.

AB was furious. On 1 July he wrote to Davis in Aden:

Herewith attached is the vile answer I have received from Disney to my courteous letter. As you may well imagine, I am not going to accept that our firm and myself are dealt with in this way by a man

In London he took his troubles to Leonard Hall, son of the First Lord of the Admiralty, who introduced him to his father. Hall received him courteously but wished to see the whole correspondence. It then turned out that the only copy of AB's letter to Khartoum had been mailed to Aden. The next letter we have is from AB at Le Paradou dated 12 July:

My dear Leonard,

Most unfortunately I had to leave London, out of sheer exhaustion, before receiving the document I sorely needed to give to your dear and noble father, who wishes to inform Ernest Bevin of our troubles in the Sudan. [AB gives a list of the correspondence he enclosed, and a summary of his complaints. He goes on:] I think it is only right to warn the British Government, with whom I have had lifelong dealings marked by exquisite courtesy and consideration, that if they persist in employing officials of the type they have in the Sudan, this territory will not remain long under the British flag. I feel strongly that an experienced and completely impartial official should be asked to proceed there to examine the position, hear the point of view of the native merchant community, inspect every government department, and when they have taken stock of the harm caused by the wrong type of official, return to London to report. A member of my staff could, if necessary, accompany him. I suggest this because, unless some precaution of the kind is taken, the state of genuine fear in which the Sudanese live under the present administration, might well prevent the truth from becoming known. I may tell you that Disney is expected in London next week, and if Bevin so wished I would be quite prepared to fly over to meet the man in the presence of whoever has the right and the power to judge and punish . . .

We have no copy of Leonard Hall's reply. It cannot have been as AB would have wished for on 2 August he wrote 'My dear Leonard, I am still smarting from the blow your letter of the 24th July gave me . . .'. And so the affair petered out. But the Sudan authorities at about this time seem to have adopted a less rigorous line towards the firm's activities, and AB liked to feel the officials there had learned their lesson.

VII

It is generally agreed that towards the end of his life AB mellowed considerably. But, as has been shown, the old fire was very much still there. A further instance is in a letter to Davis in Aden written shortly before AB's departure from Le Paradou in the autumn of 1950. It concerns the rival firm of Riès.

The firm of Riès had been founded in Aden on the opening of the Suez Canal. Like other concerns it had its ups and downs. The middle thirties had been a difficult period. One evening Jeff Collins had reported to AB that a valuable consignment of skins was coming on the Aden market next morning. AB gave him a ceiling price. Collins protested this was not enough. AB was adamant. Collins attended the sale, with the result he expected, and came back indignantly to report to AB that the skins had gone to Paul Riès. AB told him he happened to know that Riès' commitments were such that to have missed this consignment would have put him in serious difficulties. All this was back in the thirties. Subsequently the firm of Riès had prospered, and by the late forties Paul's son Maurice had become its leading partner. On 3 September 1950 AB wrote to Davis in Aden:

I have had to give serious thought again to the rapid extension of Riès' business. In every report which I have left behind for the edification of Aden during my absence in recent years I think I have written a page or more on this subject. As soon as I saw Maurice extending his field of action I sounded a note of warning. The only reply I received was that his way of doing business would soon bring about his own ruin. The same argument was repeated year after year, and I am wondering whether I shall hear it again when I return this time. Since I first uttered my warning, Riès has bought a very large house in Marseille, for which he paid several millions, has built houses in Aden on excellent sites, has entered the salt business, in which he is a very serious nuisance, and now he has snatched from under our very nose a connection full of promise with the Raffineries de Sucre St Louis. . . . As for Riès' finances, I have it from Danbhoora that his situation to-day is perfectly sound. . . . If my reports are read with the care they deserve a certain percentage of the firm's

profits will be devoted every year to the elimination of dangerous
competitors. Obviously, the earlier we start cutting the ground
under a potentially dangerous competitor the less it will cost us. . . .
When I arrive in Aden in a fortnight's time shall I be told once again
that Riès' business is badly managed? Are we going to allow him a
free field for the purchase of skins? and to continue to trade in Salt
and Sugar? I am afraid the argument that has been employed up to
now will convince me less than ever, and, for my part, I am
determined once and for all to crush him . . .

In this particular instance AB's bark was worse than his bite: the
firm of Riès continued to flourish. But as against these frustrations it
was in the late 1950s that AB brought off his last and one of his biggest
and most successful gambles. In the scare throughout the Far East at
the turn the Korean War was taking, Formosan sugar refiners were
prepared to accept almost any price in order to have funds abroad.
Ship owners were reluctant to allow their ships to call at Formosan
ports. Insurance companies refused to quote. AB stepped in, purchased and brought away a whole shipload of Formosan sugar.

29   The Final Chapter

I

We have a paper, written shortly before AB's return to Aden in the autumn of 1950, which should be quoted in full:

> I have been wondering what it is that prevents people from behaving like good business men and drawing up as exact and objective a balance sheet of themselves as possible, of what is left to them of their physical and mental powers, and where their spiritual evolution has brought them. The task is a difficult one, usually humiliating, but all the more salutary for that. I have now made the attempt. My assessment is probably not an exact one, possibly quite inaccurate. Such mental dissections are difficult, and we do not see ourselves with the critical eyes of outsiders. But here is my inventory such as in all sincerity I conceive it.
>
> Physically I have passed the peak, and my only path is downhill. My heart is much weaker, I lose breath after mounting a few stairs, I have pains in the throat and chest. My legs are uncertain, and at every step I must take care not to fall. My faculties are failing: if I take up a book my eyes begin to close. Hearing and vision are impaired. I take no pleasure in my food, and if left to myself might well eat nothing. I must be brave and admit that I am an old man with not much longer to live. Mentally I have little power of concentration. Books with the slightest content of abstract thought are now beyond me. A page or two will put me to sleep, though this is the only form of nourishment that still attracts me. I have before me piles of books which I feel essential for filling up the gaps which my scrappy education had left – links in the chain all important to one whose ardent desire was to be a complete man – I must set out on my final stage without aspiring to go higher or further. Resignation is not easy for a man of action who has been a fighter all his life, greedy of knowledge, greedy of adding to what he has created. But now I have no choice but resignation.

My spiritual evolution moves slowly. Rationalism does not satisfy me: it leaves a gap. Spiritualists' explanations are repugnant to one whose mind looks to reason and logic and who believes there is nothing without its cause. I shall continue to be torn between contradictions without, ever, finding an answer to my problems; unless of course my mind deteriorates, and, like so many old men, I take refuge in a religion that will make me hope and believe in a life after death. I hope I may be spared this lapse.

One other factor calls for my attention. Since my gift to Oxford became known – for the creation of a College for the propagation of the ideas that are dear to me, – I have been the target of numerous appeals for funds. Most of them, on behalf of individuals, are such as are seldom likely to make me wish to help. Others are more or less connected with education, the one arm left to us against the rising ideology one can best describe as levelling down. Here I would like to help with all my knowledge, my experience, and my talent for organisation.[1] But my powers are dwindling, and after the huge contributions to Oxford, to Gordonstoun, Djibouti, Aden, Sheikh Othman etc. the funds may well, if not exhausted, be reduced to a level that will not allow me to start up new projects. Only after my return to Aden shall I be able to make a decision. It means much to very many people that my firm should survive and should prosper. And that means working capital commensurate with the vastness of the enterprise.

II

For most of his last winter in Aden AB was a sick man. Many believe that towards the end of his life his state of health was aggravated by his refusal, in spite of all that HB could do, to follow his doctors' advice on diet. He might well protest he took no pleasure in his food, but he was overweight and remained so. He did however listen to his doctors over a projected visit to Addis Abeba. He was told it was doubtful whether his heart could stand the altitude and it was suggested he should spend some days at Diredawa (less than half the height of the capital) and test his reactions there. The Emperor Haile Selassie heard of the proposal and placed the Imperial Lodge at Diredawa at his disposal. AB's feelings towards Maurice Weerts had somewhat mellowed, and Weerts came down from Addis Abeba to see him. He found him in poor shape. He was fussed by the meticulous attention of the imperial guards who followed him closely in his little walks in the garden. 'On ne peut même pas faire pipi'. It was here that he repeated, somewhat wistfully, what many years ago he had written to Fenn: 'I have put my business before my family, before my friends, before everything.' After a few days he returned, reluctantly, to Aden.

Here he was heavily involved in the affairs of the firm. As he was shortly to write to Tony: 'At this very instant when I have nobody here or elsewhere who can help me I am confronted by decisions of the highest importance.' Indeed the variety of problems, great and small, was considerable. There was trouble in the Sudan where a big deal in gums had recently gone wrong. (AB was thinking of posting Davis permanently to the Sudan.) There was labour unrest in Aden. *El Amin* had run aground on a sandbank off Assab. There was a dispute with the firm's main agents in Italy, and similar argument in Beirut. The Aden authorities were obstructing the recruitment of more clerical staff from India. The young air-conditioning business was having teething troubles. There was a project (later abandoned) of building a fourteen -storey skyscraper in Ma'alla; and a building programme in Addis Abeba. There were exchange control complications. There was the question of whether or not to adopt a new type of collapsible oil drum. There was a tentative scheme to supplant Gellatly Hankey in Saudi Arabia; and negotiations with Amalgamated Code Compilers Ltd. regarding a new private code.

In mid-January 1951 HB wrote to the Warden of St Antony's: 'Anton keeps fairly well but his morale is at a hopelessly low ebb.' There had been a tiresome development with the Oxford University Appointments Board. In late 1950 talk of the insecure tenure of jobs with Besse reached the ears of Sir Percival Waterfield of the Treasury. Sir Percival, whose son was working for the firm in Addis Abeba, discussed the matter with the secretary of the OUAB; and the latter, in due course, wrote out to AB in Aden expressing misgivings at the very high rate of turnover. Sir Percival's name was mentioned. AB took the matter up with Martin Waterfield in Addis Abeba, Martin informed his father, and on 3 January 1951 Sir Percival wrote to AB to explain what had happened. AB's reply to this letter is dated 26 January:

> What you and Mr Escritt may have said or written in connection with my firm's treatment of its staff is no concern of mine. It has been my habit all my life to speak and to act as my Reason and my Conscience dictated, regardless of any man's opinion, and I am now too old to change my conception of life. It is true that there has been

a considerable amount of wastage amongst young recruits that I have taken into my firm. The reason is not far to seek. We demand a very much higher standard than the average business firm.... For all too long it has seemed to me that the order of the day in England has been 'Conformity', the training for which begins at School. I know personally of cases where boys who did not conform were bullied mercilessly by their fellows and even thrashed by the masters. Where boys of other nationalities were the victims this treatment sowed a lifelong hatred of England in their hearts which nothing could subsequently eradicate. Where British youth is concerned the craze for conformity to a pattern and the failure to exhort boys to set themselves and strive towards a higher ideal, both individually and collectively, has resulted in a standard of mediocrity which is painful to behold in a country I have always loved and admired.... The present levelling down of humanity and the widely adopted principle of 'Safety First' represent the very antithesis of my ideal and I hope that I made this sufficiently clear when I asked Oxford University to accept the College I wished to found for the purpose of inspiring young men of all nations with a higher conception of life and work than is abroad to-day. So strongly do I feel the need for Strength, Individuality and Leadership in our youth that I would like to distribute to every University student in my own country and yours a copy of Nietzsche's *Thus spake Zarathustra* ...

AB sent off copies of the correspondence to the Warden of St Antony's whom he had come to regard as his natural champion in Oxford. He was moreover impatiently awaiting the day when the College would be supplying the firm with a flow of recruits of the quality on which he had set his heart. Deakin replied sympathetically; suggested deferring talks with the Appointments Board till AB's next visit; and promised to do what he could about recruits for the firm, though warning AB that this might take some time.

In a subsequent letter to the Warden AB wrote:

The first stages of our forward march are now over, the others, possibly more difficult, may require different qualities than those you have shown so successfully in the creation of the college. But I feel confident that you possess them and that from now onwards our progress will be still more rapid and encouraging.... I long to see you in full possession of our funds and taking all decisions without having to waste your time in discussions with others.[2] You have certainly a clear vision of what we intend to do and you have my trust if that has any value for you.

III

It was now, in the last year of his life, that AB was accorded official recognition of his achievement. Late in 1950 the Governor of Aden called to sound him confidentially on the proposal to confer on him the distinction of Knight Commander of the British Empire. The award appeared in the 1951 New Year Honours, in the Colonial Office List, 'for public services in Aden'. On 4 January 1951 AB wrote to the acting Chief Secretary to the Government of Aden:

> I am deeply sensible of the honour done to me by His Majesty unworthy though I feel myself to be of such a distinction.
>
> I only hope that what I have been able to do for Aden will continue to bear fruit and remain a lasting memorial of my gratitude and affection for the place and the people amongst whom I have lived and worked for so long.
>
> Please convey my grateful thanks to His Excellency for his most kind and cordial message.[3]

An honour that was perhaps to afford him even greater satisfaction was notified in a letter from Oxford he received the following month: it was proposed to confer on him the degree of Doctor of Civil Law. His reply of 21 February to the University Registrar is also characteristic: ''*Non sum dignus*'. My life, though a full and active one indeed, has achieved nothing of an outstanding character beyond a marked success in business, which is within the reach of anybody possessing the necessary qualities, and these are the attributes of many men.'

IV

Staff troubles persisted. Resignations in February 1951 included those of the managers of two of the African branches, one of whom wrote:

> After mature consideration I have come to the very firm conclusion that I do not like the manners and methods used in this organisation

with regard to personnel policy. In view of the treatment of . . . (he lists four cases) I have decided that no amount of capability or meaning well is a guarantee of consistent and just treatment.

About the same time there was a letter from Davis on the subject which has not survived; but we have AB's reply dated 28 February:

> . . . Your advice in connection with the recruiting and training of our staff . . . cannot be understood by me except as a criticism of what we do and what we have done all our life. If I am to judge the pudding from the eating you will excuse me if I state that you have no cause to complain about my treatment of the staff . . .

But AB's relationship with the most faithful and dedicated of all his collaborators was now reaching a point of no return. For over thirty years Davis had worked through the heat of the Aden summer while AB was in Europe; and had spent the rest of his life rushing off, at short notice, to whatever parts of the globe the expanding business and its dynamic proprietor might demand. Now, in his late fifties, he was about to marry: and he and his fiancée agreed that the former pattern of life could not continue. He was not prepared to fall in with AB's plans to send him for an indefinite period to the Sudan. In early March he wrote to AB to put the point bluntly:

> . . . I have tried unceasingly for some time past now to make it clear to you that I cannot undertake to put in any long periods out East. . . . Much as I dislike to write to you that there is the distinct possibility of a break between us, I feel it only right that I should do so.

We do not know if AB ever answered this. In any case his letters to Davis lapsed. What he felt comes out in a letter of his to Tony, dated mid-May when back in Le Paradou:

> It is a well known fact by mariners that when a ship springs a leak and is in danger of foundering, the first to leave the ship are the rats. I did not know there were so many rats in my firm and the present crisis has brought home this unpleasant fact. To begin with GED, the staunchest of my associates who has been dealt with by me as if he were a brother, nothing ever having been refused to him, who, I am convinced, has become a MAN through my exertions, my tuition

and my advice. . . . That he wishes to leave the firm is after all human
if ungrateful and on this point I have no comment to make, but to
insinuate that I was the culprit is unworthy of him and a sad end to
those long years of collaboration in which our firm was built . . .
[After touching on other members of the staff AB continues] I shall
not mention here the crowd of these young men from Oxford who
believe that the perfect crease of their trousers and their affected
pronunciation entitle them to a high position, whereas they are
scarcely able to understand the slightest intricacy of our business. In
any case, though the leaks in our ship are many, she is not founder-
ing, but the signs which are not wanting show it is high time a strong
hand takes the rudder and puts her in the right channel. I wish you to
visualise, the same as I do, that in Aden where the most important
part of our business is transacted, we have, so to speak, nobody big
enough to supervise the minute details by which any transaction is
surrounded and that we have nobody either in London except
nincompoops who have never done anything to promote our interest, to plan for the future or to construct. . . . I had to state these facts,
my dear Tony, in order that you should realise the frame of mind
which is mine . . .

V

At the beginning of April 1951, on the eve of AB's last departure from
Aden, he called in Patel, his chief accountant, to give instructions for
gratuities to be paid to the families of two old servants of the firm, one
Indian and one Arab. As he said goodbye he added: 'When I come
back to Aden, if I do come back, I will take no active part in the
business. I will just keep an eye on how the boys get on.'

Back at Le Paradou there was much planning of the forthcoming
visit to Oxford where AB was to receive his degree of Doctor of Civil
Law. Normally such degrees are conferred at the Encaenia at the end
of the summer term. But it was felt that this long ceremony would be
too great a strain on AB's health. Accordingly it was arranged that in
his case the degree should be presented at the meeting of Convocation
eight days previously. The Warden of St Antony's explained what
would take place in a letter to HB dated 24 April:

The ceremony is at 2 p.m. Mr Besse would go to the Delegates' room
in the Clarendon Buildings at approximately 1.50, where he would

find the Vice-Chancellor and where he would put on his Doctor's robes. He would then walk in procession about 100 yards to the Convocation Building. The actual ceremony there would not last more than about five minutes. The Public Orator presents Mr Besse to the Vice-Chancellor in Convocation in a short Latin speech. After this presentation is over Mr Besse would be seated for a further 5 minutes during which certain formal University business is transacted. When this is done I will myself accompany Mr Besse out of the building and back to the Delegates' room where he will remove his robes. Mr Besse's part in this brief but impressive ceremony is entirely passive and he does not have to utter a word.

VI

In early June AB and his party arrived at the St Ermin's Hotel in London [4]. On the 11th they moved to Oxford to stay with the Warden of St Antony's in readiness for the meeting of Convocation the following day. Unknown to her husband, HB had arranged that his three sons and four daughters, scattered over three continents, should assemble in Oxford for the ceremony. Though never demonstrative about his children AB was greatly touched. 'I am an old man,' he said to his hostess with real emotion in his voice, 'and I am deeply grateful for having all my family around me to-day. I never thought we should be all together in one place.'

The ceremony passed off smoothly, and the younger generation (who had been found accommodation in the town) went off on their various ways. AB stayed on for the Encaenia the following week. No. 70 Woodstock Road, recently acquired by the College as Warden's Lodgings, was neither spacious nor convenient; and the prolonged impact of AB, HB, Miss Ogilvie, a French chef and a Lebanese chauffeur meant a certain strain on its resources. Luckily the weather was fine and warm, and AB spent much of his time in a chair in the garden reading *The Times*; not the City pages, he was careful to explain, but the leading articles and the foreign news – his business being based on international politics. Lady Deakin notes:

His mind was not impaired, but his movements were. All his life he had been proud of his prowess as an athlete; now he would resent any attempt to give him a hand to raise him from a deep settee. I found it wiser to go out of the room and leave it to HB or Miss Ogilvie to help him.

On the day of the Encaenia AB attended the morning ceremony. When, however, the distinguished company were assembled outside New College hall for the formal luncheon he abruptly decided he had had enough. HB appealed to the Warden of Wadham to persuade him to stay on. Sir Maurice Bowra felt he should be allowed to do as he wished. AB meanwhile in his doctor's robes had started to walk away. HB in desperation turned to Lord Simon, who followed AB down New College Lane and eventually found him a taxi.

Ten minutes later the Deakins, at lunch in their Lodgings at 70 Woodstock Road, were bewildered at AB's sudden appearance, still in his doctor's robes. AB himself was completely unperturbed and gave his hostess a lesson on how to prepare salad dressing.

VII

After the Encaenia AB returned to London. His birthday was on 26 June. Lady Deakin writes:

> The last time I saw him was on his birthday. Bill and I went specially to London to go with him to see the Spanish dancers, and we were supposed to dine together afterwards. He enjoyed the theatre enormously – he was convinced he had Spanish or Catalan blood in him. But on coming out he had a malaise and the dinner arrangement had to be dropped. He believed the smoked salmon and glass of champagne we had had before the theatre had upset his stomach

But the following evening, his last in London, he was well enough to dine with the Godbers in St John's Wood. There was telephoning that morning between Shell and St Ermin's Hotel about sending a car for him, but something went wrong. After waiting half-an-hour for AB to turn up in his own car, Lord Godber phoned St Ermin's to find him impatiently expecting a car from Shell. A car was sent off at once and in due course AB arrived, somewhat ruffled. He maintained his displeasure throughout dinner, but then, as he was apt to do when he felt he had gone far enough, he offered to supervise the making of the coffee.

Next morning, Thursday 28 June, AB and HB set out by road for Gordonstoun, spending one night on the way. It was planned, after the Gordonstoun visit, to embark at Aberdeen for a tour of the Norwegian fjords as guests of Wilhelm Wilhelmsen of the shipping line. AB felt unwell on the Thursday evening, but the restful Friday night at Gordonstoun seemed to restore him. On the Saturday he was able to watch the exercises of the school's Life Saving Company along the shore, and was most impressed. 'This,' he told Kurt Hahn, 'calls for all the qualities so necessary in war; but it is to save life, not destroy it.' All day this happy mood persisted. After dinner he asked his host to come for a walk; and as they walked, very slowly, through the mellow Scottish evening he talked about England. He acknowledged his debt to the independence and integrity of young Englishmen who had helped him build up his business.

But these pioneer virtues are growing feeble, though the Commonwealth will need them more than the Empire ever did. . . . People keep saying I gave all that money for education because I am happy about England. I gave it because I am not happy. England is the pillar of the world. It is crumbling. It must not crumble . . .

That evening, the night of 30 June/1 July he became very ill. He was moved to the school sanatorium and a specialist was summoned from Aberdeen: but AB never fully recovered consciousness and on the afternoon of 2 July he died. The doctor noted.

He had pneumonia at the bases of both lungs. . . . I found evidence of paresis on the left side of the face and in the right leg . . . evidence of thrombosis on the left side of the brain. There was no doubt about the palatal paralysis . . . due, I thought to a recent small cerebral thrombosis. . . . The fatal factor was the palatal paralysis.

When the news reached Aden shops and offices were closed in sign of mourning; memorial services were spontaneously arranged in the Catholic and Protestant churches, and in the principal mosque. In Gordonstoun the memorial service was held in the Michael Kirk, with the school Colour Bearers present and an address by the Headmaster Kurt Hahn. Meanwhile HB had telegraphed to the members of the family now dispersed; Tony arrived by air to be with his mother while arrangements were made for a charter plane to convey the coffin to Provence. A guard paraded at Kinloss Naval Air Station to offer military honours when, in the presence of the Lord Lieutenant of Morayshire, the Last Post was sounded as the coffin was carried on board. The plane came down at Croydon to refuel; and here HB and Tony were joined by Peter who had rushed from London airport where he had landed from New York little more than an hour before.

The other members of the family were waiting at Le Paradou; it was barely four weeks since, united for the first time for many years, they had seen their father receive his honour from the University of Oxford. In their presence he was laid to rest in the spot he had long since chosen as his burial place, in a fold of the wooded hills above Le Paradou. Among AB's papers was found a copy of the *Illustrated London News* for 23 June 1951. On a margin he had written, in his tiny handwriting, a verse from Alfred de Musset:

Le livre de la vie est le livre suprême
Que l'on ne peut ouvrir ni fermer à son choix
On voudrait le garder à la page où l'on aime
Et la page où l'on meurt est déjà sous nos doigts.

Appendix A : AB's Reading

AB was a voracious reader. Right up to the end he would retire to his desk with a book and sit there for hours – marking, doodling, copying, making notes. He read with the deliberate aim of filling the gaps in his education; but what really mattered was the aesthetic and, above all, the emotional satisfaction that reading gave him. He took pains to keep up with the times, and became familiar with a whole range of modern authors. But he would come back, again and again, to the books which he had read as a young man and out of which he had forged his ardent philosophy of life.

One of his commonplace books has been preserved, a cheap quarto notebook of the type used by schoolboys and small shopkeepers at the time of World War I. What is tantalising is there are no dates. There is only the handwriting. AB's own spidery and microscopic script, so familiar to all and so alarming to most of his correspondents, did not get set till the mid-twenties. The first entries in the commonplace book are in meticulous copperplate as taught in the schools, the later ones in the handwriting we find in AB's later letters to his brother-in-law Joseph Selignac. It seems likely that the book was started during AB's service in the army, when his friend Bernard began to guide and encourage his reading; and was continued intermittently till after World War I.

The first entry is a long one copied from M. Guyau's *L'Irreligion de l'Avenir*, concerned with female emancipation as one of the benefits hoped to accrue from the decay of religious belief. But more than half the book is taken up with Pascal, La Rochefoucauld and La Bruyère, all entered in the early copperplate. Then we have the younger Dumas (the foreword to *Ami des Femmes* has a note by AB 'This is very well written but I feel the ideas are wrong'). Further there are Maeterlinck, *The Thousand and One Nights* (in Mardrus' translation), Charles Kingsley, Albert Schweitzer, de Pourtal/2es (*Vie de Liszt*), Richard Burton, Sully-Prudhomme, de Musset, Verlaine. Towards the end of the book are a number of love poems, some of them copied in feminine handwriting. One poem is written out, in alternate lines, by AB and his lady partner. Who she was seems impossible to find out for certain. She may have been Madame Jules Siegfried.

There is another notebook, dated Brussels 1920. This contains extracts from, or references to, Rabindranath Tagore, Wu Wei (the Taoist philosopher), Fitzgerald's Omar Khayyám, Arnold Bennett, Edward Carpenter, Popper, Spinoza, Goethe, Seneca, Plato, A. Gide, Emerson, Georges Duhamel, Tolstoi, Claude Bernard, Lord Acton, Balzac and Corneille. This little notebook obviously dates from the time when AB was searching for a motto. One page is headed by the one he finally chose – *Plus est en vous* from the Von der Aa family memorial in the Grathaus in Bruges. Underneath are some of the alternatives that he considered: *All ich Kann* (van Eyck); *Mieux je serai* (Beaumont); *Mieux qui pourra* (E. Lemaitre of Laon); *Nec prece nec pretio* (P. Hachette, 1647).

AB would mark with a five-pointed star passages that especially appealed to him. Among them are 'The evil that we do brings us less persecution and hatred than do our good qualities' (La Rochefoucauld); 'Man must firmly believe that the incomprehensible will become comprehensible' (Goethe); 'Only a gifted man can keep a secret, only the best of men can keep a promise' (*The Thousand and One Nights*); 'A beautiful woman with the qualities of an honourable man is the best of what we can find in the world' (La Bruyère. AB once remarked that this applied to HB); 'To be with those one loves is enough – dream, talk to them, not talk at all, think of them, think of trifles – as long as one is with them it does not matter' (La Bruyère); 'Do not take too much trouble to be all that good: excess of effort here will bar your way to true wisdom' (Wu Wei); 'When one has set oneself an aim in life it is bitter to find it impossible . . . once it is impossible to follow one's aim then life has nothing left' (Balzac). Some of AB's marginal comments are characteristic. On one of La Bruyère's aphorisms he noted, and emphasised with his star: 'A woman really in love will *never* accept a valuable gift from the man she loves; a man who respects the woman he loves will never offer her one.'

One regrets that AB did not continue with his commonplace books; in later years he copied and doodled on odd bits of paper. In all this, as in so much else, HB was his close partner. One quotation among many in her handwriting is 'The true disaster in a troubled world is not the malice and folly of the wicked but the weakness of the good' (quoted by Prince Max of Baden). An amusing incident arose from a piece by Lord Carnock beginning: 'That rectitude need not necessarily be disagreeable or industry arrogant; that patience and modesty are not incompatible with a radiant rapidity of mind . . .'. This AB sent to a friend, who dabbled in calligraphy, for an illuminated copy to be mounted and framed. It came back headed by the monogram 'AB'. He was highly annoyed: he had intended it as a reminder for HB.

II

Some of AB's favourite authors do not figure in the notebooks – notably Anatole France for whom his admiration was profound and lasting. Again there is nothing from Nietzsche in the early notebooks, and the one slip found among his papers was evidently copied out in later life: '. . . For the creators are hard. And blessedness must it seem to you to press your hand upon millenniums as upon brass – harder than brass, nobler than brass. Entirely hard is only the noblest. This new table, O my brethren, put I over you – BECOME HARD.' All the same it is reasonably certain that AB's cult of Nietzsche began in early manhood. It was not, as with so many of his contemporaries, a phase that he was to grow out of. The Nietzschean concept of 'creation' inspired his dedication to his firm. The appeal of the injunction 'Live dangerously' comes out in all sorts of ways, in the risks he took in his business, in his rock climbing, his manner of driving a car, his swims.[1] And, it has been suggested, the precept 'Be hard' came to serve as justification for some of AB's less likeable qualities – the vindictiveness when his vanity was wounded, the disregard of the feelings of others, what one of his own sons has described as 'the frightening lack of human kindness', so oddly at variance with a persistent inner desire to be loved.

III

Once he had found and adopted his motto *'Plus est en vous'* it seems, from the evidence of the notebook, that he was looking for a short poem to go with it. He was impressed by some lines from Richard Burton's *Kasida*, copied out and then recopied after an interval of years.

> Do what thy manhood bids thee do,
> From none but self expect applause
> He noblest lives and noblest dies
> Who makes and keeps his self-made laws .

But later he came across Kipling's *If*, and this seemed to epitomise his whole philosophy of life. He decided to translate it into French – a task that took up hours and hours of dedicated effort over a long period of years. Repeated revision resulted in a final version of forty-one lines. Meryem one year took a copy to Paris and had it recopied, illuminated and mounted by a Left Bank craftsman as a birthday present to her father. For the rest of his life it stood framed on his desk.

If

If you can keep your head when all about you
    Are losing theirs and blaming it on you;
If you can trust yourself when all men doubt you,
    But make allowance for their doubting too;
If you can wait and not be tired by waiting,
    Or being lied about don't deal in lies,
Or being hated don't give way to hating,
    And yet don't look too good, nor talk too wise:

If you can dream and not make dreams your master;
    If you can think – and not make thoughts your aim;
If you can meet with Triumph and Disaster
    And treat those two imposters just the same;
If you can bear to hear the truth you've spoken
    Twisted by knaves to bait a trap for fools,
Or watch the things you gave your life to, broken,
    And stoop and build 'em up with worn-out tools:

If you can make one heap of all your winnings
    And risk it on one turn of Pitch-and-toss,
And lose, and start again at your beginnings
    And never breathe a word about your loss;
If you can force your heart and nerve and sinew
    To serve your turn long after they are gone,
And so hold on when there is nothing in you
    Except the Will which says to them: 'Hold on'.

If you can talk with crowds and keep your virtue,
    Or walk with Kings – nor lose the common touch;
If neither foes nor loving friends can hurt you;
    If all men count with you, but none too much;
If you can fill the unforgiving minute
    With sixty seconds' worth of distance run,
Yours is the Earth and everything that's in it,
    And (which is more) you'll be a Man my son!

If

Si tu peux, impassible, rester maître de toi,
Quand tous perdent la tête et, dans leur désarroi
T'accusent; de leur doute, en leur âme en détresse,
Comprendre et pardonner le soupçon qui oppresse;
Si tu peux, inlassable, attendre sans faiblir
Être en butte au mensonge et ne jamais mentir,
Poursuivi par la haine, mais ne jamais haïr;
De paraître trop bon, ni te poser en sage,
Bâtir en Utopie sans trop croire au mirage,
Garder toujours en ta pensée profonde
L'impérieux besoin d'une tâche féconde;
Si tu peux mépriser en leur valeur surfaite,
Imposteurs tous les deux, Triomphe ou Défaite;
Si tu peux sans colère ouïr des scélérats
Tendre pièges au sots, en prenant comme appâts
Ta belle vérité dans ce but travestie;
Voir l'idéal auquel tu consacras ta vie
Crouler anéanti, et sans perdre courage,
Ta main peut empoigner des outils hors d'usage
Et ton dos se courber pour rebâtir encore;
Si tu peux, en un tas, réunir tout ton or,
Risquer le tout sur un seul coup de pile ou face,
Perdre, puis repartir, sans rien sinon l'audace,
Sans jamais proférer un mot sur ce malheur;
Si tu peux obliger nerfs, muscles, ton coeur
A te servir longtemps après qu'ils sont perdus,
Stoïque résister ainsi, jamais rendu
Quand plus rien n'est en toi, en suprême abandon
Sinon ta volonté, hurlant toujours 'Tiens bon';
Si, parlant à la foule, gardant ta dignité,
Tu peux causant aux Rois être en simplicité;
D'amis et d'ennemis dédaignant la blessure,
Estimant chacun d'eux mais selon sa mesure,
Tu peux, tel un champion, par un dernier effort
Pour gagner la victoire, en un suprême essort
Remplir à déborder, éperdu inlassable
Chaque seconde en la minute inexorable,
Regarde autour de toi, tout alors t'appartient,
La terre généreuse et ce qu'elle contient,
Suis donc ta voie, de quelque titre l'on te nomme,
Sois fier, mon fils, car mieux encore tu es un Homme.

Appendix B : AB's Business

AB suffered a stroke in the summer of 1948, as a result of which he feared that he might no longer be able to keep up his personal control over his huge business. Accordingly he compiled a sixty-eight page review of the firm's activities as a guide to his successors. What follows are long extracts (in AB's original wording) from this document, covering exports, branches and agencies, overseas markets and source of supply, imports and the main departments of the Aden head office.

SECTION 1 – EXPORT COMMODITIES

Hides

For many years, our firm has been the chief exporting organisation of hides and skins from Ethiopia, and if we have now lost our supremacy, the fault lies with X. It should be our firm and lasting policy to bring fresh life into the branches and see to it that through our agents our total amount of purchases is maintained at such a level that our firm secures, at the very least, fifty per cent of the whole hide production of Ethiopia. Prices may be high or they may be low, but whatever their level our purchases should never stop. We must always keep in close contact with the market. It is necessary to pay a premium for those lots containing a large percentage of mediums and lightweights. My instructions were disregarded and these lots naturally went to the competition. When buying hides, you must not weigh until you are certain they are absolutely dry. The test is very simple. If, when you try to open the hide – it remains open, you can be sure it is not completely dry. If the hide springs back into the folded position, then it is dry and may be safely weighed. There was a time in Addis Abeba when the sellers were in the habit of sprinkling water on the hides, or even soaking them in liquid mud. This practice may still be extant and should be watched. I hope Mr Davis will let me have the information for which I asked him as I am convinced that I shall find that

214

arch-scoundrel Y at the bottom of the trouble. The policy regarding ordinary Ethiopian hides applies equally to the butcheries, but instead of buying through native or Arab dealers we should operate direct with the butchers themselves.

Skins

Goatskins

It seems to me that were we satisfied with a small profit we should control the quasi-totality of that trade. When dealing with skins it is always possible to discover defects and therefore the door is open for disputes and claims for allowances, which are heavy when dealing with American tanners. I therefore repeat here that wherever we have branches our agents should be instructed to operate steadily regardless of cost once we can assure ourselves the quality is of the best obtainable. As regards Addis Abeba itself, I feel that we should see to it that our head sorter there is sufficiently backed by the Manager to avoid intimidation by Y. We know from experience that seventy-five per cent of the goatskins X shipped were obtained through the instrumentality of Y's son, and we also knew to our cost the loss our friends in the States have incurred through the bad quality of these deliveries. Next to the skins from Ethiopia come the Berberahs which originate chiefly from British Somaliland. In this country also we have proved conclusively that whenever we decided to stop operating completely (the price having risen too high) we have made a fatal error.

Our agent at Hodeidah has always secured the very best. In short, the policy of the firm should be continuous, indefatigable purchasing of nothing but the best whilst making frequent offers in order to ascertain whether or not we are acting wisely.

Sheepskins

Our Blackheads are so popular in the USA that our only policy can be to instruct our agents in Somaliland to continue to buy the best in their various branches. If our agent of the Benadir Coast could pick up the best in his territory, I am certain that part of these could be mixed with our Blackheads. In spite of the fact that I am advocating continuous purchasing of the best, we should not leave the bad quality skins to our competitors, since experience has shown that however poor the skins they will find buyers at Yeovil.

Leopard skins

Not so many years ago we had a quasi-monopoly in Leopard skins. I remember a time when our purchases averaged a thousand pieces a month. Thanks to the stupidity of a high official of the Benadir Coast regulations were enforced which prevented the purchasing, but not the killing. These skins thus obtained crossed the southern frontier and went to Mombasa. The leopard skins from this part of the country are of such a high quality as to command a premium over the Ethiopian skins which are considered to be very inferior.

Gazelle skins

These skins were shipped annually by the firm to the extent of about two and a half million, until such time as an Italian official prevented the transport of the skins to the Coast, with the idea, I believe, of protecting the herds. But Nature had her revenge, for when we were authorised to resume our purchases there were no gazelles to be found! They were probably killed off by inherent disease made more virulent by over-prolific breeding. The moment herds increase, and a large quantity can be exported, it will be up to our London Office to contact outlets in Germany where we used to have clients who worked at a rate of half a million skins a month.

Antelope skins

There is a ready market in France and the USA for Antelope skins and provided Feinberg keeps us acquainted with the rate at which they can be sold, our Mogadiscio agent should be instructed to buy. There are two kinds of Antelope skins – one in much greater demand than the other.

Cheetah skins

A parcel of these skins was recently consigned to the States but I am not aware of the price it fetched.

Others

I mention here merely as a memo that snakes and lizards can be secured from the Benadir Coast and I think that otters can be had in Ethiopia.

Coffee

At the time of writing, I am not aware whether difficulties, such as the handing over of our dollars to the Imamite Government, are imposed upon us. I am not aware, likewise, whether A is continuing his nefarious activities in coffee, but I am certain that abnormal conditions cannot last and in the near future the situation should become normal. Arrangements must then be made, either directly or through the instrumentality of our Hodeidah agent to secure the bulk of the Matari, Sharkieh and Aboree crops. In a word we must have a monopoly of all the highest class districts. In Ethiopia the coffee from the province of Harrar is gradually gaining a reputation which makes it possible for us to demand a higher price than that generally obtained for the best Yemeni types. Indeed, some of the coffee grown in this area can be mixed with the beans from the Yemen without anyone being able to detect the admixture. The coffee coming from Lakempti and from Aroussis, sold under the name of Djimma, is nearly as good as the Harrari, while Sidamo provides nothing but an inferior quality. This means that we must have an expert in Addis Abeba for undoubtedly, as years go by, the importance of the crops from these districts will increase.

Incense

Though the following is past history, it is well that I should recount it here for the sake of those who have not followed the trade from the beginning. Originally, incense was produced on what is known as the Aromatic Coast, i.e. the Maharra country. This stretches from the Hadramaut Coast, beginning at Cochin, onwards up to Muscat. From there the trees producing the gum were exported to Somaliland, where they found a soil as good. Until our firm sent agents to Kishin the incense was shipped to Bombay at the time of the favourable monsoon, where it was graded and sorted by Indian merchants. They then offered it in competition to us, nearly always defeating us since we could not reduce our price to their level. But we persevered in spite of the loss we incurred at the beginning and gradually built up a reliable clientèle. In order to keep these customers it is imperative that our cleaning and grading should always be perfect. The natives of Somaliland mix all sorts of rubbish with their incense such as small stones, earth and inferior incense which is black. They always take care, however, that the top of the bag is clean and consists of nothing but pure incense. It is therefore our custom to bring all we purchase into our own warehouse and open it up, bag after bag, then, after reconsidering the rate at which the sale has been concluded, beat it down to a reasonable level. This process can take days, but by patient efforts the right quality of incense can be obtained.

Myrrh

This is another gum which comes mainly from British and ex-Italian Somaliland. Its quality varies greatly and however tempting the price one should refrain from buying unless the product is really fresh, has the strong smell peculiar to it and, when broken, exudes a kind of sticky liquid.

Beeswax

Beeswax can be obtained from the Yemen and from the Sudan, but chiefly from Ethiopia. The chief method of adulteration in Ethiopia is to mix with the wax earth, insect bodies, banana pulp, etc., and this wax must be refined. The refining process is a very simple one and we have a big installation at Addis Abeba. It consists of a huge cauldron one-third filled with water in which the wax is placed. The water is then heated until the wax melts – rising to the surface since it is lighter than water, while the impurities sink to the bottom.

Gums

Kordofan gums

I am too much of a layman to express an opinion on the subject of the different qualities of Kordofan, but the fact remains, that we should always, whatever the circumstances, keep in close contact with the market. I believe that by judicious purchasing we should be in as good a position as our competitors who have been established in the Sudan for generations. The only means of reaching our goal is by steady purchases from the Sudan and continuous investigations by our London Office of all the outlets. Kordofan, like Beeswax, is constantly required by certain firms and it is with these firms that we should try to become connected. I have noted with pleasure that we have succeeded in contacting new markets in India and this should be carefully followed up.

Opoponax

Another gum closely allied to Myrrh. Opoponax has a scent which is pungent almost to the point of being unpleasant. A valuable essence is extracted from this gum which is used in the manufacture of perfumes.

Gum Arabic

The Gum Arabic which comes from the Benadir Coast and Somaliland is generally of a reddish colour and never fetches a high price for it cannot be utilised, as can the gum from the Sudan, in the production of sweets and confectionery.

Methi

There is yet another kind of gum which comes from Somaliland and is consumed solely in Egypt, where it is used in lieu of chewing gum. Provided one buys at the very beginning of the season and the Methi reaches Egypt before the competition has had an opportunity of securing supplies considerable profits are obtainable.

Sundries

Ambergris

This product is a disease of the Sperm whale and is an article about which so little is known. It should always be consigned to Hasslauer in

Paris, care being taken when purchasing to avoid those lots which are black in colour and in which the smell is almost non-existent.

Civet

I feel it my duty to state once more that as long as the civet is adulterated (and it is always adulterated in Ethiopia), perfumers cannot extract from the product we ship them the Civetone they use as a fixative for all expensive perfumes. It pays them better to buy synthesized Civetone, a product more costly but more reliable than impure civet. Considering that the perfumers are prepared to pay practically any price for clean, unadulterated civet, any other man but Z would have succeeded in convincing the producers that it would pay them better to avoid admixtures when collecting the civet from their cats.

Trocas, Mother of Pearl:

Meru, a town in the Seine et Oise is the greatest centre in the world for the manufacture of buttons. Trocas can be bought in Massawa and Port Sudan, but unfortunately for us, A in the former place has proved to be unreliable and the Port Sudan product is very uncertain. This should be modified for we shall need Trocas as cargo for our ships whenever they proceed to Genoa. As a rule, the freight rate exacted is extremely high and companies avoid shipping it on account of the bulk and the unpleasant smell. It is therefore valuable to us since, as we use our own ships, we have no such qualms.

Dom-nuts

The same applies to this product, purchases of which should never be interrupted.

SECTION 2 – BRANCHES AND AGENCIES

Addis Abeba

If this branch of ours had been well managed and Aden's instructions followed to the letter it would today have been if not more important then at least as important as Aden itself. In Addis Abeba the activities of the firm could be developed in a multitude of ways. The branch could be organised in similar lines to Aden and different departments created with a capable man in charge of each. To mention but a few there are Cotton goods, Photographic and Pharmaceutical Materials, Automotive, and diverse other articles of import, such as Galvanised Iron Sheets, etc. With good specialists in the above lines and a competent secretary capable of assuming the responsibillity of the correspondence and filing, added to our present native staff, Addis Abeba, with the right leadership, should be capable of almost unlimited development. It would be a task which would fill every moment of the General Manager's time, especially if, as I hope, we are able to expand our trade in cereals and oil-seeds, the importation of sugar and other articles.

Dessie

This agency comes next in importance to Addis Abeba and is vital to the welfare of the firm. There was a time when Bati Goatskins were known to our competitors by name only. We had a virtual monopoly of them but thanks to X's disregard of the instructions given him to create an organisation of our own by appointing sub-agents in all the outlying villages where the skins were collected, our competitors began to take an interest in these skins, and made advances to the native dealers who soon built up the very organisation I had in mind for the firm. No alternative was left to us but to employ the native medium also, and today, after many years of work in the Bati district, we are still obliged to pass under the Caudine Forks of their exactions in order to obtain supplies which have become indispensable to our goatskins trade. Dessie is also an important centre for all kinds of cereals and there was a time when we could collect Horsebeans by the hundreds of tons, jowaree – also by the thousand – and lentils and haricot beans in large quantities. It may be noted that Dessie is a very important centre also for the distribution of Shell products and, last but not least, Salt. In a word, it is a branch which should extend constantly and its potentialities justify the presence of the very best men that can be detached from our staff. Life there is by no means unpleasant, the altitude and climate being very similar to that of Addis Abeba. The agent should have a strong, reliable car – a Jeep for instance – which would allow him to pay frequent visits to the outlying villages in which collections of skins are made by his sub-agent and, possibly, a certain quantity of imports sold.

Diredawa

This is a branch which has never been managed properly since the departure of Khamdar. It is a matter for regret as it could play an important role in our Ethiopian organisation. As representatives of the Shell; having a monopoly of salt; being in a better position than any one else to provide cotton goods, I cannot foresee any firm competing with us if we have an agent there of average business acumen. We could also operate in many sundries which would prove profitable.

Djibouti

Until Monsieur Siriex took charge, the maladministration of this colony led us in Aden to consider Djibouti as an agency of small importance, in spite of the fact that all the goods collected in Ethiopia pass in transit there and it has a small market for cotton goods and sundries, but now, having made up our minds to extend our activities to shipping, and supposing we obtain the agencies of the American Export Line and the other shipping lines we represent in Aden, Djibouti is likely to take a very important place amongst the branches of our firm. It is my intention to develop it to the utmost and to build there the house, the workshops and the offices we shall assuredly need. I deem it imperative that our agent there should be a Frenchman, as with the xenophobia peculiar to all Frenchman he would know how to meet the difficulties he is bound to encounter with French officials. Once arrangements at Djibouti have been completed it will be time to see whether we can create an organisation which could deliver Bills of Lading from Addis Abeba to ensure that the Bulk of the trade in Ethiopia passes through our hands.

Berbera

In view of our Blackhead trade it is imperative for us to have in this branch an agent who is reliable and who possesses knowledge, business acumen and above all, honesty. Berbera is one of those agencies whose accounts cannot be checked in a satisfactory manner as the bulk of the purchases concluded, if not all, are made against cash with no receipts ever being demanded. The agent should also take charge of the management of the sub-branches, Burao and Hergeisa, including leopards, as well as myrrh and opoponax.

Jigjiga

This is a place which undoubtedly produces the best and heaviest of the Blackheads as well as an interesting collection of hides, and it is also a prominent market for textiles. We have been consistently unlucky in our choice of agents.

Benadir Coast

Our branch at Mogadiscio has always been a great asset to the firm and today it is becoming even more essential. The shipment of goods accumulated in Mogadiscio should be effected by our vessels and our agent there informed in advance in order to have every thing in readiness and so that he may activate or delay his purchases of hides, skins, gums, tallow, cereals, oilseeds etc. accordingly. On the return voyage the ships should carry cars, tyres, radios, cotton goods, machinery etc., etc.

Hodeida

The political situation overshadows everything in the Yemen. The new Imam is cruel, vindictive, physically rotten to the core, does not believe in progress and will do his utmost to prevent any being attempted in his territory. The poverty in a land which could be transformed into a paradise is unbelievable. From the Yemen we receive, through our agent in Hodeida, coffee and skins. Both of these articles have already been dealt with in another part of this report. We import sugar, cotton goods, cigarettes and sundries. On this subject of importing, I would like those responsible for the management of the firm to satisfy themselves with a small profit only on these articles, which can be dealt with in very large quantities. We have no other method of retaining the bulk of the trade and creating freight our ships and dhows constantly need.

Jedda

We are very unfortunate in Jedda. We should continue our researches either in Jeddah or in the Hadramaut for a reliable and already experienced man to replace the ... now representing us.

Port Sudan

Though our firm has had a branch at Port Sudan for some time, I feel that we know little or nothing about the potentialities of that country. I therefore long for the day when we have a man sufficiently great to open up branches and agencies wherever they may be required in order to collect at first hand the gum, the hides, the skins, the dom-nuts, the mother-of-pearl, the trocas, the cereals and possibly, the cotton this huge country produces.

Hadramaut

Our agents there are very satisfactory and we do not intend to expand there as the amount of trade could not justify the opening of two branches.

Eritrea

This country is the poorest part of Ethiopia. Still it was a necessary link with our other Ethiopian branches and I feel sure that we could have taken a large share of the importing business transacted in Asmara. Unfortunately for us Q has proved to be a most despicable individual. ... The chief export, indeed almost the only one, from Asmara is the Eritrea kid-skins which I feel will remain in continuous demand, provided that they can be offered at a price which will allow American tanners to make a generous profit. Another town in Eritrea which means a great deal to us is Massawa. Time after time the representative of the Halal Shipping Co. has offered cargoes for the first ship intended for Genoa.

SECTION 3–MARKETS AND SOURCES OF SUPPLY

Japan and Germany

These two countries, now on their knees, are being raised again by America on the one side and Great Britain on the other. This is inevitable. I am convinced that whatever chains we may bind them with they will eventually break away and regain their former place in the economy of the world. I am so absolutely certain of this fact that I suggest that as soon as we can find the right type of man, we open a branch in each of these two countries. From Japan we can obtain an unlimited supply of textiles and undoubtedly in the near future, many other kinds of products. From Germany we can get all types of machinery and find there an outlet for our goat and sheep skins and for our hides.

Italy

As the Italians are not a self-righteous people their Government policy merely invites them to 'combinazione' in order to evade the many regulations. They are not to be blamed for this attitude as in all Latin countries the citizens are subjected to much heavy taxation and so many fiscal obligations that were anyone to comply with these restrictions, however strong his firm and his financial position, he would soon find himself in the bankruptcy courts, and the great law of life is that above all one must live – the weak are pushed to the wall. The English are privileged in this respect for their rulers (not to mention Sir Stafford Cripps) have discovered a formula to fleece every citizen – allowing him at the same time to live just above starvation level. A day will come however, when Englishmen will find they have to choose between cheating the Government or closing down their businesses. There will always be an unlimited market for our hides of very inferior quality, which can be worked at a profit in Italy. Italy will always be a country in which we can obtain the best price for our trocas, Mother of Pearl, and Dom-nuts. As regards imports, I should say that Italy today stands a good chance of taking an important place in the world of textiles, machinery and electrical equipment. When dealing with Italians, one should always bear in mind their mentality and every clause of every contract concluded with them should be adhered to rigidly, or one must be prepared for trouble.

France

The state of this country and gradual infiltration of communism makes it impossible for it ever to compete in world markets. This is a matter for regret, as the great producing centre is Alsace where, thanks to family connections, we are better placed than anybody else. It would be impossible indeed to find more honest men than our Marseille agents, Monsieur Meister and Monsieur Di Domenico. The former is in charge of the administrative side of the business and the latter is the technical expert. I can think of no one more qualified to deal with hides and skins than Di Domenico. But these two men, have an important drawback which cannot, alas be corrected. They take no interest whatsoever in anything outside their own particular sphere, i.e. hides and skins.

England

Where London office has failed, and failed us time and time again in the past, has been in the choice of the staff sent out to Aden. The collaborators sent us this last time have proved to be almost useless, and useless members of the Aden community are most objectionable. In the first place, they are not happy, and unhappiness spreads like a contagious disease. In the second, we cannot afford to waste our time on people with insufficient intelligence. I am not at all satisfied with our offices in London, and I shall be very glad to know whether the owners of the building are prepared to let us have the floors we need; the fact that there would be then plenty of space for all would make the working conditions very much more pleasant. Further improvement could be included: less smoking, a few attractive paintings to detract from the somewhat austere aspect of the office walls, and encyclopedias and books of reference made available to all members of the staff. For many years past I have been criticising the way the London Office has been handling imports of coffee, gums and other articles as indeed our share has been much below the importance our firm merits. As regards shipping there seems to have been an improvement since we dispensed with the services of the firm formerly working with us. The banking arrangements made of late have been quite satisfactory. I am convinced that had we had reliable brokers who could have canvassed the dealers and concerns and last but not least the great clubs using coffee on a large scale, we would have created a clientèle faithful to us.

India

Chaghanlal Kasterchand is as good as agent as we could find in India and we are privileged in having his services at our disposal, but I have been wondering from time to time, considering the magnitude of our transactions in textiles and other products with that country, whether it would be better to open a branch of our own there. It has always been one of my ambitions to control a mill which would work solely for us. Once two or three types of cloth had been chosen, I am sure that the amount of business which would be transacted would be large enough to keep the mill busy all the year round.

USA

It appears to me imperative that we have an agency of our own in New York to take charge of our total purchases and sales in the United States. I am afraid we shall never have on our staff a man with the necessary, but most rare, qualities to take charge of that colossal task and therefore some other means must be devised. Though the importance of the cotton goods trade seems to be receding, the potentialities of the USA are so immense that it may revive and flare up at any moment. We must be well prepared for this eventuality. Our business in cars, lorries, air-conditioning apparati, fluorescent lighting, radios, typewriters, etc., requires nothing but an administrative brain which a man of Heins' ability should have little or no difficulty in supplying. As regards the financial side of our New York branch, our Mr Davis should approach our bankers in that city and endeavour to obtain from them information as to the possibility of an overdraft in case of the need arising between the time of making a payment and the receipt of our transfers in dollars against our sale of skins, coffee, gums, beeswax etc., etc. I feel that our transactions in coffee should go through the branches as I deem it advisable to have everything of this nature transacted at source.

SECTION 4 – IMPORT GOODS

Salt

Not so long ago I seem to remember that our friends at the Banque de l'Indochine – undoubtedly prompted by that arch-scoundrel A – hinted that they were no longer receiving the accounts as regularly as before. As this agency is so valuable to us in many respects it is essential that all the work connected with salt is done perfectly. The news received about B's behaviour is most annoying and I feel that X's attitude towards that scoundrel is the cause of all the present trouble.

Cigarettes

To me, cigarettes, like alcohol, are taboo and I continue to wonder from whence came this dirty, nauseating habit of swallowing tobacco smoke and blowing it into the air, to add these nauseous fumes to an already poisoned breath. Here at the Paradou where the scent from every blade of grass is aromatic, where the fragrance of the flowers always surrounds you, where the earth itself is perfumed, to see men – and still more women – smoking and soiling the air which we breathe makes me ponder anew on the 'blessings' of civilisation. Still, it is not our job to reform mankind and, having accepted this important agency, we have no alternative but to do it full justice.

Automotive

This is a department to which the firm has never done justice, while with a reliable man at the head, a man possessing both technical knowledge and business acumen, it is capable of immense development. We hold the agencies of the Chrysler group, of Austin and now, if the promise that has been given me is confirmed, of Lancia. In its own way each of these groups is the best of its class. With such a range we should be in close contact with the native and European population, and we should have selling agents who could supply their needs, but unfortunately such brokers as we need are rare and the ones we have managed to find have proved to be unreliable. Our organisation should be provided with spare parts for all the cars and lorries we represent. They should always be at hand, ready for any breakdown. This entails a fully qualified man being constantly on the job.

Air-Conditioning

We were the first in the field and I believe could have remained so had our Mr Fletcher had more time at his command. The future of this apparatus is assured and a time will come when no European and no rich native will be satisfied until he has at least one room in his house equipped for air-conditioning – which will mean a peaceful night whatever the temperature outside.

Lighting

I have not followed as closely as I might have done Mr Fletcher's efforts to introduce into Aden, either with the municipality and the Government, or with the large offices, a system of lighting which is undeniably a great step forward compared to all other methods of illumination. I refer to Fluorescent lighting. I am sure it is solely a matter of time before we have an opportunity of testing its qualities in our own home and offices, and once it is installed we shall be in a position to demonstrate to potential buyers its undoubted advantages over any other type.

Radio

Philips Radio is second to none and I have yet to meet a single buyer who has obtained a radio of this make through us, wishing to complain about it.

Dyes, etc.

It would be expecting too much to hope that the arrangements I have made to represent at the same time the English Group, the ICI, the Swiss form CIBA and the French FRANCOLOR will last, but as long as they do, we should see to it that the indents we send are equally divided to prevent any of these concerns making claims on the others. It is my firm conviction that the day Germany is free to sell she will prove not only a large, but an active and successful competitor to the combines mentioned above. We should make certain that all the buyers, even those at Sheikh Othman, buy through us. I have been very alarmed whilst in Basle to see that these people, who have always been treated fairly by us, continue to send their orders to CIBA direct and that concern refuses to give them up. All the firms mentioned are not only manufacturers of dyestuffs, but they also make other products, some of them medicaments of the highest repute, e.g. Paludrine. Having the whole of Arabia, including Aden, as well as Ethiopia and Somaliland to provide, we have a large field of action for these drugs. A day may come also when we will be asked to provide manure.

Kodak

Correspondence between London and Aden on this subject shows clearly the growing demand for these products and now something should be done to find men who have had enough experience in photographic materials to canvass dealers, remain in close contact with them and see to it that every order they have to give comes through us. Though Kodak is undeniably a reliable and powerful firm, I do not think that once the Germans begin competing they will be able to keep up to the standard of the latter.

Cotton Goods

This is a department which has developed steadily and on a considerable scale since we were entrusted by the Government with the distribution of their supplies. This work gave us a unique opportunity of realising the magnitude of the trade in the various parts of the world where we have established branches. We have now in embryo an organisation which should be strengthened and extended in such measure as to prevent the competition out-pacing us. It is to be feared that Manchester will lose its privileged position now that Japan is resuming her former activity. I take it, though I am by no means sure, that we can maintain a steady flow of business in Mahmudi of our own brand and that it is possible from time to time to buy yarn of a higher count than that obtainable from India or Italy. The kind of cloth we can get from America should now be obtained from either China or Japan; but for fancy articles I believe Manchester to be more competitive and in any case infinitely more reliable, as has been proved by our last purchases from Hamilton.

Shell

The agency of this powerful concern has been of such a great help in the formation and growth of our firm that I feel it is imperative that we should continue at all times, as I have always done, to collaborate as closely and on as friendly terms as is possible with them.

Granted that we have achieved wonders, for when their agency was entrusted to us they were selling a maximum of two hundred cases a month only (less than one-half of one per cent of the total quantity marketed in the area) and that at a discount of at least one rupee a case. Five years later their share had risen to seventy-two per cent sold at a premium and our sales amounted to more than half a million cases a year. This surprising result could never have been achieved, however, if we had not received their help, enjoyed their trust and been given every facility to follow our ideas. The fact of being their agents in the Red Sea and adjacent countries had greatly increased our prestige with the various governments and has undoubtedly been instrumental in obtaining for us other most reliable agencies.

It is my desire, expressed here that we never show greed or pettiness when discussing terms. I feel certain that whenever we consider we are unfairly treated it will be enough to appeal first to Cairo and finally, if necessary, to London to see the errors righted at once.

I would have liked, before detaching myself from the firm, to finish the task I set my hand to, i.e. to give our friends such a hold over Ethiopia as for ever to preclude the possibility of any other concern interfering. Our tanks at Assab, once the pipeline is laid, and our tank lorries thence to Dessie and Addis Abeba should economise a great deal for them on the transport Massawah Addis Abeba; our tank wagons should ensure safer and better deliveries from Djibouti where we must aim at control of the tanks now in the hands of that dishonest concern, the CMAO. I shall leave our friends no peace until this is an accomplished fact even if I have to erect new tanks there with our own money. I have no doubt that in this respect I shall be given the maximum help by the French Government.

SECTION 5-DEPARTMENTS

Shipping

When one is young, and endeavouring to acquire a knowledge of the fundamentals of geometry, it is essential in dealing with theorems and consequent problems, to anticipate their solution, before entering into explanations. I shall proceed on the same lines and will suppose our organisation so perfect in every respect that it is able to answer, with ease and every degree of accuracy, all the calls and demands of business which must inevitably be made upon it. We now have, or to be more accurate, we shall soon have, four ships, fourteen dhows, twenty to thirty lighters, five tugs and a floating dock which are manned and organized by a staff possessing experience, knowledge and administrative acumen. For the time being therefore, I think it unnecessary to add to our fleet of steamers, although it is within the bounds of possibility that when our two latest ships are in commission, a new and vigorous avenue of trade will be opened to us and more vessels of the same type may prove to be a good investment. Our yards will, of course, maintain their present activity and will continue to build as many lighters as our stock of wood allows. With regard to this question of timber, we are not served in a satisfactory manner by our present suppliers, and it is now time that steps be taken to explore the possibility of purchasing wood on the Malabar Coast. Certain sections of our floating dock need re-plating and as it is vitally important that this dock should always be in perfect order it is imperative that we equip our marine workshops with the machinery required for the re-plating of ships, as nowadays vessels are so overworked that accidents are the rule rather than the exception. Because of such breakdowns, which are due also to the delays of building and the shortage of steel, we ought to be in a better position than anyone else in Aden to repair them. The opening up of Djibouti will necessitate our sending to this port a number of lighters and a tug. We shall have to arrange also for a competent staff and a manager with personality and initiative, capable of making important decisions, for he will have to contend with many problems. We shall have as an active and a dangerous competitor the organisation of CMAO. This concern is powerful and has such influence in high quarters, that I should not be surprised if our very good friend, Governor Siriex, is hurriedly transferred to another colony. We should thus lose the invaluable assistance of this man, whose successor might not be so well disposed to our firm.

Workshop

I long to see with my own eyes the improvements made by our Mr Millar in the workshop. There is so much to do to bring it up to date, to organise, distribute, check tools, stores, all the machinery, to maintain an intelligent discipline and create in our labour – both European and native – enthusiasm, devotion, loyalty, and pride in the fact that they belong to our organisation. I wish to know whether we are now allotted enough electric current and want to be shown a specification of the machines still needed to allow us to carry out any kind of work proposed to us, either from the sea or the land.

Garage

I was criticised when it was decided to put Melhem Daou at the head of our garage. But the critic did not pause to think of the result of his own experience not so long ago when two Englishmen had to be dismissed in ignominious circumstances. In our household we all, without exception, consider Melhem as a gentleman in the highest sense of the term and we certainly do not know a more expert and considerate driver, or a more thorough and competent mechanic. He is one of these men who, though shy and modest, are capable of rising to any situation. I deem it advisable to order from London as quickly as possible all the types of machinery our competitors, the Arabian Trading Company, possess. Our garage should be, if not better, at least as well equipped as the best.

Buildings

V; the latest comer, whose natural dullness seems to have become more marked during his last stay in Aden, was unable to state whether the building erected above the skins godown had been completed or if one, two, three or four months will still be required before the apartments can be occupied.

Hotel

Until everything is in working order and runs smoothly this project will be a white elephant. But it has never been my habit to abandon a scheme once undertaken and I have no intention of doing so in this case until everything is perfect and runs to my satisfaction. The materials accumulated seem to be sufficient for opening up the hotel, serving meals, looking after the bar which should become popular if well organized.

Finance

A balance sheet prepared from our books has undoubtedly its value but I consider it insufficient. I shall ask our best accountant to prepare for me what I would call a grocer's inventory, i.e. a complete list of everything the firm possesses, from the smallest screw to the largest ship. We shall have to estimate the value of each separate item and rectify our books, if necessary. The decision is prompted by my desire to leave the firm almost completely and I must know its exact position. I shall have to transfer another £750 000 to complete the £1 500 000 promised and I hope this huge withdrawal will not affect the vitality of the firm. Once our true position is known it will be time to determine whether we should invest our surplus of available capital in another ship – new buildings, factories, etc., etc. Moreover, there is so much to be done and in so many directions for the enlightenment and the comfort of our staff that good use will certainly be found for surplus capital at all times.

Appendix C : AB's Writings

AB was possessed by an urge for self-expression. Quite apart from his huge correspondence he was a prolific writer. Some of the pieces found among his papers seem to have been written for himself with the aim of clarifying his ideas. Such a one is the undated note on 'My Socialism'.

My socialism is simply love of one's neighbour, of humanity. I want to abolish poverty and enable everyone to live by his work, give everyone enough elbow room. Humanitarianism is not the old style philanthropy. Philanthropy only helps here and there, but real love of humanity seeks to amend the state of things by process of law. If that is socialism so much the better. In equality, absolute equality, I do not believe. Neither in stars or in men is there equality. There always have been and always will be individuals who by their own gifts and a combination of extraneous circumstances beyond their control can and do achieve more than others; there will always be a hierarchy among men. But hierarchy means order, organization, discipline, knowledge, obedience, not the exploitation of man by man. That is why I do not accept communism. Lenin as soon as he was in power, began to arrest leading personalities. The longer I live the more I realise the true role of the individual in the evolution of humanity. But, I repeat, higher gifts and so-called good fortune are no justification for the exploitation of the less gifted and fortunate. I do not believe one can do away with private ownership. The personal relation, that real price of affection that binds the owner to his possession, is good in the interest of common progress. Communism is possible, but only among brothers in a family or in a religious, and friendly, community; it could only be kept by real love. I do not accept class war; there is a difference of class and status; there are degrees among people, but that does not mean War. It means the organisation of natural inequalities and of those due to historical development.

The sentiment of universal fellowship, a noble emotion, is in some danger of perversion into a creed which repudiates the order of values amongst men, a temper which hates hierarchies, and distinction of merits, breeding, rank or character and would bring about equality by levelling down. That paves the world for dictatorship. Utopian visions of self-determination are a dangerous guide for students of world affairs because they distract attention from the invidious task of upholding law and order in lands where freedom and self-government are coming to birth.

II

More often the purpose was didactic, to bring the essential facts to the notice of those concerned, to advocate a particular policy, to propagate those ideas which AB so strongly had at heart. Mention has been made of his reports to Sir Stewart Syme following his visit to Sana'a in 1931 and to Addis Abeba in 1937. There was the Symposium on the Djibouti Railway in 1943; and a paper on the world economic position in 1947, stressing, in its conclusion, the paramount importance of close Anglo-American co-operation. Many of AB's papers have not survived, including one written in the early thirties, on the impact of soviet oil products on Western markets. Copies of this, as of most of the others, were sent to AB's contacts in the upper hierarchy of Shell. The trouble was that the recipients were very busy men and the papers extremely long. AB was disappointed that the reception was not more enthusiastic.

A more personal note is struck in 'The Qualities of a Merchant', completed in the summer of 1941 a few weeks after his return to Aden. The ideas of course had been maturing in his mind for many years, and their expression may well have crystallised during the enforced idleness of the previous autumn and winter at Le Paradou. One story is that he originally intended it for publication; whether or not that is true it certainly never appeared. But it is important as a statement of AB's business ideals and as a picture of what he so ardently desired himself to be seen to be. Here are extracts:

When I came to Aden forty-odd years ago merchants were, and maybe still are, held in contempt by officials and officers, towering, socially, above them. 'Boxwalla' was the kindest epithet used for a merchant. Shipping agents and bank managers were regarded as the aristocracy of these common folk but were nevertheless considered to belong to the 'boxwalla' clan... except when their help was required.

Being young and innocent I was ready enough to believe, until I knew more of them, that officials and officers were not made of the same humble clay as ourselves; but unfortunately I soon came into contact, when I was first astonished, then appalled by their abysmal ignorance, their utter and complete indifference to anything and everything that had not an immediate bearing upon sport, drinks, pay, promotion, gossip and politics of the approved variety. Science, with the exception of a few scattered notions collected and memorised to enable them to pass examinations in their youth but long since forgotten, Art, General Knowledge, Political Economy – the social problems that loomed so large – all these were tabooed subjects. Like Religion and the King, it was bad form to discuss them, and to be branded a 'highbrow' was to be condemned. Not one in a hundred knew any language other than his own, and many were inarticulate even in that.

It did not take me long to discover that in business, on the contrary, unless you kept your mind constantly alert, curious and receptive... unless you added psychological instinct to technical knowledge, thus enabling you to differentiate instantly between a rogue and an honest man, unless you sharpened your wits, steeled your will, conserved by clean and sober living, *mens sana in corpore sano*, you were a defeated man before you started. I continued to learn all the time, and after more than forty years of struggle I am still confronted with problems which baffle me...

The first requisite for a business man is Honesty – infrangible, uncompromising Honesty. Temptations are many and great in business and unless Honesty constitutes, and remains throughout, the bedrock upon which the merchant builds his firm the foundations will crumble. It must be apparent in everything he does and says – in every word, in every act, in every gesture.

After Honesty, come Hard Work, Pride in the well-accomplished task, Indomitable Will, Generosity and Indulgence to others. Hard work and the discipline it imposes forms character. Pride in the work to be done adds the incentive. An Indomitable Will is the mainspring, for without it the ever-recurring difficulties, disappointments, set-backs, calumnies and deception (often on the part of people who had our trust) will break us. Generosity and indulgence towards others, less privileged than ourselves, will take the sting out of the competitive spirit which, alas! is essential to a successful business career.

On the intellectual plane it is necessary to maintain an insatiable curiosity – to amass knowledge through books, conversation, and, best of all, hard experience; to preserve logic and the power of reasoning; to look at facts with unprejudiced eyes; to study all questions with imaginativeness; to study political economy and its inexorable laws, realising that economically all parts of the world are interlocked. A revolution in Cuba will affect the price of sugar in Java; a poor cotton crop in the USA will send prices of that commodity in India and consequently of the finished article in Japan skywards.... Examples of cause and effect are innumerable and tend, all of them, to prove the inter-dependence of markets the world over. Hence the necessity for a merchant to act as the antenna of a radio, sensitive to all the news that comes to him.

But that is not all. Man has achieved little by himself. In business, as I believe it to be true in every walk of life, a merchant must be surrounded by collaborators, his staff. It is in the choice of these men, in the ideal he inspires them with, in their devotion, their understanding, their sense of responsibility, that his success will reside. He must make them feel the interest he takes in their welfare. As soon as circumstances permit he should provide for their future; he should give them every opportunity to express grievances, to discuss with him the aims of the firm, the motives behind each move. By acting thus he may hope that when the time comes for him to place the torch in another's hands the flame may continue to burn as brightly as before.

For the majority Commerce means the pursuit of wealth. This may be true, but is it not equally true that an official or military career is chosen, with rare exceptions, by men without special qualifications who desired a sheltered life, and are not those men just as keen on obtaining ever larger salaries? But just as among more highly principled officials and officers a career is chosen as a means to develop personality, attain mastery over oneself and to satisfy that craving for 'creation' which is to be found in all leaders and men of action, so does this apply in equal measure to the man who chooses the profession of Merchant. Once their feet are firmly set in the chosen path the urge to create becomes stronger, more impelling, as they proceed. The best of them forget their ego, become disinterested and find their greatest satisfaction not in 'making money' but in 'Service', their greatest joy in the contemplation not of a successful Balance Sheet but of the child of their creation, grown from the embryo of an idea, nurtured, watched over, studied, weighed, caressed in their minds until its once vague shape attains form and stands before them materialised and alive.... They feel like an athlete whose muscles are ready to answer the call the moment it is made. They see Respect in the eyes of those who approach them and realise they are Men, and recognised as such.

The Americans' definition of a leader: 'A man who has to draw the line between himself and his subordinates is not a boss.' A true leader, whether he be an official, an officer or a merchant of the higher order, has not to draw that line ...

I should like to find more merchants who answer this description – who take a pride in their profession not because it brings Money, but because it is more useful to humanity than any other, because it demands superior qualities of the mind and heart, because it requires greater and longer-sustained effort. Never should they allow themselves to be treated as inferior members of the social order... Their whole attitude should be inspired by the beautiful lines of Rabindranath Tagore:

This is my prayer to Thee, my Lord –

Strike, strike at the root of penury in my heart.

Give me the strength to make my love faithful
in service.

Give me the strength never to disown the power or
bend my knees before insolent might.

Give me the strength to raise my mind high above
daily trifles.

And give me the strength to surrender my strength
to Thy will and love.

III

Finally, here are extracts from AB's paper on Education, composed in 1949.

Practically all human knowledge in the medieval period was concentrated in a few towns, scattered throughout Europe, such as Cambridge, Oxford, Parma, Paris, Salamanca, Bologna, Salerno and Pisa. The universities they housed were co-heirs to the knowledge accumulated formerly in the abbeys and monasteries, and they were therefore linked with each other....

It was natural that this teaching, and the knowledge derived from it, should have been primarily of a religious nature, covering exegesis – the interpretation of sacred texts, the significance and performance of rites and ceremonies and the technicalities of precedence, finance and lay organisation. All too often schisms and struggles for supremacy ensued, so bitter as to involve the settlement by bloodshed of questions which in our generation seem futile. But throughout it all, like certain plants which grow imperceptibly and relentlessly until in the end they dominate all others, Science grew up, fostered by the spirit of scholarship, which, avid of detail and trained to study facts, was nevertheless capable of seeing them in their true perspective. Yet instead of the Divine, as interpreted by the teachings of traditional and progressive morality, and the Human, as represented by Science, merging and flowing together in one great stream, these two currents have, up to the present pursued two different courses...

The great savants are not unaware of the force of sentiment; being more acute than the average man, they know that nothing great or strong can be created without it. One has only to study their lives and see the truth of that. But the others, whose intelligence is not vast enough to comprehend that discoveries and mathematical speculation are essentially part of one harmonious whole, who limit their vision to some specific line of research, of whatever order or importance it may be – mathematics, physics, chemistry, etc. – without a thought for the outcome, or for its moral implication, repudiate sentiment, which they hold to be harmful because it cannot be bound by a formula...

We must nevertheless admit that the religious scale of values, shaken by the attacks of Science on archaic dogmatism, is cracking, and those sentiments, founded upon a belief in the Divine, upon which the past lived, are thereby deadened to a dangerous degree, and with them are thereby deadened those qualities which make possible our relations with each other and with the community as a whole – love of our neighbour, self-control, disinterestedness. Popularized versions of scientific publications penetrate the masses, where, as is only too often the case, ideas, imperfectly understood and pushed to extremes, bring about a moral disintegration which intensifies as it spreads. Is not this the explanation of the degeneracy and spinelessness, of the unconscious egoism, indifference and lack of ambition and of the virtual disappearance of manners, civic spirit and patriotism which seems so widespread today? Is it not the explanation of the fatal tendency to level downwards, which gives the impression that Humanity, instead of advancing, is in full retrogression, under the impulse of forces which appear to us base, because they are essentially material? . . .

AB then quotes Emerson:

Let a Stoic open the resources of man, and tell men they are not leaning willows, but can and must detach themselves; that with the exercise of self-trust, new powers shall appear; that a man is the word made flesh, born to shed healing to the nations; that he should be ashamed of our compassion, and that the moment he acts from himself, tossing the laws, the books, idolatries and customs out of the window, we pity him no more, but thank and revere him; and that teacher shall restore the life of man to splendour, and make his name dear to all History.

AB continues:

What can we do save seek to influence our children by inspiring them with the spirit of revolt that is in us? . . .

It is not enough to clutter up the mind with an unselected jumble of facts, forcibly absorbed in order to satisfy examiners and obtain diplomas. We all know by experience with what alacrity, with what joy even, we subsequently clear our heads of all but the essentials. When I see my small sons committed, in their turn, to the curriculum that I followed, and that my forefathers followed before me, I can only cry from my heart; 'Stop, stop. . . . Open the window, let in the fresh air and blow away this odour of stagnation.' . . .

Could we not take immediate and practical steps to show students the possibilities of each of the many careers open to them, not merely in their own spheres, but in their vital relationship to the well-being and economy of the country – shipping, oil, chemistry, high finance, industry and commerce, electricity and its applications, law, architecture, government, etc? It is certain that the big shipping companies, petroleum companies, chemical industries, banks and industrial and engineering concerns would co-operate by sending specialised lecturers, and that eminent lawyers, well-known architects or officials chosen by the Government, would willingly give talks to the students and encourage questions on their professions. Is it not high time to give them a working knowledge of the complexity of our modern society, and train them thus to consider from an international angle problems which are no longer soluble on a purely national basis? and, still more to use, in considering them, that same scale of moral values which is equally applicable to the nation, the family and the individual? ...

Given teachers who are also converts, and lecturers duly chosen from the élite of all countries, men known for their international breadth of outlook, it should not prove too difficult a task to influence the students and to convince them, not merely by economic arguments, but by promoting in a practical way the ideal of universal brotherhood, that the creation of a world free from fear, and from the three other evils marked in the speeches of those supermen, Roosevelt and Churchill, is in their hands and dependent on their efforts. Under such conditions the development and strengthening of character can proceed hand in hand with the acquisition of knowledge, by special methods which would include tests of physical endurance and sense of responsibility; but for such the school would have to be specially adapted and dedicated; it is hopeless to expect anything of this sort from the ordinary school curriculum.

Notes

CHAPTER 1   1899

1. See Maps. The Settlement comprised Crater (the old town), Steamer Point, Tawahi, Ma'alla, Sheikh Othman and Little Aden across the Bay.
2. Bury, G. Wyman, *The Land of Uz* (Macmillan, 1911) p. xxi.
3. Wellstead, J. R., *Travels in Arabia* (John Murray, 1838) p. 385.
4. Because of the ebb and flow of casual labour, Arabs from the Yemen and Somalis from across the sea, exact figures have always been difficult to assess.

CHAPTER 2   THE YOUNGEST CORPORAL

1. Then about £400. Up to World War I the French franc was 25 to the £.

CHAPTER 3   PASSAGE TO ADEN

1. We have seen from his own letters that this was not strictly true, though the sums had been very small and to ask for them had been painful.
2. This was what Rimbaud had had from Bardey nineteen years previously. In September 1880 he had written home 'I am badly paid – I have only five francs a day plus food, lodging and laundry.' (Rimbaud, Arthur *Œuvres complètes* (Paris: Gallimard, 1954) p. 325.
3. He was wrong aboout Marcel Besse, who in due course took a doctor's degree and became a leading light of the Montpellier School of Pharmacy.

CHAPTER 4   THE FIRM OF BESSE

1. Burton, Richard, *First Footsteps in East Africa* (1856).
2. See Appendix A on AB's reading.
3. Richard Burton had noted: 'The European degenerates rapidly as do his bull-dogs, his game-cocks and other pugnacious animals in the hot, enervating and unhealthy climates of the East' (Burton, ibid.).
4. A few years later he wrote to one of his staff: 'In Aden I have often stopped activities and through the channels of our native friends spread rumours meant for my competitors; and often succeeded in bringing prices down.'
5. In 1948 AB compiled a marathon review of the firm's activities. By that

time, of course, the import side had been greatly developed and diversified. But the general pattern remained the same. An abridged version of the review is given in Appendix B. Those interested in the problems of, for instance, Ethiopian beeswax or Hodeida Whiteheads can there see what AB had to say about them.

CHAPTER 5   WORLD WAR I

1. AB was pioneer of all the modern amenities that came to Aden. His was the first private motor car; the first electricity; the first modern plumbing when piped water became available; the first refrigerator; and the first air-conditioning.
2. There is an account of it in Sir Tom Hickinbotham, *Aden* (Constable, 1958). See also the article *A Sad Little Sideshow* in *The Times*, 19 July 1965.
3. Monfried, H. de, *Aventures de Mer* (Paris: Bernard Grasset, 1931).

CHAPTER 6   STONER

1. All his life AB had, from time to time, trouble with his eyes. He himself explained that in his early days in Arabia he had dabbled in the pearl trade, and the long hours spent poring over a microscope in artificial light had left permanent damage.
2. This was one of Mme. de Coppet's charities to which AB had subscribed 1500 frs (£60).

CHAPTER 7   THE CRISIS

1. Emile was a hard bargainer, and argument over the settlement was to go on for the next six years.

CHAPTER 9   THE EARLY TWENTIES

1. AB's debt to Raymond Bernard comes out in the names given to the two boys – Peter Raymond and Antonin Bernard.
2. For a most informative account of dhows and their running see Villiers, Alan, *Sons of Sinbad* (Scribners & Sons, 1940).

CHAPTER 10   SHELL

1. Bunkering arrangements were kept separate from normal trading: it was to be one of AB's great disappointments that he never handled bunkering either for Shell or for APOC.
2. The cans themselves were of great importance to the villagers, who had all manner of uses for them. Shell cans, with their Gazelle marking became

very well known throughout the area. 'If we stress this matter of packing,' AB was to write, 'it is because it is absolutely the determining factor in the conditions of our market.'
3. Figures supplied by Shell.

CHAPTER 11   A SECONDMENT

1. Louise le Brozec and Ina Marek ('Petrouchka') were two of the secretaries.
2. On another occasion EM had noted: 'Aden is a most peculiar place, and people who live there (with very few exceptions) become obsessed. This takes the form of lethargy coupled with intense personal animosity, and its effects cannot be calculated by those breathing a wider air.'

CHAPTER 12   THE DEPRESSION

1. Waugh, Evelyn, *When the Going Was Good* (Duckworth, 1947) pp. 152–7. 'Monsieur Leblanc' is of course AB. Waugh's only inaccuracies are on AB's dress after bathing. He never wore *crêpe de chine* shirts – only airtex cotton. And he would not wear, or allow his staff to wear, socks with shorts. His mercerised cotton stockings were specially made for him in India. But Waugh is correct in recording that a drive in a car with AB at the wheel was a hair-raising experience.
2. Stark, Freya, *The Coast of Incense* (John Murray, 1953) pp. 39–41. 'M. Besse . . . is more than charming: he is a Merchant in the style of the Arabian Nights or the Renaissance . . . a wonderful person who lets life play upon him as if he were an instrument responsive to all its variations.'

CHAPTER 13   STAFF

1. Nizan, Paul, *Aden, Arabie* (Paris: Maspero, 1960).

CHAPTER 14   THE TITLE DEEDS

1. It ran as under:

Mes yeux
sont bleus.

Un feu
de joie
en moi
s'étend
si gent-
iment.

c'est doux!

Car je comprends
Que ça, c'est grand, –

Le sent-
iment

EN TOUT.

2. AB was now Ford Agent.

CHAPTER 15   THE INDIANS AND THE ARABS

1. M. G. Patel became Chief Accountant when Parekh retired.
2. After 1937, when Aden was taken out of the Bombay Presidency and became a Crown Colony under Whitehall, the trend of official policy was towards the employment of local Arabs both in government offices and in local firms. But it took a long time to have any effect. There were not the Arabs available with the qualifications possessed by the Indians.

CHAPTER 16   PROGRESS

1. Millar, Hugh, *Notes on Aden-Type Arab Dhows* (MS in the library of St Antony's College, Oxford).

CHAPTER 18   THE ABYSSINIAN WAR

1. The French franc was not devalued till the end of September 1936 when the sterling rate dropped from 76·75 to 105·75.
2. But André warned his father it was no good trying to send parcels. The French had to be very careful as the Italians were complaining of misuse of the bag.

CHAPTER 20   ARABIAN AIRWAYS

1. Twenty years later, long after AB's death, two large crates were found at the back of a Besse godown in Ma'alla. Inside were Pobjoy engines. With the help of an RAF engineer, for whom Pobjoys had a vintage interest, they were set up and started. They were splendid engines for fitting into speedboats.

CHAPTER 21   STAFF AGAIN

1. Rather more than £700.

2. André was at that time in charge of the Djibouti office; and at one stage AB sent him instructions to reduce by one quarter the salaries of six junior members of the staff who might be thought to bear some responsibility. André wrote back that, as branch manager, the responsibility was his, and suggested that instead his own salary be cut by half. But he was brusquely instructed to mind his own business and do as he was told.

CHAPTER 22   WORLD WAR II

1. Hostilities were to last much longer than anyone imagined and the Le Paradou party ran out of funds. Luckily the Marseilles agents, Meister and Di Domenico, were able to look after them until the liberation.

CHAPTER 23   ADEN IN WAR-TIME

1. Stark, Freya, *Dust in the Lion's Paw* (Murray, 1961).
2. See Appendix C on AB's writings.
3. He contributed substantially to local Free French funds, and gave them the original Monospar. But the ill luck dogging his flying ventures persisted, and the Monospar crashed within a month of being handed over. AB's services to the Free French were to be recognised by the award of the Legion of Honour in 1949.
4. Among the stories going round were (1) AB was the illegitimate son of a wealthy Belgian who financed him, (2) he had murdered his first wife, (3) Mohamed Aly was his own son by an Arab woman in Hodeida and (4) his main source of income in 1944 was from refuelling Japanese submarines in the Indian Ocean from his dhows. There was also the Union Club crack on his immunity from sharks when bathing: 'No sensible shark would ever think of taking on a shark that size.'

CHAPTER 24   THE FIRM IN ETHIOPIA

1. In 1943 AB found an outlet for some of his frustration by composing a satirical 'Symposium on the Djibouti Railway', the point being that the only party with no say in its running was the unfortunate merchant who wanted to move his goods.
2. At one stage he was playing with the idea of buying the Aden salt works. That, in the end, he decided not to do so is an example of his foresight. The past profitability of the Aden salt works had been due to exports to India and Japan. In the post-war years India became an exporter of salt and Japan became self-supporting.
3. £33 000. British and East African shillings were equal in value.
4. Sir David Barran has confirmed that the cause was his interest in the Besse accounts.
5. While we have no corresponding figures for AB's area it may be noted that in 1932 his commission from Shell amounted to 148 190 Rs (£11 342). In 1947 it was 882 349 Rs (£66 176). In 1951 it was to be East African

shillings 3 500 000 (£175 000).

6. A tribute to the reliability of the service is that when in due course the new Ethiopian currency was introduced the entire government stock of old silver MT dollars was sent down to the coast in an imposing convoy of Besse Lancias with an Ethiopian army escort.

CHAPTER 25 POST-WAR

1. Later the French Ministry of Education had second thoughts, and in the summer of 1948 a senior official was sent down to Le Paradou to reopen the discussions. But by then AB was committed to Oxford.
2. In 1948, at the time of the Berlin blockade, AB was to write from France to Weerts in Addis Abeba:

   Very few people here seem concerned with the immediate future which I myself find alarming. There is nothing here to stop the Russian hordes; and for our country to be occupied under the pitiless ferocity of the GPU would make us feel the German occupation had been Paradise.

CHAPTER 26 ST ANTONY'S I

1. AB was difficult to fit; a number of letters have survived on the problems he set the bootmakers.
2. See AB's paper on education in Appendix C.
3. The wish that the gift should remain anonymous is entirely in keeping with AB's character. But he was also aware of the inevitable repercussions in the area where he traded once it was revealed that he had donated so large a sum to a foundation in England.
4. AB seems originally to have envisaged an active role in the affairs of his foundation. There has been preserved an extract of a letter to him from Clyde dated August 1948:

   I shall also, as at present contemplated, be the man who, in conjunction with the University Authorities and the Warden and Directors of the College, shall have the task, under you, of introducing your ideals into their work, and of helping in the organisation of those courses of lectures which we contemplate and which shall be designed to give to your college those wider horizons and that individual character which are derived from you.

5. The Colleges were Worcester, Wadham, St Edmund Hall, Exeter, Pembroke, Lincoln and St Peter's Hall (now St Peter's College).

CHAPTER 27 ST ANTONY'S II

1. The first headings in this form are: Public Spirit; Sense of Justice; Ability to state facts precisely; Ability to follow out what he believes to be the right course in the face of Discomforts, Hardships, Dangers, Mockery, Boredom, Scepticism, Impulses of the moment . . .

2. See Appendix C.
3. The original Council of Management consisted of Sir David Maxwell-Fyfe (Chairman), the Vice-Chancellor, Maurice Hill and Roy Borneman. To these were subsequently added the Provost of Worcester, Dr Ifor Evans, R. A. Butler and the Bishop of London. F. W. Deakin, on his appointment as Warden of St Antony's, also became a member of the Council. R. A. H. Clyde continued as Secretary till mid-1950 when he resigned and was succeeded by P. C. Hailey, the Bursar of St Antony's.
4. To confirm his own impressions, AB sent specimens of Deakin's and also of Kurt Hahn's handwriting to C. E. Magnat, a graphologist of Geneva with whom he was in touch. Unfortunately the latter's reports have not survived, but there is ample evidence that both were extremely favourable.

CHAPTER 29   THE FINAL CHAPTER

1. AB had shown great interest in suggestions put up by Professor Julian Huxley for the education of specially gifted children.
2. It took some time to dismantle the various committees set up by the lawyers. This was to be accomplished in 1953 when St Antony's College received its Charter.
3. AB died before his investiture could take place; and his insignia were handed to HB by the Governor on her return to Aden towards the end of 1951.
4. It was now that AB presented to the British Museum his collection of South Arabian antiquities, acquired over his long years in Aden. Many of them – calcite and bronze sculptures, statuettes and fragments – are on view numbered 130882 to 130914 in the Department of Western Asiatic Antiquities.

Index